Measuring the Harlem Renaissance

Measuring the Harlem Renaissance

The U.S. Census, African American Identity, and Literary Form

MICHAEL SOTO

UNIVERSITY OF MASSACHUSETTS PRESS
Amherst and Boston

Printed in the United States of America

ISBN 978-1-62534-250-8 (paper); 249-2 (hardcover)

Designed by Sally Nichols
Set in Adobe Garamond Pro
Printed and bound by Sheridan Books, Inc.

Cover design by Sally Nichols
Cover art: Lionel Pincus and Princess Firyal Map Division, The New York Public Library. "Population distribution map." *The New York Public Library Digital Collections.* 1945. http://digitalcollections.nypl.org/items/b9f2b588-8fb6-d39b-e040-e00a180679bc

Library of Congress Cataloging-in-Publication Data

Names: Soto, Michael, 1970– author.
Title: Measuring the Harlem Renaissance : the U.S. Census, African American identity, and literary form / Michael Soto.
Description: Amherst : University of Massachusetts Press, [2016] | Includes bibliographical references and index.
Identifiers: LCCN 2016031027| ISBN 9781625342508 (pbk. : alk. paper) | ISBN 9781625342492 (hardcover : alk. paper)
Subjects: LCSH: American literature—African American authors—History and criticism. | American literature—20th century—History and criticism. | Harlem Renaissance. | United States—Census—History. | Harlem (New York, N.Y.)—Intellectual life—20th century. | Modernism (Literature)—United States. | African Americans in literature.
Classification: LCC PS153.N5 S6465 2016 | DDC 810.9/896073—dc23
LC record available at https://lccn.loc.gov/2016031027

British Library Cataloguing-in-Publication Data
A catalog record for this book is available from the British Library.

for Américo Benjamín

Contents

Preface

As I write this I can look out of my office window to see the downtown San Antonio skyline, a view dominated by high-rise bank buildings, River Walk hotels, the Tower of the Americas, and the Alamodome sports venue. The seventy-five-story Tower was completed in 1968, just in time for the HemisFair world's fair, an event that endowed the city, finally, with a twentieth-century outlook. Twenty-five years later, the Alamodome was constructed to host large-scale concerts and sporting events and to house an as-yet-unrealized National Football League franchise. Between them, on the eastern edge of downtown, runs U.S. Interstate 37, carved out of the San Antonio geography during this same period in a process that displaced hundreds of families and that cemented, quite literally, the historical divide between downtown and the predominantly African American East Side area. Just northeast of downtown I can also see Fort Sam Houston, a large military outpost that for decades has done much to heal the city's racial fractures.

Beginning a book about the so-called long Harlem Renaissance with brief and incomplete reflections about the racialized geography of a South Texas city strikes no one, I hope, as too far misplaced. After all, Harlem holds a grip on the American cultural imagination as the paradigmatic

African American urban enclave; its story shapes my view of San Antonio society in untold ways. Nor does it shape my view alone. In 2014, when the U.S. Department of Education awarded the local United Way with a Promise Neighborhood grant to support renewal in the East Side, numerous references to Harlem, and specifically to the Harlem Children's Zone, which inspired the national program, seasoned homegrown reporting and political discourse. Similar rhetorical gestures by now look familiar: as Harlem went a century ago, so went the rest of black America in the following decades—never mind that the facts of life in San Antonio bear little resemblance to those of New York City.

For at least a century, Harlem has been known by many metaphors, many symbolic restatements—test tube, Mecca, city of refuge, Negro metropolis, cultural capital of black America, "a raisin in the sun"—that recommend part (Harlem) for whole (black America) social and cultural analysis. Even when Langston Hughes, who gave us the raisin metaphor, lampooned the notion that creative literature might play a role in the day-to-day lives of Harlemites—"ordinary Negroes hadn't heard of the Negro Renaissance," he quipped in *The Big Sea,* "And if they had, it hadn't raised their wages any"—he nonetheless looked forward to a day when his humorous dismissal might no longer apply, when serious literature might take on equally serious cultural work.

It is to Hughes and to his fellow creative writers that I look for guidance when taking up sociohistorical questions about Harlem and the wider American landscape. *Measuring the Harlem Renaissance* interrogates the basic assumption of most Harlem Renaissance scholarship and much of its literature: that a clear connection exists between social life and cultural production; that historical experience gives birth to literary and artistic expression. Part of the allure of Harlem Renaissance literature, for scholars and for more casual readers, is its constant engagement with questions of sociohistorical importance. Yet the social facts behind these questions are routinely taken for granted, with no recourse to empirical evidence that has been collected for decidedly nonliterary purposes.

Much closer at hand, stacked high on my desk, are the numerous Census Bureau volumes, photocopies of New York City and New York

State government reports, and printouts of the computer spreadsheets that I've assembled to better understand Harlem social life during the early part of the twentieth century. The novels, poems, short stories, and plays of the Harlem Renaissance line the bookshelves along my office walls; these are joined by decades of scholarship on the subject, beginning with Franck L. Schoell's "La 'renaissance nègre' aux États-Unis" (1929), a *Revue de Paris* overview of the ongoing movement, and Melvin B. Tolson's "The Harlem Group of Negro Writers" (1940), his retrospective Columbia University master's thesis. Such early ventures are joined by Nathan Irvin Huggins's seminal *Harlem Renaissance* (1971), David Levering Lewis's feisty *When Harlem Was in Vogue* (1981), and too many of their scholarly heirs to count here.

As I look back and forth between my bookshelves and my desk and the view outside, I'm tempted to yoke the images together with a sweeping rhetorical gesture. But I'll resist. What strikes me most about the bird's-eye view of my adopted home city is the wide discrepancy between the facts on the ground and the hazy, romanticized versions of San Antonio handed down by such writers as Sidney Lanier or even Jack Kerouac. No such problem emerges from a consideration of Harlem, progenitor of what James de Jongh aptly describes as a "vicious" modernism. And yet the book that follows is no mere catalog of a doctrinaire realism that arose in response to urban squalor, nor does it imply (I hope) a narrow range of literary responses to social reality. Anyone familiar with more than a handful of Harlem Renaissance texts knows that they veer from social realism to avant-garde surrealism, from detached imagism to syrupy love sonnets. Here's why: there is no such thing as Hughes's "ordinary Negro." The social landscape of Harlem was so complex, so intriguing during the heyday of the renaissance that bears its name that no one approach, to literary representation or to social analysis, could ever hope to offer but a partial and provisional view of the facts on the ground.

Let me conclude here by thanking a number of kind people and institutions for their role in supporting this book along its winding path. Drafts of selected portions of *Measuring the Harlem Renaissance* were presented as papers to the American Literature Association, the American

Studies Association, the South Texas College Black History Month Distinguished Speakers Series, and the University of Texas Heman Sweatt Symposium on Civil Rights; I am grateful to the conference and symposia participants for their engaging comments. I would like to thank as well the members of the African American Literature and Culture Society and the Washington Irving Society for their valuable feedback. A crash course on Geographic Information Systems led by Ian Gregory at the Digital Humanities Summer Institute in Victoria, British Columbia, enhanced my thinking and mapping skills.

Many thanks go as well to my friends, colleagues, and students at Trinity University for their help along the way. As the cliché goes, there are far too many names to list here. But a few must not escape mention, particularly those who shared their insight and encouragement and who reviewed drafts of the manuscript: Victoria Aarons, Christine Drennon, Carey Latimore, Arturo Madrid, Claudia Stokes, Amy Stone, and my many Harlem Renaissance seminar students. Trinity University provided generous financial support in the forms of Faculty Development funds, a Mellon Foundation travel grant, and a Summer Research Stipend; Mark Brodl and Duane Coltharp helped smooth the processes along. The staffs at Emory University's Stuart A. Rose Manuscript, Archives, and Rare Book Library, the Schomburg Center for Research in Black Culture, and the Beinecke Rare Book and Manuscript Library at Yale University have also been kind with their assistance. At the Trinity University library, Sean Connin, Jeremy Donald, and Anne Jumonville Graf have been especially generous with their time and talents.

The writing of this book took an unexpected detour after I was elected to the Texas State Board of Education. Although my time in public office was brief, it was refreshing to discover how many passionate advocates for learning there are in Texas and beyond. Although my board colleagues and I routinely disagreed, I am glad that we were able to do so with civility and sometimes even camaraderie.

At the University of Massachusetts Press, I thank senior editor Brian Halley for his generosity and zeal and the anonymous manuscript reviewers for their intelligence and insight. Brian led a clear, efficient, and rewarding process; my faith in scholarly publishing has been renewed. I thank as well copyeditor Mary Bellino; my prose benefited greatly from her expert eyes.

I owe a great debt of gratitude to my family. My parents, Josefina and Paulo Soto, my brothers and their families, and my in-laws in the Peña Sanchez family never fail to offer unconditional love and support. To my wife (and in-house GIS expert), Celina Peña, and sons, Alejo and Américo, I owe the very best moments of my life: you inspire me each and every day.

Finally, I dedicate this book to my son, Américo Benjamín: one day when you read these pages I hope that they inspire you to encounter for yourself the people, places, and words that they describe.

Measuring the Harlem Renaissance

Introduction

The True Measure of a Renaissance

The census man,
The day he came round,
Wanted my name
To put it down.
—*Langston Hughes, "Madam and the Census Man" (1949)*

The census and American slavery go hand in hand. We tend not to see the two as mutually constitutive institutions, but America's founders devised the decennial census partly to adjudicate the Three-Fifths Compromise, which split the legal difference between unenfranchised property and full-fledged personhood. An apologist for slavery might see it in these terms: if a slave must be taxed as property, then he or she should also factor in congressional apportionment. Slavery's opponents saw the situation in another light: states should not be rewarded with political clout by denying the fundamental rights of others. An accurate census tally would assure both sides that their position was safeguarded by the machinery of the federal government. Alexander Hamilton, a key architect and fervent booster of the Constitution, spoke of the compromise as a necessary evil when in 1788 he urged his fellow New Yorkers to ratify the foundational document: "Would it be just to compute these slaves in the assessment of taxes, and discard them from the estimate in the apportionment of representatives? Would it be just to impose a singular burden, without conferring some adequate advantage [to slaveholding states]?"[1] And thus the constitutional framework enshrined both slavery and the decennial census in an awkward dance of competing interests.

To better understand and appreciate African American cultural formations from the late nineteenth to the mid-twentieth century—the so-called long Harlem Renaissance[2]—this book proposes the following: African American identity as we today understand it solidified roughly a century ago as the product of and in response to (1) the U.S. census, (2) demographic statistical analysis, and (3) the conceptual linkage of abstract geopolitical space and racialized social identity. I examine African American literature through the lens of census history to tell the story of how U.S. officialdom—in particular the Census Bureau—placed persons of African descent within a shifting taxonomy of racial difference, and how African American writers and intellectuals described a far more complex situation of interracial social contact and intraracial diversity.[3]

That I even bother with the phrase "Harlem Renaissance" should raise doubts among some readers. The overburdened label, bequeathed to us in 1940 by Langston Hughes,[4] does a disservice to the national scope and internationalist ambitions of the era's black thinkers and writers. As Brent Hayes Edwards importantly reminds us, we must guard against the parochial view that overemphasizes "U.S.-bound themes of cultural nationalism, civil rights protest, and uplift in the literary culture of the 'Harlem Renaissance'" at the expense of the black internationalism that spread from Harlem and Paris and Port-au-Prince to the far corners of the globe.[5] To signal the label's inadequacy, Edwards scrupulously places quotation marks around "Harlem Renaissance" whenever he can't avoid the phrase. But as the anthropologist John L. Jackson Jr. demonstrates, Harlem is also a "quotation-marked-off place" in the sense that it functions as a conceptual shorthand signaling urban American blackness to a worldwide audience caught in the media web spun from Madison Avenue and Hollywood: "Every application of the name supplies, implies, and applies oversaturated and highly charged assumptions about the neighborhood and its inhabitants as either the epitome of racial potentiality or the embodiment of squandered opportunities."[6]

The notion of a Harlem Renaissance easily displaced the Negro Renaissance label, long before "Negro" fell out of widespread use, precisely because the last century perfected the science of assigning racial measurements all the way down to the neighborhood level, even down to the city block. "Harlem" became a metonym for "blackness" because of its unique location in space and time. Harlem was the laboratory for the new racial science, so much so that the journalist Roi Ottley could declare in 1943 that the neighborhood resembled "a sort of test tube in which the germs of Negro thought and action are isolated, examined, and held up to the full glare to reflect Black America."[7] Harlem conveys race and space simultaneously, a move that signals atavistic racial categories but demystifies claims of filial origins based on an aboriginal geography or shared bloodlines. The racialization of Harlem allows us to see "race" as a modern and modernizing concept. In Harlem more than anywhere else, black persons of all nationalities tried on a newfangled "African American" identity. Although the social-scientific conferral of full-fledged citizenship occurred well outside the confines of the Harlem Renaissance, both geographically and temporally, in Harlem during the renaissance the conceptual linking of racial identity and geospatial evolution accelerates and comes into sharp focus.

The federal census and racial labels exist for the same fundamental reason: the conditions of modernity—an expansive nation-state, huge waves of immigration and inmigration, unprecedented urban density—demand vast bureaucracies and an efficient understanding of difference to make sense of individual and collective identities. Premodern societies, in which all individuals know firsthand all other members of the social group, have little need for censuses or for abstractions such as "race" or "nationality." "The census's abstract quantification/serialization of persons," to borrow language from Benedict Anderson, yields a grammar that enables belonging to an "imagined community" such as a race or nation. During the nineteenth century, Anderson points out, national censuses became increasingly obsessed with cataloging individuals according to racial difference, but difference alone stood without meaning in the absence of strict quantification, such that "the particular always stood as a provisional representative of a series, and was to be handled in this light."[8] The constitutional requirements of the U.S. census (apportionment, direct taxation) quickly grew to encompass all manner of data gathering, so that by 1850 the Census Bureau tracked "color" difference along with profession, real estate value, literacy, and "whether deaf and dumb, blind, insane, idiotic, pauper or convict." The Census Bureau then tabulated these data geographically by state and county, so that subnational social trends might be visualized and so that the nation's political elite might identify social concerns and allocate resources strategically (if not always charitably).

As we will see in chapter 1, these same policymakers directed census employees to track an increasingly byzantine system of race/color classification to promote a white supremacist agenda. Decades would elapse before political actors, military strategists, cultural shapers, and everyday folk fully assimilated the modern nation-state's insistence that full-fledged citizenship and bureaucratic processes go hand in hand in a complex give-and-take of social privilege and sacrificed individualism. And still more time was required before the tools of geospatial understanding, particularly in the wake of the Voting Rights Act of 1965, allowed activists and academics to deploy social-scientific analysis in support of the civil rights cause. Throughout the century-long process, the "Negro" becomes an enfranchised U.S. citizen and an object of social-scientific concern simultaneously, in a mutually reinforcing imaginative enterprise.

By way of introduction to my larger project, chapter 1, "Measure for Measure for Measure," briefly traces the history of how the U.S. census positioned African American identity, with an emphasis on three intellectual paradigms that define partly overlapping eras.[9] During the first era, early census practices embedded racist hierarchies and aligned national unity with nativist concepts of "racial" purity, all the while formalizing subnational racial categories that in earlier eras signaled a quasi-national geographic reach. The racial hierarchy that privileged Europe over Africa was folded over and imported to the United States. Here I investigate in particular Abraham Lincoln's reliance on the first-ever map of U.S. racial demography, a map that embodies contradictory aims in the president's evolving understanding of African American citizenship. During the second era, the late nineteenth and early twentieth centuries, diverse and shifting labels were grafted onto African American identity; these were deployed to buttress with scrupulous statistical data the racist pseudoscience of eugenics. Here my focus is the present-day use of historical census data to pin down Jean Toomer's vexed racial self-identity, along with W. E. B. Du Bois's largely successful effort to ground the nascent field of African American studies in social-scientific empiricism and at the same time to counter the eugenicist position on racial declension. During the third and ongoing era, a social constructionist understanding of census categories and data has emerged. My point of emphasis will be the reaction to how Barack Obama, filling out the government form at his Oval Office desk, self-identified on the twenty-third U.S. census in 2010. The event formalized his status as the nation's first "Black, African Am., or Negro" president. A table listing the categories deployed to identify "race" (or "color" as it was often labeled) throughout the history of the U.S. census is included as an appendix to the book.

The second chapter, "Harlem Society," centers on affinities between Harlem Renaissance literature (especially prose fiction) and key developments in twentieth-century social theory, particularly game theory and feminist critiques of the pathologizing of African American family life (as evidenced by, for example, the infamous Moynihan Report of 1965). I examine motifs of sexual competition in narratives of intra- and interracial romance; color discrimination within and beyond the African American social context; gender balance within the Harlem enclave and in other locales throughout the United States; and the performance of sexual propriety and indecorum in Harlem society and literature. In this chapter I also introduce what I call "imaginative social engineering": the handling of social questions in literary expression to test new, sometimes utopian modes of social organization. In the examples I investigate, Harlem Renaissance writers deploy the strategy to imagine environments less bound by gender-biased or heterosexist social pressures.

The third chapter, "Harlem Diversity," explores the institutionalization of racial difference in social-scientific literature and stores of data, alongside cultural efforts to demystify and dismantle institutional racial categories. I look specifically at Harlem Renaissance celebrations of collage-like physical diversity within the "black" population; at the Census Bureau's awkward efforts to track intraracial diversity during the late nineteenth and early twentieth centuries; at the difficulties associated with the transnational analysis of U.S. Afro-diaspora populations; and at the national and linguistic diversity of the "African American" population, with special focus on Harlem between 1910 and 1930. Against this sociohistorical backdrop, I introduce yet another Harlem Renaissance motif: depictions of literary characters who pass not as white, but as Latino.

The fourth chapter, "Harlem Modernity," takes up the theme of intraracial diversity in a movement often credited with cementing a unified racial consciousness. I look closely at how the idea of a "Great Migration" of African Americans from the rural South to the urban North derives from a wide array of academic disciplines (such as anthropology, biology, and religious studies) and how the notion filtered into literature and the visual arts; at the curious set of references to "blue vein" societies amid the onset of the suntanning craze; and at the strategic functions of a motif that I call the "racial blazon," the cataloging of a literary character's racialized physical features. I argue that the racial blazon shows striking similarities to post-Reconstruction era legal definitions of blackness and whiteness and underscores the difficulties embedded in the Census Bureau's enumeration practices.

The fifth chapter, "Harlem Geography," traces the cultural history of Harlem in the American spatial imagination. I focus particular attention on the influence of Manhattan's urban grid in nineteenth- and twentieth-century social theory and social analysis; on the emergence of Harlem as the paradigmatic African American urban enclave in social and cultural history; and finally (in the epilogue) on the role of arbitrary census tract geography in imposing static notions of ethnic and racial difference onto the social landscape.[10] I argue that the census tract, at one time an awkwardly nativist intellectual construct, has allowed social chroniclers to consider Du Boisian problems of racial identity in geographic terms.

My approach to literary texts emphasizes the extent to which writers shape ongoing conversations about racial identity, both formal and informal. The modernizing tendencies of census data gathering and their geostatistical outgrowths inform, but only provisionally, incompletely, and imperfectly, membership in a racial group with ancestral ties to Africa but having more immediate claims to social belonging in the United States. Despite the best efforts of Census Bureau statisticians and the cultural historians who follow their lead, precisely *who* counts as African American has always defied simple measure. African American writers launched a bevy of rhetorical strategies, ranging from age-old motifs to wholly new modes of organizing narratives, to complicate Americans' understanding about racial difference and to update the language of social belonging.

Much of New Negro identity was negotiated in response to national social and cultural institutions. If African American literature arose in response to the social and cultural pressures of a post-Reconstruction, Jim Crow regime, as Kenneth W. Warren is, I think, correct to propose,[11] then New Negro cultural patterns are necessarily preoccupied with subject formations that are defined by the several states and especially by the national apparatuses of the United States. (Whether or not the social conditions enabling African American literary emergence are behind us, as Warren argues, is a question too tangled to explore here.) The Harlem Renaissance very obviously took inspiration from, for example, W. B. Yeats and the Celtic Renaissance, but the postcolonial self-fashioning, as I have described elsewhere,[12] very much had national cultural ambitions and institutions in sight. The Harlem Renaissance thus provides an intriguing example of the paradox of globalization: global economic and cultural systems disseminate and sustain seemingly intractable nationalisms and ethnic fundamentalisms, and early twentieth-century Harlem was hardly immune to the forces of tribalism and globalization. New Negro intellectuals understood their roles because they had seen them performed elsewhere and by others, whether these were Yeats or Amy Lowell or some long-forgotten cultural gatekeeper. It is now well known that the Négritude movement relied on a similarly paradoxical source for its Pan Africanist orientation: the cultural nationalism of the Harlem Renaissance.[13]

There are many places in this book where even my most fervent intentions are stymied by a simple fact of social analysis: the most reliable and readily available sociohistorical data typically derive from national bureaucracies. Those who live by the census die by the census. The "grammar" of the modern nation-state, to borrow again from Anderson, relies on apparatuses that measure national subjects in pursuit of full bureaucratic if not political inclusion. "The fiction of the census is that everyone is in it," Anderson reminds us, "and that everyone has one—and only one—extremely clear place."[14] As much as I rely on the Census Bureau to carry out this study, I've also come to share Anderson's jaundiced view about the fictional dimension of census data. Long after the Fourteenth Amendment did away with the Three-Fifths Compromise that once sullied the Constitution, the Census Bureau formally tallied persons of African descent in ways that render statistical analysis across different racial and ethnic groups, at least until well into the twentieth century, difficult if not impossible. The difficulties are especially pronounced when it comes to understanding the social impact of diaspora, of travel across the black Atlantic to these United States.[15]

Throughout *Measuring the Harlem Renaissance,* I propose that the movement's writers and thinkers lead us to new ways of understanding the relation of both social history and literary culture to social reality. Just as important, these writers and thinkers serve as imaginative social engineers; that is, they force us to rethink social reality not only in terms of the self-evident features of the present, but also in terms of what's possible in the future given slight adjustments to prevailing social patterns. They guide us to a theoretical space inhabited most famously by Theodor Adorno, whose maxim "It should be otherwise" insists that even the most rarified, sublimated work of art contains within it a transformative political vision.[16] Even the harshest critics of the Harlem Renaissance, including many of its firsthand participants, tend to measure its failures in terms of the slow pace of American social change. David Levering Lewis's proposed "belated subtitle" for *When Harlem Was in Vogue* (1981)—"Civil Rights by Copyright"—might be dismissive, but the phrase points simultaneously to textual worlds and to quotidian reality, to the space shared by social and cultural history.[17]

Although I hesitate to describe this book's central ideas as theories of African American literary expression, I will offer three conclusions that are more fully explained elsewhere in the book. In each case, national bureaucratic apparatuses, and the census in particular, play key roles. First, geography matters. The urban way of life that grew out of Harlem and that came to be recognized as universal throughout the United States redefined the African American experience and the literature that arose from that experience. The so-called Great Migration of African Americans from the rural South to the urban North—a kind of fugitive slave narrative writ large—played *the* pivotal role in African American modernity, but not always in the expected ways. As a general rule, modernity's abstracting of lived human existence carved out new spaces in which local, self-evident associations such as those found in small southern communities were necessarily replaced with legal and social inventions. In other words, blackness and whiteness as we now understand them are specifically modern phenomena; for roughly a century, Harlem served as the epicenter of racial abstraction.

Second, and although this goes without saying, gender matters. Even though feminist scholars have revolutionized Harlem Renaissance studies since the 1980s, gender figures into the structuring and reception of Harlem Renaissance literature in ways that often go unnoticed. The constructedness of gender identity has inspired critics of women writers such as Zora Neale Hurston and Nella Larsen for decades now, and a similar approach has more recently animated research into sexual identity in the work of, say, Countee Cullen and Gladys Bentley. Throughout this book, I take for granted the notion that "One is not born, but rather becomes, a woman," to evoke Simone de Beauvoir's famous reckoning of gender construction.[18] Since Beauvoir's seminal work, feminist literary critics (such as Sandra Gilbert and Susan Gubar) and linguists (such as Deborah Tannen) have demonstrated beyond all doubt that literary structures and even language itself reproduce women's consignment to the second sex. With pathbreaking insights such as these firmly in place, and extended to Harlem Renaissance writers, I am able to address the dissociative foundations of gender and sexual identity within the context of elaborate social systems that complicate binary notions of male- or heteronormative identity formation. In other words, key works from the Harlem Renaissance insist on befuddling either/or binary systems of social identity. I am most obviously inspired by multiagent game theory because I was first led there by Harlem Renaissance fiction.

Third, skin color matters. Readily discernible variation in skin color is a fairly recent phenomenon in the history of human evolution, but it has still played a crucial role in defining human identity in the modern world. When the first so-called great migration of humans out of Africa took place some eighty thousand years ago, humans ventured into regions in Europe and Asia with less direct sunlight than previously encountered, beginning the evolutionary process that left some with paler skin than the earliest humans.[19] But only during the last few centuries have modern means of intercontinental travel given voyagers access to areas for which they weren't naturally adapted; this in turn allowed for contact between humans with wholly different skin colors. Unprecedented contact with cultural others involved rigid hierarchies in technical know-how and coercive power. Modern forms of chattel slavery grew out of such contact between lighter and darker "races." Indeed, modern chattel slavery required a brutal cultural classification according to racial phenotype, and skin color was the most obvious among many options for identifying visual difference. For as long as lighter and darker races have come into contact with each other, "miscegenation" has been a fact of human existence.[20] Harlem Renaissance writers routinely investigate the legacy of sexual violence in American social history, and they often dismantle the fiction of racial purity by deploying narratives of miscegenation, mulatto identity, and racial passing. In most of these cases, writers focus precise—often absurdly precise—interest on skin color; their handling of racial phenotype curiously parallels legal and biological systems of racial classification. Indeed, the several motifs of racial difference I explore throughout this book draw liberally from the very discourses that Harlem Renaissance writers wish to undermine.

A Race by Any Other Name

When referring to persons of African descent, I will use the term "Negro" throughout much of this book for three reasons. First, most of the writers mentioned in this study self-identified as Negro; they wrote, as they usually put it, "Negro literature." As the Census Bureau struggles to explain with each decennial census, there are still those who refer to themselves as Negro with only the merest trace of irony. Second, the Census Bureau has used the term to signal the combined black and mulatto population since the mid-nineteenth century and up to the most recent (2010) census. Until well into the twentieth century, the Census Bureau reported on the domestic Negro population without regard to national origin; before 1940, one was simply Negro, not a native-born or a foreign-born Negro. The word "Negro" thus connotes an international, polyglot society—it describes the diverse reality of Harlem social life—in a way that "African American" fails to do. Third, growing up in a largely bilingual environment on the Texas–Mexico border during the 1970s and '80s, I routinely heard black persons of all nationalities referred to as *negro* without a hint of malice.[21] The word "Negro" may be somewhat awkward to type, but less so to read and not to hear when spoken with a Spanish accent. For these reasons, whenever the preferred contemporary phrase "African American" groans under the weight of imprecision, I will resort to another—and I hope clearer—option. Specifically, when a literary text or census report depicts "Negro" life, I too will favor the outdated racial label. It would be wrong and far-fetched to presume that this book will alter the way individuals handle racial taxonomies in the United States or elsewhere, but I hope that continual references to "Negro"—along with a host of additional racial categories, from African American to Afro-diaspora to black—will force the reader into a mindful relationship with her or his use of social identity markers.

1

Measure for Measure for Measure

Three Eras in American Racial Census Taking

The Great Emancipator and the Geostatistical Imagination (1790–1860)

In the U.S. Capitol building, above the Senate chamber's west staircase, hangs Francis Bicknell Carpenter's *First Reading of the Emancipation Proclamation by President Lincoln* (1864; fig. 1.1). At nine feet tall and fifteen feet wide, the painting depicts a larger-than-life Lincoln surrounded by his war cabinet as the president reads the first draft of the historic document. Carpenter considered emancipation to be "an act unparalleled for moral grandeur in the history of mankind"; Lincoln, according to the painter, declared the Emancipation Proclamation "*the central act of [his] administration, and the great event of the nineteenth cen-*

Figure 1.1. Francis Bicknell Carpenter, *First Reading of the Emancipation Proclamation by President Lincoln,* 1864. Courtesy U.S. Senate Collection.

tury."[1] To record the moment, Carpenter spent six months at work in the White House, interviewing his subjects, sketching studies of the persons and things found in the painting, and composing what he hoped to be the pinnacle of his professional career.

Perhaps ironically, we remember Carpenter more for his memoir, *Six Months at the White House with Abraham Lincoln* (1866), than for his work as a painter of historical subjects or even as a portrait artist. The memoir, a rare inside look at the Lincoln presidency less than a year before his assassination, offers a hagiographic portrait of the president, one that continues to influence assessments of the man's moral worth. In Carpenter's memoir Lincoln emerges as tragically burdened by the demands of history, but not so much that he can't let out the occasional guffaw; Lincoln is attentive to a diversity of opinion but unwavering in his core convictions and unflappable in the face of political intrigue; he is privately religious and unfailingly kind, even to strangers. Lincoln epitomizes the great moral cause of equality for all.

Carpenter achieves his task by deploying a rhetorical strategy that has its painterly analog, but that is more properly considered linguistic: the literary blazon, the verbal cataloging of a subject's physical features to reveal his inner moral worth. Lincoln possessed a "gaunt but sinewy" frame in Carpenter's estimation and was "inclined to stoop when he walked"; his "head was full medium size, with a broad brow, surmounted by rough, unmanageable hair"; and his "complexion was inclined to sallowness"—hardly a flattering portrayal. At the same time, Lincoln's mouth was "expressive of much firmness and gentleness of character," and his "eyes were blueish-gray in color,—always in deep shadow, however, from the upper lids, which were unusually heavy, (reminding me, in this respect, of [Gilbert] Stuart's portrait of Washington,)—and the expression was remarkably pensive and tender, often inexpressibly sad, as if the reservoir of tears lay very near the surface."[2] In this early example of a rendering that merges traditionally feminine and masculine traits, Carpenter insists that Lincoln's physiognomy replicates his personality, so that tenderness and sadness and firm resolution irrepressibly show themselves on the president's features. In literature as in heraldry, the blazon testifies to the subject's purity of bloodline, and in this curious revision of the "blood will out" cliché, Carpenter even suggests, although Washington had no direct descendants, a lineage connecting the nation's two greatest presidents. What genealogy cannot furnish, art readily supplies.

In the passage immediately preceding this blazon, Carpenter explains the painting's second most prominent still-life object (after the Emancipation Proclamation draft): a depiction of the "Map Showing the Distribution of the Slave Population of the Southern States" (1861) created by the U.S. Coast Survey.[3] Carpenter writes: "Visitors to the Executive Chamber, during the administration of Mr. Lincoln, will remember the lithographic map, showing the slave population of the Southern States in graduated light and shade, which usually leaned against the leg of his desk or table, and bore the marks of much service. The States and counties most abounding in slaves were indicated on this map by degrees of blackness, so that by a glance the proportion of whites and blacks in the different States at the commencement of the Rebellion could be easily comprehended."[4]

The map (fig. 1.2) shows a county-by-county, graduated image of slave density in the South in ten-point increments: a white county has a slave

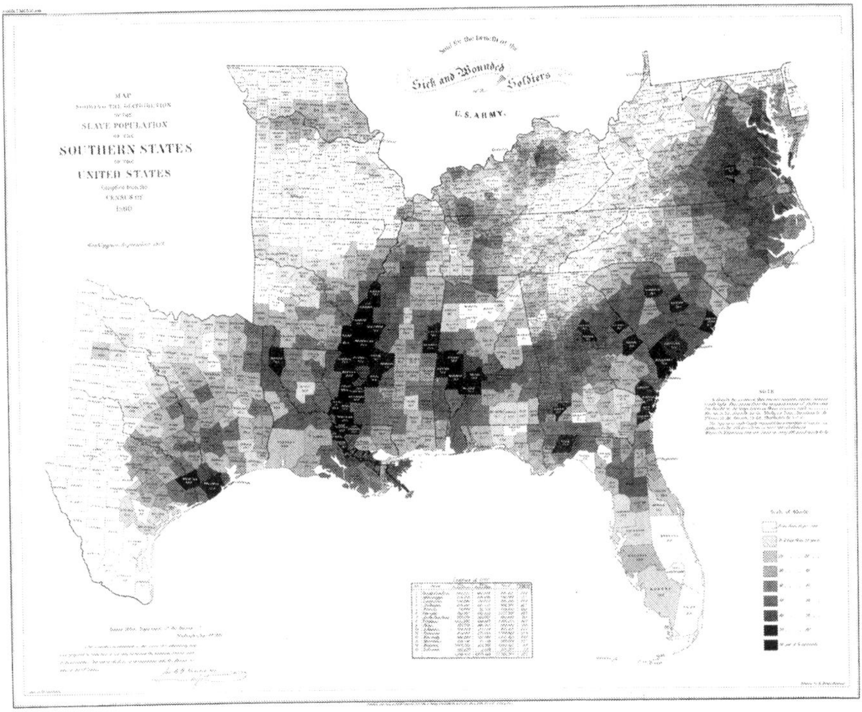

Figure 1.2. U.S. Coast Survey, "Map Showing the Distribution of the Slave Population of the Southern States," 1861. Courtesy Library of Congress, Geography and Map Division.

population of less than 10 percent, a light gray county has a slave population of 10 to 20 percent, and so on, until the darkest counties indicate a slave population, according to the "Scale of Shade" key, of "80 per ct. & upwards." Beneath a county's name is printed the proportion of slaves in its population; Amelia County, Virginia, just west of Richmond, for example, has a slave population of 72.6 percent, resulting in a near-black hue that requires white lettering for the label to be visible. On the bottom center of the map, a table shows the free population, slave population, total population, and percentage of slaves of each southern state. On the bottom left is certification of the map's accuracy by Joseph C. G. Kennedy, superintendent of the census.

As he worked on this section of the painting, Carpenter borrowed the map without informing Lincoln, who later discovered it in the painter's makeshift State Dining Room studio: "One afternoon the President came in alone, as was his wont,—the observation of the daily progress of the picture appearing to afford him a species of recreation. Presently his eye fell upon the map, leaning against a chair, as I had left it after making the study. 'Ah!' said he, '*you* have appropriated my map, have you? I have been looking all around for it.' And with that he put on his spectacles, and, taking it up, walked to the window; and sitting down upon a trunk began to pore over it very earnestly." According to Carpenter's anecdote, Lincoln deployed the map as an instrument of wartime intelligence: the Commander in Chief studied its gradations to determine the likelihood that the so-called Kilpatrick-Dahlgren Raid of Union cavalry into Virginia might yield wartime spoils in the form of emancipated slaves. "It is just as I thought it was," the president inferred, "He is close upon —— County, where the slaves are the thickest. Now we ought to get a 'heap' of them, when [Gen. H. Judson Kilpatrick] returns."[5] (The botched raid badly misfired when Confederate troops killed Colonel Ulric Dahlgren and found on his body documents revealing a scandalous plan to torch Richmond and to assassinate Jefferson Davis.)

The historian Susan Schulten has pointed out that the map's aesthetic features serve still other purposes: "Its minimalism and absence of decoration and color suggests neutrality and transparency: it appears simply to translate population data into graphic form." The sheer force of social-scientific truth telling, Schulten adds, masks the map's ideological underpinnings. The "very decision to map the relationship between slaves and the general population reflects a belief that slavery was behind the rebellion. And . . . the map enabled Lincoln to follow the progress of his military, which after January 1863 had officially become an army of liberation."[6] Seen in this light, the map of southern slavery fits perfectly into Carpenter's larger project to define Lincoln as a martyr for freedom's cause, as the Great Emancipator.

We have no reason to doubt that the Coast Survey map allowed Lincoln to unite military strategy with moral imperative, that it symbolized the war's grand cause of human justice. That the map was so popular in the North—and explicitly "sold for the benefit of the sick and wounded soldiers of the U.S. Army," according to its heading—reinforces the idea that the twin goals of military victory and abolition were inseparable. The four slave states that remained loyal to the Union, and that were not subject to the Emancipation Proclamation, complicate but do not diminish this understanding of the Coast Survey map.

Even his contemporaneous detractors knew Lincoln to be a shrewd and pragmatic politician, one quick to avail himself as necessary of the hard-knock politics of bureaucratic machinery. The map's very existence, according to Schulten, stemmed from Lincoln's desire for compensated emancipation.[7] During the first two years of the Civil War, right up to January 1, 1863, when the Emancipation Proclamation, an executive order emancipating southern slaves "upon military necessity," took effect, Lincoln pressed for gradual, compensated emancipation, a gesture meant to retain the loyalty of the four border states and to encourage the peaceful return of Confederate states to the Union.[8] Such an approach would require geographic precision because Lincoln, a conservative Constitutionalist, believed that each state must arrive individually at a negotiated settlement to free its slaves.

The map very likely allowed Lincoln to see quickly the regional economics of such compensation, which would surely require a large overall price tag. As the historian Eric Foner notes, slaves at the start of the Civil War, when considered only for their monetary value, "exceeded the combined worth of all the banks, railroads, and factories in the United States"; they represented America's single greatest asset at the time.[9] The table at the bottom of the map would yield statewide figures, indicating that Virginia, because it had the largest number of slaves, required the greatest compensation; the map itself would further specify that the counties nearest Richmond, the darkest on this part of the map, would prove most expensive to compensate.

For both political and economic reasons, Lincoln hoped to convince the border states to agree first to gradual, compensated emancipation. It is in these loyal jurisdictions that the abolitionist cause might have taken hold more easily than in the deep South, and the small number of slaves there would prove relatively inexpensive to liberate in this transactional way. In a March 6, 1862, message to Congress, Lincoln urged legislators to provide incentives to states to agree to compensated emancipation as "one of the most efficient means of self-preservation" of the Union. He presented the effort as a simple matter of arithmetic: "In the mere financial, or pecuniary view, any member of Congress, with the census-tables and Treasury-reports before him, can readily see for himself how very soon the current expenditures for this war would purchase, at fair valuation, all the slaves named in any State."[10]

In a follow-up letter sent eight days later to Senator James A. McDougall of California, Lincoln included a ledger detailing the slave population in each border state; at a rate of $400 per person, freeing the 1,798 slaves of Delaware would require $719,200, "less than one half-day's cost of this war." Freeing all of the border state and District of Columbia slaves would cost $173,048,800, slightly less than eighty-seven days of war expenses. Lincoln then asks, "Do you doubt that taking the initiatory steps on the part of those states and this District, would shorten the war more than eighty-seven days, and thus be an actual saving of the war expense?"[11] Throughout that summer and into the fall of 1862, Lincoln pressed border state legislatures and the Congress to push ahead with gradual, compensated emancipation; even with an offer of financial compensation, a delayed implementation of twenty years or more, and a guarantee that the federal government would not interfere with the right of individual states to allow chattel slavery, not a single state legislature, and very few slaveholders in Washington, D.C., took up Lincoln's piecemeal offer.

Even after the Emancipation Proclamation took effect in 1863, when plans for a gradual, compensated transition no longer applied, Lincoln may have viewed the Coast Survey map as something beyond a tool of military intelligence, moral stimulus, or financial accounting. In fact, the map may well have had a more sinister effect when judged by today's standards. Revisionist scholars have long seen Lincoln as less than saintly; indeed, the historian George M. Fredrickson's assessment leans heavily on the ambivalence toward Lincoln of W. E. B. Du Bois, who supplies the title to *Big Enough to Be Inconsistent* (2008), and of Frederick Douglass, whose nuanced appraisal concludes the slender volume. Before describing Douglass's genuine appreciation of the martyr for Emancipation,

Fredrickson shares the former slave's more skeptical understanding of Lincoln, who stood, in Douglass's words, "ready and willing at any time during the first years of his administration to deny, postpone, and sacrifice the rights of humanity in the colored people to promote the welfare of the white people of this country."[12] Lincoln often viewed slaves as abstract "problems" not in the Du Boisian sense, but rather as glitches in the political system, and the Coast Survey map assists anyone who wishes to view slavery in the abstract, as data points rendered with visual elegance.

The language of geospatial data analysis—its brute simplicity, its tendency to strip away all competing information in favor of a single spectrum of knowledge—suggests another "problem" in Lincoln's Coast Survey map. The racialized subjects represented by the map had yet to achieve full citizenship, even in Lincoln's estimation; their density in parts of the South, especially along the great corridor of the Mississippi Delta, symbolized a grave threat to the Union. When Lincoln appraised military efforts in light of geospatial demography, he saw "slaves" and (according to Carpenter at least) "heaps" of wartime bounty, not the free-thinking individualist portrayed by Douglass, not the slave become a man.[13]

Much of Douglass's and Du Bois's and eventually Fredrickson's ambivalence toward Lincoln stems from the president's scheme to colonize newly emancipated slaves in Africa, Haiti, or Central America, an effort born of political expediency and perhaps an unreconstructed worldview. As Lincoln framed the issue for a "committee of colored men" gathered at the White House in late 1862, colonization represented the only avenue for African American political, economic, and social self-determination. In the United States, the president offered, biological differences create too high a hurdle for racial equality: "We have between us a broader difference than exists between almost any other two races. Whether it is right or wrong I need not discuss, but this physical difference is a great disadvantage to us both, as I think your race suffer very greatly, many of them by living among us, while ours suffer from your presence."[14] Seen from this condescending vantage, the dark ink that depicts slave density in the Coast Survey map looks like a deep fissure tearing the Union in two. As the central artery of the national body politic, the Mississippi River should unite North and South, not split them apart. Healing the nation would require colonization.

As someone who cut his political teeth in Illinois, arguably the most racist state in the antebellum North,[15] Lincoln did not require census data or the Coast Survey map to arrive at negative, racialist opinions about African Americans. Still, census data during the antebellum period skew toward the disenfranchisement embedded in the Constitution's Three-Fifths Compromise. Following the language in Article 1, Section 2 of the Constitution, censuses prior to 1850 enumerated for the purposes of representation and direct taxation "all free Persons . . . excluding Indians not taxed" and added to these "three fifths of all other Persons." The first census schedule of 1790 thus lists "Free white Males" and "Free white Females," "All other free persons" (used to designate free persons of color), and "Slaves." The same data, with minor variations in age ranges, were collected and reported through the 1840 census.

Beginning in 1820, the census schedule called for the enumeration of "Free Colored Persons," the closest approximation to the identity that we now label African American. Marshals entrusted with gathering the results were given no instructions on how to distinguish between slaves and free colored persons; census reports are equally silent about the distinction. Marshals were required to interview heads of households; in theory, these would include both slaveholders, who would report on the slaves in their possession, as well as free colored persons, who would report on their families. As a practical matter, the results were so lopsided that the latter category hardly registers in early compilations of the U.S. population. In 1820, for example, there were 233,524 free colored persons and 1,538,038 slaves, a sevenfold difference.

In a move with profound implications for modern racial demography and identity, the 1850 census schedule, which Congress specifically wrote into the legislation authorizing the census that year, introduced a new category for "color," and within this category it offered the options "white," "black," or "mulatto." These racial markers had been in popular use for centuries, but prior to 1850 they had never guided the formation of U.S. government policy. A sinister motive, one that would play out for most of the next century, lies behind this move toward a more complex racial taxonomy: as the political scientist Melissa Nobles demonstrates, policymakers collected the data because they wished to prove the racial degeneracy of free blacks and especially the mulatto progeny of racial mixture.[16] Social scientists required definitive statistics to demonstrate, as they believed, that mulatto offspring had higher mortality rates than "pure" whites or blacks; by showing a dwindling mulatto population, they determined to prove, statistically, the "fact" of interracial degeneracy.

The official recognition of mulatto identity thus derives from a pseudoscientific belief that the mixed offspring of "pure" races are more susceptible to disease and less likely to reproduce than "pure-blooded" blacks or whites. Gathering data about mulattoes would demonstrate with statistical precision the theory of racial degeneracy. Yet any "scientific" data garnered from the new census category might serve competing ideological ends; that is, abolitionists might demonstrate the cruelty and deformity of slavery using the same data that slavery's apologists might use to verify white supremacy. Perhaps to steer clear of political controversy, the census report for 1850 simply distinguished between "Free colored" (the number rose to 434,495) and "Slaves" (3,204,313).

The 1860 census, which obtained the data represented in the Coast Survey map, instructs enumerators for the first time, if only vaguely, how to reach racial designations in their work: "Under heading 6, entitled '*Color,*' in all cases where the person is white leave the space blank; in all cases where the person is black without admixture insert the letter 'B;' if a mulatto, or of mixed blood, write 'M;' if an Indian, write 'Ind.' It is very desirable to have these directions carefully observed." The instructions divulge a crucial piece of census history: until the late twentieth century, census enumerators, rather than the person counted, assumed responsibility for assigning racial identity on census schedules. The instructions posit race or "color" as a given—one simply *is* "white" or "black" or "mulatto" or "Indian"—but as we will see in the following section, the contextual cues for reading a person as white or black play a critical role in the labeling process.

The census of 1860 proved a watershed for yet another reason: for the first time, census officials released detailed, county- and city-level data about the color of the population. That is, data about the number of whites, blacks, and mulattoes, collected since 1850, figured prominently in the census report for 1860. In fact, several pages of the introduction to the Eighth Census are given over to a discussion of the "future increase of the African race in this country." Within this discussion, which is startlingly accurate in its prediction of the African American population through the year 1900 (though less impressive when it comes to overall U.S. population forecasts), we find tacitly racist statistical reasoning and patently racist moralizing. Addressing the "declension of the free people of color," the report identifies as causes "their greater indifference as a class to virtuous moral restraint" and the "unfavorable moral condition" that results. The census report goes on to point out, without identifying direct demographic evidence, "that corruption of morals progresses with greater admixture of races," and predicts the "gradual extinction of that [free colored] people." To be mulatto, the report concludes, is "more unfavorable to vitality, than a condition of slavery"; like the vanishing Indian before him, the mulatto faces "rapid absorption and extinction" in the swift progress of U.S. social change.[17] An entire class of the population, the predominantly mulatto free persons of color, an invention of the U.S. legal system, is thus dismissed as morally and physically wanting, as diseased and doomed to perish.

The earliest geostatistical maps served epidemiological ends, allowing scientists to track the spread of disease and in so doing to pinpoint their source of origin and to mitigate negative outcomes. This epidemiological line of thinking—seeing spatial evidence for a problem to be eradicated—may well have informed Lincoln's assessment of the Coast Survey map. If so, he was guided in this direction by the mapmakers. The map's execution was not only seemingly neutral and transparent in its visual design; it was also strategically selective in its use of data. Just as epidemiological maps gain instructive power by filtering out needless data—today we call this "noise"—the Coast Survey sifted through mountains of available demographic information to present a compelling case about southern slave density. That is, the map does not present racial distribution (except indirectly and imprecisely), nor does it offer evidence of the geographic extent of blacks versus mulattoes versus whites. In fact, to arrive at its statistical results, the Coast Survey map actually *omits* the South's entire population of free persons of color: they simply are *not there.*

If we deploy census data to look more closely at the example of Amelia County, Virginia, we discover that the slave population accounted for 71.3 percent of the county population rather than the 72.6 percent depicted on the map. That's because Amelia County's free colored population of 189 (55 blacks and 134 mulattoes) was not used in the Coast Survey's calculations; rather, the mapmakers measured the county's 7,655 slaves (5,914 blacks and 1,741 mulattoes) against its 2,897 whites. In Amelia County, dubious statistical practices yield only small differences in the final, slightly skewed results. Elsewhere, however, the Coast Survey's narrow aim distorted results far more dramatically. In coastal Accomack County, Virginia, situated between the Atlantic Ocean and Douglass's cherished Chesapeake Bay, 3,418 free colored persons, fully 18.4 percent of the county population, were left out of the Coast Survey's calculation. The map shows a slave population of 29.6 percent, but in reality, when we account for the missing free colored persons, the figure stood at 24.2 percent. Not one of Virginia's free colored persons is represented in the Coast Survey map. It's as if 58,042 Virginians vanished into the ether, or migrated to a far-off colony. For the purposes of the map, that is precisely what occurred.

Jean Toomer, W. E. B. Du Bois, and Other Purebred Mulattoes (1870–1930)

With their 2011 edition of Jean Toomer's *Cane* (1923), Rudolph P. Byrd and Henry Louis Gates Jr. unleashed a small storm by concluding, "based upon an analysis of archival evidence previously overlooked by other scholars, that Jean Toomer—for all his pioneering theorizing about what today we might call a multi-cultural or mixed-raced ancestry—was a Negro who decided to pass for white."[18] The controversy spilled over into the pages of the *Chronicle of Higher Education,* where Byrd and

Gates repeated the charge of passing, and into the *New York Times,* which quotes Gates as saying, "Everyone on his family tree was black and didn't claim to be anything else. Only Jean tried to cross over."[19]

Cultural historians have long associated Toomer with the U.S. census, a link that began innocently enough when George Hutchinson pointed out in 1991 that "both [Georgia Douglas Johnson] and Toomer could remember a period in which racial definition in Washington society was less rigid, less distinctly bifurcated into 'black' and 'white' worlds, than it had become by 1920, the last year in which the 'mulatto' designation was included in the U.S. census."[20] What appears to be the fleeting reference to a happy coincidence has in fact a far more jaded source. To expand on his point about the mulatto census category, Hutchinson cites Joel Williamson's *New People: Miscegenation and Mulattoes in the United States* (1980). In that assertive social history, Williamson points out that the "census of 1920 was the last count of mulattoes made in the United States," and from this Williamson concludes that "insofar as the Bureau of the Census was concerned, all Negroes did look alike."[21]

Williamson's conspiratorial tone has since crescendoed, finding its way into studies of Toomer that see the Census Bureau's unbending agenda as antithetical to Toomer's polyethnic "New Americanism." In his *Dialect of Modernism* (1994), for example, Michael North argues that the withered options on post-1920 census schedules "may have made the choice of racial allegiance for someone like Toomer a good deal starker" than before. Discussing the collage aesthetic in *Cane,* and again citing Williamson, Rachel Farebrother subsequently offered that the disappearance of "mulatto" from census racial categories "reflects a shift from recognition of biracial and interracial identity to the complete segregation of the population according to the one drop rule, which was accompanied by the rigid enforcement of racial difference through Jim Crow laws. Toomer was fully aware of the hardening racial boundaries." Against this winnowing conformity to a black/white racial binary, Farebrother asserts, Toomer's avant-garde poetry and prose proposes instead "a liquefaction and softening of racial boundaries," a rendering of the racial order that defies bureaucratic compartmentalization.[22]

This brings us back to Byrd and Gates, who, rather than take up Toomer's shifting and sometimes contradictory statements about racial identity, instead scoured the public record for hard evidence about the Toomer family background and thus about Jean's racial allegiance or disloyalty. To answer their "vital question"—"Was Jean Toomer a Negro who passed for white?"—Byrd and Gates pored over census records from 1850 to 1920 to determine that "Jean Toomer's mother, father, grandfather, and grandmother all self-identified as Negroes." Then they looked to the 1917 draft registry, which lists Toomer as Negro. Then it's on to the 1920 census, which "shows Toomer boarding with other lodgers in the house of an Italian couple on East Ninth Street in Manhattan. He is assigned New York as a birthplace, suggesting that someone else responded on his behalf, in his absence. His race is listed as 'white.'" On the 1930 census form, "Toomer is listed as a resident, with many others, at 11 Fifth Avenue, in Manhattan. Because of the accuracy of other data contained in this document—including his birthplace, his parents' states of birth, and his occupation as a freelance writer—it is likely that he furnished these details himself. His race is listed as white." A later draft registry identifies Toomer as Negro, but a marriage certificate lists Toomer and his wife, the writer Margery Latimer, as white.[23]

According to Byrd and Gates, "These documents reveal that Jean Toomer self-identified as Negro in 1917, when he first registered for the draft. Then either he or a roommate decided to identify him as 'white' in the federal census of 1920. Similarly, Toomer self-identified as 'white' in the 1930 census and a year later on his marriage license with Margery Latimer. . . . In the course of twenty-five years between his 1917 and 1942 army registrations, Toomer was endlessly deconstructing his Negro ancestry."[24] The inconsistencies, Byrd and Gates concluded, demonstrate Toomer's unwillingness to commit to his true, ancestral racial heritage; instead, Toomer eagerly passes as white when given the chance. As if selecting from among the clichés offered by the tragic mulatto stereotype, Toomer chooses his wife's racial identity over that of his parents and grandparents.

There are, however, a few glitches in Byrd and Gates's analysis.

The first stems from a misunderstanding of census and draft registry policy and a subsequent misreading of census documents. Most important, we cannot attribute agency on the part of a person counted in a census enumeration, particularly with respect to racial identity. Before 1970, census enumerators were solely responsible for determining the racial identity of a person counted, and in most decades they were specifically instructed on how to reach such a determination. Very often the instructions governing one census were superseded by contradictory instructions for the following census. In 1920, for example, the instructions required the enumerator—not the person counted—to record "all Negroes of full blood" as "black" and to record "all Negroes having some proportion of white blood" as "mulatto." In 1930, they were instructed to record as "Negro" any "person of mixed white and Negro blood . . . no matter how small the percentage of Negro blood." These contrast sharply with the instructions for how to determine nationality or language use during the same censuses; these less visible data required the enumerator to ask specific questions of the person counted. The instructions for the 1870 census indicate just how fluid and contingent racial interpretation can be. That year, enumerators were instructed to "be particularly careful in reporting the class *Mulatto*. The word here is generic, and includes quadroons, octoroons, and all persons having any perceptible trace of African blood." The instructions further emphasized that "important scientific results depend upon the correct determination of this class."

With these instructions, the Census Bureau struck a balance between the language of subjective interpretation ("perceptible") on the one hand, and popular notions of precise blood fraction ("quadroons, octoroons") on the other hand. In other words, census enumerators determined "race" or "color" based largely on visual cues, but presumably also based on the enumerator's subjective understanding of the wider circumstances in which data were collected. To assume that Toomer's parents and grandparents "self-identified" as Negroes and that Toomer "self-identified as 'white' " grossly misapplies the data found on the census schedules.

The same cannot be said of Toomer's identification as Negro on his draft registration cards. In completing the 1917 draft registration, Toomer responded *in his own hand* to the simple question "Race (specify which)?" with "negro." Beginning in 1918, draft cards provided respondents with a choice of racial categories, first "White / Negro / Indian," and later "White / Negro / Oriental / Indian Citizen / Indian Non-Citizen." Draft cards in 1942—the so-called Old Man's Registration because the effort collected information about seasoned industrial workers rather than potential combatants—simply asked respondents to list their "race" without offering specific options.[25] Put simply, the draft cards rather than the census schedules provide a clearer window into how Toomer racially identified himself to the federal bureaucracy.

A closer look at the census schedule for 1920 reveals additional errors of historical interpretation on the part of Byrd and Gates.[26] Although Toomer shared a roof with "an Italian couple of East Ninth Street in Manhattan," the pair were not his landlords; rather, they were among the fifty or so other lodgers at the corner of East Ninth Street and Fifth Avenue, just two blocks north of Washington Square Park. (The census schedule shows the address as 6/8 East Ninth Street.) The young Italians were Daniel Martin, a musician, and his wife, Marie, both immigrants to the United States in 1906. On the schedule, the Martins are listed first among a group that includes Toomer, but still other groups at this address can be found further up the page and on the next page; no one at this address is described as head of household, as we might expect of a resident landlord. Like Toomer, most of these lodgers are fairly young, with well over half in their twenties or thirties; most are U.S.-born, but over half are the second-generation children of immigrants. Those who are employed typically work in a skilled trade or in a clerical profession: there are two stenographers, two translators, two medical students, and eight salespersons, including Toomer, whose occupation is listed as "salesman" and whose place of work is listed as "grocery."

All of the residents at 6/8 East Ninth Street are identified as "white"; in fact, of the one hundred persons counted by this census enumerator, Frank B. Guest, on January 21 and 22, 1920, every single person is listed as white. The sheer preponderance of those who appeared white at this and nearby addresses—including the lawyer and future New York Supreme

Court justice Samuel Seabury and the writer Alleyne Ireland—would incline Guest to assume that the olive-skinned Toomer was also "white," whether or not Guest interviewed Toomer in person. In a densely populated area such as Manhattan, residential segregation no doubt guided enumerators' decisions. Indeed, out of all 1,034 persons who lived in Toomer's census tract (Manhattan CT 59) in 1920, only three (0.3 percent) were Negro males and eleven (1.1 percent) were Negro females. (The Census Bureau did not report a distinction between "black" and "mulatto" at the census tract level.)

The 1930 census yields similar data about the contextual cues that would incline the enumerator, Franklin Howard, to record Toomer as "white" when he visited 11 Fifth Avenue and four additional apartment buildings on April 29, 1930. Howard collected data about roughly a hundred people on that Wednesday, almost all of whom are listed as white. Two of them, both servants on East Tenth Street, are listed as "Neg." for "Negro." Out of the 2,652 people who lived in Manhattan CT 59 in 1930, just five (0.2 percent) were Negro males and 13 (0.5 percent) were Negro females. The fifty or so people who shared an address with Toomer were mostly born in the United States, although a large number, nearly half, were second-generation Americans. These "guests" at 11 Fifth Avenue tend to represent the professions, with an architect, two attorneys, and a physician joining an artist (Alexandre Sach de Paris, a Romanian-born painter) and six writers, including Toomer, whose profession is listed as "writer" and his industry as "free lancer." Once again, the enumerator would likely assume that Toomer, like everyone else at 11 Fifth Avenue, was white.

It makes perfect sense that a writer such as Toomer, whose work underscores racial fluidity and who in vignettes from *Cane* such as "Fern" and "Bona and Paul" even brings up the difficulties of interpreting racial identity, would inspire critics to see him as somehow betrayed by the Census Bureau when it dropped the "mulatto" category after 1920. It also makes some sense that Byrd and Gates, whose prolific careers saw them emerge as authorities on African American literary culture, would want to authenticate, however uncomfortably, Toomer's racial background.

But both camps are equally guilty of still another historiographical error: the sin of omission.

That Toomer was a grocer (he worked for New York's Acker, Merrall & Condit Co.) rarely enters into discussions of his life and career. An obsession with how the census places Toomer into one or another racial category also ignores the unique feel of his Greenwich Village environment and downplays the sociological dimension of his existence. Never more than 350 feet from the headquarters of the avant-garde journal *Broom,* housed in the basement of a brownstone owned by his future wife, Marjorie Content, Toomer was continually surrounded by first- and second-generation Americans who fit the upwardly mobile profile popularized by Horatio Alger and Mary Antin.

That Toomer shared a roof with so many writers in 1930 has also gone unreported. The writers include Harold P. Davis, a journalist originally from Maine; Montague Glass, the Anglo-Jewish creator of the Potash and Perlmutter characters; the Tennessee-born novelist Charles B. Parmer; and Philip G. Wylie, the science fiction writer whose best-selling novel *Gladiator* (1930) later inspired the *Superman* comic books. Another writer listed at the same address, just above Toomer on the schedule (which suggests that they lived in adjacent apartments), is the mysterious Nels Jargenson, the divorced son of a Denmark native and a World War I veteran. Jargenson's occupation and employer are the same as Toomer's (writer / free lancer), but there exists no evidence of his life in print except perhaps as "Nels Jorgenson," a minor fictional character in Dashiell Hammett's *The Thin Man* (1934). The clustering of so many writers at one single location is not unusual, and in fact Toomer's neighborhood had previously been home to Mark Twain and Willa Cather, among many others; writers and artists no doubt cherished the cosmopolitan feel of the cafes at the Hotel Brevoort and the Hotel Lafayette, located less than a block from Toomer's doorstep.

The explosive population growth in this small part of Manhattan (from 1,034 in 1920 to 2,652 in 1930) was driven almost entirely by a surge in the number of native-born whites, who account for 1,409 of the census tract's 1,618 new residents during this time (table 1.1). As these data reveal,

Toomer's neighborhood of choice was increasingly white and decreasingly immigrant during the decade when Harlem came to be identified as the "Negro Metropolis." At the turn of the century, the immigrant enclaves west and south of Washington Square encroached on the pricier homes north of the square, including Toomer's apartments; as the social historian Caroline F. Ware somewhat crassly put it, "the substantial, middle-class complexion of the 'American Ward' was rudely destroyed by the erection of tenements . . . encircling, invading, and finally overrunning the Village in the closing years of the nineteenth century and the early years of the twentieth."[27] This "encircling" and "invading" is better characterized as an ebb and flow, one that depended on wider economic patterns.

TABLE 1.1. Manhattan census tract 59 population, 1920–1930

CENSUS CATEGORY	1920	1930	GROWTH RATE
White Male (native-born)	346 (33.5%)	1,028 (38.8%)	297.1%
White Male (foreign-born)	80 (7.7%)	279 (10.5%)	348.8%
Negro Male	3 (0.3%)	5 (0.2%)	166.7%
Other Male	3 (0.3%)	7 (0.3%)	233.3%
White Female (native-born)	388 (37.5%)	1,115 (42.0%)	287.4%
White Female (foreign-born)	203 (19.6%)	203 (7.7%)	100.0%
Negro Female	11 (1.0%)	13 (0.5%)	118.2%
Other Female	0 (0.0%)	2 (0.1%)	n/a

Source: Minnesota Population Center, National Historical Geographic Information System: Version 2.0. Minneapolis: University of Minnesota, 2011.

During the boom years of the 1920s, a gentrifying mix of real estate speculation and high rents brought to the Village a new crop of twentieth-century bohemians and pretenders who found nearby tenements quaint and who associated ethnic diversity with radical ideas about art and politics. In fact, because the rehabilitation of older buildings into luxury apartments was bounded in upper Manhattan by Negro Harlem, an influx of real estate capital poured into Greenwich Village redevelopment projects after World War I—a full $18 million between 1920 and 1930 alone.[28] Jean Toomer was one among many Villagers lured there by the charm and romance of its recent past, along with the latest in fashionable creature comforts.

It might be said that my splitting hairs with Toomer scholars owes much to the influence of W. E. B. Du Bois. Fresh off the publication of his groundbreaking study *The Philadelphia Negro* (1899), Du Bois, at the same time that he was working on *The Souls of Black Folk* (1903), set out to systematize the empirical study of the African American population. From his position in the Atlanta University sociology department, Du Bois carried out an ambitious program, practically inventing the field of Negro sociology with scores of conferences, seminars, field studies, statistical analyses, and publications for academic and lay audiences. As he put it in an address to Boston's Twentieth Century Club, Atlanta University was at the time "the single American institution of learning that is making systematic and conscientious study of the American Negro."[29] Because he had grappled with the problem firsthand, Du Bois understood well the importance of gathering solid data, information that could be trusted and compared across historical and geographic divides. He sought publicly and behind the scenes to make the U.S. census the key instrument for furthering what we now call African American studies.

Du Bois explained his reasoning and outlined a broad research program in his *Southern Workman* essay "The Twelfth Census and the Negro Problems" (1900). The research plan was to take place within a three-tiered institutional framework. The primary data collection would occur during the decennial census, and Du Bois indicated that "special pains should be taken to count and classify returns as to Negroes somewhat minutely and elaborately in a special census volume." The data would be handed off to a "Special Committee for the Study of the Negro Problems" composed of distinguished scholars and civic leaders, both black and white; this group would then "have general oversight of a series of social studies into the condition of the American Negro."[30]

With a proposed budget of up to $500,000, the group would outsource research questions to diverse teams of social scientists, and the committee would ultimately determine the scope and shape of public reports. Du Bois's grand blueprint never came into being; however, the Census

Bureau was already undertaking a similar effort, spearheaded by a Cornell University statistician, Walter F. Wilcox, and published as *Negroes in the United States* (1904). Wilcox, who later introduced his Cornell student Jessie Redmon Fauset to Du Bois, commissioned Du Bois in late 1902 to write one the volume's entries, "The Negro Farmer." *Negroes in the United States* would serve as the benchmark and model for similar studies published by the Census Bureau in 1915, 1916, and 1932; together these volumes underpin the emergence of African Americans as an object of statistical inquiry and the rise of African American studies as an academic discipline.

Although *Negroes in the United States* doesn't explore African American society at quite the level of depth envisioned by Du Bois, it nevertheless presents a comprehensive look at the subject. In "The Twelfth Census," Du Bois calls for examinations of 1) occupations and wages, 2) land, property, and taxation, 3) education, 4) crime and punishment, and 5) the right of suffrage. *Negroes in the United States* takes up the first three items to some extent, and paints the most complete demographic picture of the subject up to that time.[31] Perhaps as important for our contemporary understanding of African American identity, Wilcox's approach conforms entirely with Du Bois's stipulation in "The Twelfth Census" that "pains should be taken to count the Negro population thoroughly; to class those of African descent together and not to confound with them groups socially so diverse as the Japanese and Indians, to have especial care taken with the age classifications and the statistics of conjugal condition where large errors creep in among the Negro statistics for obvious reasons."[32] Each of these aspects of Du Boisian methodology deserves attention, but for the present I wish to focus on the first: the classification of all persons of African descent under a single banner, whether this be "black folk" or, as Du Bois more often put it, "Negroes."[33]

Throughout *Negroes in the United States,* Wilcox considers the reliability of his data. For example, he points out that "when [the enumerator] classifies by observation alone (and it must be borne in mind that he usually sees personally only a small portion, perhaps not more than one-fifth, of the persons about whom he reports), he must judge some families to be negro that are really white and some to be white that are really negro"; most of the errors, he continues, will be of the latter sort, the mistaking of Negroes for white. Seen in this light, some measure of bureaucratic "passing" seems unavoidable. On the specific question of intraracial color distinctions he sides squarely with Du Bois. Although Wilcox dutifully reports data on the number of mulattoes, he dismisses the number's accuracy. For one thing, the "percents of mulattoes to all negroes in some states differ so widely from census to census as to cast grave doubts upon the results." When it comes to the tortured congressional requirements placed on the 1890 census, Wilcox observes that "no competent authority will claim that a census can obtain trustworthy information regarding the intermixture of the two races in the detail in which it was called for by the law of 1889."[34] But Wilcox has little doubt concerning the ontological value of the mixed-race category: in his view, there exists a species of American known as the mulatto, and the census confirms that between one-ninth and one-sixth of all Negroes in the continental U.S. deserve the label.

Du Bois, on the other hand, tended to deploy the concept of the mulatto rhetorically, even when the veneer of demography reinforced the potency of his message. In *Souls,* for example, he decries the "two millions of mulattoes" who testify to the sexual violence perpetrated against female slaves.[35] Here Du Bois cares more about the magnitude than the specificity of the tally. In subsequent years he would point to the elaborate West Indian racial caste system as a means to discredit the political philosophy of Marcus Garvey. (Du Bois held that Garvey was blinded by a fixation on intraracial color difference.) In his role as foundational social scientist, however, Du Bois rarely even mentions intraracial color difference, and he never makes a distinction between blacks and mulattoes the basis of social analysis. The problem of the previous century, he put forward, was the problem of *the* color line, singular. In 1930, the U.S. census recorded Du Bois as a "Negro" for the first time in his life; prior to that point, he had been counted among the "mulatto" population. But throughout his career, including his early career as an activist scholar, Du Bois insisted that the civil rights agenda required intraracial solidarity and interracial cooperation.

Du Bois and Wilcox were entirely correct to distrust mixed-race census data, which emerged from a pseudoscientific belief in interracial degeneracy. Although racist social scientists hoped to demonstrate that mulatto offspring were less healthy and less likely to reproduce than their racially "pure" parents, the facts as they actually emerged told another story: the proportion of mulattoes among the overall Negro population grew from 11.2 percent in 1850 to 13.2 percent in 1860, fell slightly to 12.0 percent in 1870, and rose again to 15.2 percent in 1890. (Although enumerators were instructed to collect data concerning the mulatto population in 1880, the Census Bureau did not report figures for that year.)

The pseudoscientific efforts to collect mulatto population data, led by people like the Massachusetts physician Edward Jarvis and the Alabama physician Josiah Nott, reached their apex with the 1890 census, which advised enumerators to "be particularly careful to distinguish between blacks, mulattoes, quadroons, and octoroons." The instructions further clarified that the "word 'black' should be used to describe those persons who have three-fourths or more black blood; 'mulatto,' those persons who have from three-eighths to five-eighths black blood; 'quadroon,' those persons who have one-fourth black blood; and 'octoroon,' those persons who have one-eighth or any trace of black blood." Partly because the Census Board distrusted the mixed-race data gathered in 1890—and partly because *Plessy v. Ferguson* (1896) rendered subtle racial distinctions largely moot within the context of American social relations—the "mulatto" category disappeared from the 1900 census. Subsequently, race statisticians, Census Bureau officials, and their congressional allies struggled to restore the "mulatto" category in 1910 and 1920.[36] Beyond 1920, the category disappeared altogether from census schedules and from enumerator instructions, although since 1970 several thousand individuals have self-identified as mulatto on their census forms.

Simply considering the racial categories available on census schedules doesn't go far enough to indicate fully how shifting and contingent bureaucratic identity labels can be; we must keep in mind as well that census enumerators were charged with interpreting the racial identity of the individuals they counted until 1970, when respondents first self-selected their racial identity.[37] As we see with the 1890 census, the instructions' vastness and variety pose inherent interpretive difficulties. The instructions in 1910 identify as "black" "all persons who are evidently full-blooded negroes" and as "mulatto" "all other persons having some proportion or perceptible trace of negro blood." Adding to the potential confusion, in 1930 and 1940 the instructions included lengthy and elaborate explanations for how to consider Negro–Indian hybrids. The 1930 instructions put it this way: "A person of mixed Indian and Negro blood should be returned a Negro, unless the Indian blood predominates and the status as an Indian is generally accepted in the community." The language of interpretive discretion—"distinguish," "evidently," "perceptible," "generally accepted"—simultaneously presumes the objective truth of a dubious ontological proposition (the existence of "pure-blooded" whites, Indians, or Negroes) and leaves much room for variation and human error.

In a study titled *Negro Population, 1790–1915* (1918), the Census Bureau acknowledged that "perceptibility [of racial difference] is dependent upon the ability of the enumerator to perceive, and this ability varies from enumerator to enumerator."[38] Indeed, the Census Bureau admitted in 1921 that the previous year's census left "considerable uncertainty" regarding the "classification of Negroes as black and mulatto," given that the distinction was left to "the judgment and care employed by the enumerators."[39] It turns out that the racial identity of the enumerator played a role in determining the racial background of the person counted. In 1928, the Census Bureau reported that it was giving up on the distinction between "black" and "mulatto" partly because "it was suggested that the increase in the percentage mulatto shown by the 1910 census [over the 1890 census] was probably the result of the employment of large numbers of Negro enumerators and that this might explain the decrease in the percentage mulatto between 1910 and 1920," since there were fewer Negro enumerators in 1920 than 1910.[40] In other words, "Negro" enumerators were more likely than "white" enumerators to identify the same person as "mulatto" rather than as "black." Negro enumerators, apparently, saw race more often as a widely varied spectrum and indicated "mulatto" identity with greater frequency—just how much greater frequency is unknown. (The Census Bureau makes no mention of mulatto enumerators in its self-assessment.) Racial identity, as we frequently see in fiction, is in the eye of the beholder.

The parallel cultural myth, that a Negro can better tell than a white person when a fellow "Negro" is passing as "white," appears to have some basis in census history. Whether or not social science confirms cultural mythology, this much is certainly true: Census Bureau practices, though cloaked in the aura of statistical truth, are conditioned by cultural practices.[41] The Census Bureau would not think to count the number of "blacks" or "mulattoes" if the culture did not already posit the existence of such creatures; for that matter, the Census Bureau would not think to count a person as "white" if "whiteness" were not already offered by the culture as an objective fact. The census thus defines social reality and conditions cultural practices at the same time that it is conditioned and defined by them. Du Bois knew well that social reality mirrored cultural practices, but as an agenda-driven social scientist he also understood that the civil rights cause required clarity of vision. Toomer, by contrast, felt under no obligation to make life easy for cultural historians with a sociological bent. The best that we can do now to honor the range of possibility supplied by both Harlem Renaissance figures is to understand that the tactical or accidental use of identity labels is governed by an intricate web of historical, legal, and social pressures. No one simply *is* this or that race or ethnicity; we are made into ourselves and we can remake ourselves within limits.

The Pre-Postracial President and the Politics of Racial Self-identification (1940–2010)

The twentieth century saw four important census trends that bear directly on this study. First, the census validated the social-scientific approach to race and ethnicity, even while noted cultural anthropologists and well-known creative writers discredited the supposed biological basis of racial difference. Beginning in the late nineteenth century, presidential administrations began appointing census directors based on their long and distinguished track records in the statistical sciences, although political patronage continued to play a role with a few appointments. Since 1950, every Census Bureau director has had an extensive research background; most have been highly regarded academics, and a few had backgrounds in corporate or think-tank research. Even when a director lacked a background in statistics or economics, he or she relied heavily on the bureau's increasingly professionalized staff. In this sense, the evolution of the Census Bureau mirrored the professionalization of the academy.

The continual effort to perfect enumeration, statistical sampling, and social analysis within the Census Bureau and among those who deploy its data sidesteps ontological questions (Who is "white"? What does "Negro" mean?) and places attention instead on less labyrinthine issues that boost short-term policy analysis (What was the undercount among rural Hispanic males? What is the mean level of educational attainment among urban African American women between ages 25 and 34?). This is precisely the effect that Du Bois and Wilcox sought to achieve: the most accurate possible count of America's widely accepted racial groups. Because the post-Depression era welfare state relies on census data for the allocation of resources, social advocacy and civil rights organizations reacted predictably.

Second, civil rights organizations began leveraging the scientific imprimatur of the census at the same time that they actively lobbied to bring Census Bureau practices in line with a civil rights agenda. For example, the very first number of *The Crisis* (November 1910) quotes two references to census data in its "Opinion" page compilation, and the magazine cited census data repeatedly, as unimpeachable fact, during Du Bois's tenure as editor.[42] (There are even cases in which Du Bois cites the data that he compiled for *Negroes in the United States.*) National Association for the Advancement of Colored People (NAACP) leadership maintained a steady correspondence with Census Bureau officials, perhaps none more than Charles E. Hall, who for decades served as the bureau's Specialist in Negro Statistics and who was a leading Negro figure in Washington politics. Hall prepared the important Census Bureau compendium *Negroes in the United States, 1920–32* (1935), a massive publication (845 pages) that grew out of the original, less exhaustive volume put together by Wilcox and Du Bois.[43] (Hall's study, it should be noted, dispenses with the "mulatto" category.)

Such lobbying has continued. In anticipation of the 2000 census, the NAACP convention of 1998 adopted a resolution launching a cooperative effort with the Census Bureau to achieve a thorough count of the African American population. In 2010, the NAACP undertook an extensive push—the Yes We Count Census Campaign—to publicize the importance of the census and to encourage full participation in the tally. Still other civil rights organizations, from the League of United Latin American Citizens (LULAC) to the United Sikhs, have lobbied the Census Bureau to alter its racial and ethnic categories or to improve its outreach and enumeration methods.[44]

Third, and important for my argument about the Harlem Renaissance era, the shift toward racial self-identification in the 1960s has had profound sociocultural consequences. One outcome of this shift is that we can now assume census records to be reasonable approximations of individuals' racial self-identity. At least once per decade, the census requires Americans to ponder which of the Census Bureau's racial categories best fits their family background and present-day sensibility. Another outcome is that social advocacy and civil rights groups now lobby their own constituencies as well as Census Bureau officials. The NAACP gains clout if the nation possesses large numbers of persons who refer to themselves as something along the lines of "colored people"; LULAC represents a larger constituency if more Americans claim a "Latin American" background. Both groups invest precious resources to ensure that their constituencies participate fully in the decennial census; some of their leaders advocate for a pared-down self-reporting of racial identity based on the premise that a multiracial option might dilute political influence.

Fourth, racial self-identification in the U.S. census introduces an existential dimension to demography at the personal and social levels. Civil rights groups reflect upon their own names and sometimes fidget over how these measure up against the preferred tags of officialdom; these same organizations stress racial and ethnic group cohesion no matter how comfortably they fit within a bureaucratic nomenclature. At the individual level, racial self-identification turns out to be a ritual to test the strength of bonds between self and family, between the present and various genealogical pasts.

To some extent, all four of these trends played out when, on March 20, 2010, President Barack Obama filled out the census questionnaire at his Oval Office desk. The national media reported the event and located great significance in Obama's choice: he marked "Black, African Am., or Negro." The man who in *Dreams from My Father* (1995) reflects poignantly on the ironies and paradoxes of his mixed-race background—he describes himself alternately as "black" and "brown," and he acknowledges that Americans often project "the mixed blood, the divided soul, the ghostly image of the tragic mulatto" onto his person—claimed a singular racial identity even though the census form allowed the option of checking multiple categories simultaneously.[45]

Public reaction to the president's choice was swift and quite often severe. When the conservative columnist Abigail Thernstrom wrote in the *Wall Street Journal* that Obama's choice effectively "disowned his white mother and, by extension, his maternal grandparents who acted as surrogate parents for much of his boyhood," she—wittingly or not—deployed the tragic mulatto motif that more often serves liberal voices of racial authenticity. At the other end of the political spectrum, the legal scholar Patricia J. Williams saw the president's choice as less from among myriad categories than one of being "black/non-black," suggesting that African Americans have less room to racially self-fashion than other traditionally nonwhite persons. Seen in this light, Obama could only disavow his black father; any claim of whiteness on his part would sever his father's branch from the family tree. It would mean disappearing in the hazy ether of a postracial society, a space that is purely theoretical to persons of African descent: "Most who appear phenotypically 'black' enjoy neither the privilege nor the inclination to play around on a government form designed to track and remediate generations of prejudice."[46] Both Thernstrom and Williams view choosing one or another racial category as irresponsible, either to one's twining family tree or to one's racial comrades. The responsibility, then, is either to the past or to the present (and future), not to both. Had Obama chosen otherwise on the census questionnaire, he would no doubt be lauded or vilified for yet another set of reasons.

We prefer to think of our presidents and poets as somehow transcending overly simple distinctions such as the ones posed on census forms. The writers of the Harlem Renaissance surely represent the humanist resistance to bureaucratic pigeonholing. And yet the retrospective diagnosis of the Harlem Renaissance as a narcissistic failure, popularized during the Black Arts era, gains in persuasive power when considered in light of the grim realities of a society that required brute oversimplification as a counterweight to plain old brutality. The following chapter brings us back to the heyday of the Harlem Renaissance, a moment when the social sciences began to understand individual psychology, individual character, as governed by predictable but hardly simplistic rules of behavior. Indeed, when we consider multiple facets of identity simultaneously, the game rapidly becomes complex indeed.

2

Harlem Society

Practicing Theory

Games People Play

You have seen how a slave was made a man; you shall see how a man was made a statistic. What happens when one's self-understanding requires an appreciation of bureaucratic abstraction? How does literature respond beyond the obvious, anti-bureaucratic satire of, for example, Dickens and Twain? This chapter explores the Harlem Renaissance's fascination with observable social identities, namely, skin color and gender, and with quantifiable outcomes of social behavior, most obviously heterosexual marriage. At times the wish to measure, even in fiction, follows tantalizing pathways. Wallace Thurman and Zora Neale Hurston were particularly adept at deploying, in their trademark jaundiced way, the tools of fiction to explore issues that preoccupied twentieth-century social scientists. This much—that Hurston and Thurman were keenly interested in racial and gender attitudes—is already well known. What is striking about their work is the extent to which they also deployed the tools of social science, including the emergent discourse of game theory, within a fictive context.

When the Macaulay Company, a New York publishing firm, brought out Thurman's first novel, *The Blacker the Berry*, in March 1929, it promised a book that exposed for the first time, according to the dust jacket, "the peculiar conflicts that exist within negro society." And the dust jacket acclaims the author "a novelist of the first magnitude."[1] Thurman's novel traces the early life of Emma Lou Morgan as she travels from Boise to Los Angeles to Harlem, always in search of personal and professional fulfillment. Along the way, she encounters the "peculiar conflict"—intraracial color prejudice, or "colorism"—because her skin is, according to the novel's third-person narrator, "too black": she appears to have been "dipped, as it were, in indigo ink when there were so many more pleasing colors on nature's palette."[2] Unable to find a job worthy of her intelligence or ambition, Emma Lou instead works as a maid for a white Broadway actress. Unable to find a suitably genteel social niche, Emma Lou instead entertains suitors who gladly use her for a body that they won't be seen with in public. Emma Lou is her own severest critic, for she has studied and internalized the racial hierarchy that privileges proximity to whiteness above all else. She wallows in self-pity and self-contempt, finding neither happiness nor a settled home because she projects, rightly or not, a distaste for blackness on everyone else's words and deeds.

With its initial publication, *The Blacker the Berry* gently stoked the fire of controversy set in previous years by Carl Van Vechten's *Nigger Heaven* (1926) and Claude McKay's *Home to Harlem* (1928), novels that similarly delve into the seedy depths of Harlem life. Reviewing Thurman's novel in *Opportunity* magazine, Eunice Hunton, an activist in the Pan African Congress and later a pioneering district attorney, lashed out against its "immaturity" and "gaucherie."[3] Alain Locke, the so-called dean of the Harlem Renaissance, went a step further in calling Thurman's novel "sophomoric in style and downright exhibitionist in psychology."[4] Even critics who weren't put off by the book's overt sexuality or by its sharp critique of intraracial prejudice, who in fact applaud Thurman for taking up the touchy subjects, sometimes found the book poorly written. An anonymous *New York Times* reviewer found *The Blacker the Berry* a kind of second-rate *Home to Harlem* because Thurman's narrator fails to inhabit satisfactorily Emma Lou's consciousness, writing that Thurman "gives the effect of objectivity where subjectivity is demanded."[5] More recently, Emily Bernard cites the novel's "multiple weaknesses" in her analysis of its "complex rendering of white characters."[6] Bernard W. Bell finds that the narrator offers a "simplistic sociopsychological explanation of the effects of racism primarily for the benefit of white and middle-class readers."[7] Thurman considered his own novel "lousy" and "scorched with propaganda."[8]

The notion that *The Blacker the Berry* misses the mark artistically because it is "scorched with propaganda" might place Thurman among the many contemporaneous writers who were or still are deemed "too political" or "too sociological" in some quarters: John Dos Passos, Mike Gold, Grace Lumpkin. But even considering Thurman's stint as managing editor of the left-leaning *Messenger,* no one would ever locate Thurman within the tradition of proletarian fiction represented by this short list. Still, here I would like to insist on the novel's interest in a more conservative branch of economic theory just beginning to crystallize around the time of its initial publication. Specifically, *The Blacker the Berry,* in its "objectivity" and "sociopsychological" leanings, enacts a sophisticated version of game theory when the discipline was just in its infancy, a full decade and a half before John von Neumann and Oskar Morgenstern's *Theory of Games and Economic Behavior* (1944) brought it into sharp focus for academics and lay readers alike.

Humanists may bristle at game theory's relentless drive to quantify human behavior, or the implication that self-interest drives decision making, but even the most simplistic definition of the discipline leaves room for human agency and, although the agents are mere mathematical models, "self"-determination. That's because game theory relies on narrative—its structure and the gaps implied by narrative structure—to explicate human behavior. A game (to quote one popular textbook on the subject) represents "any interaction between agents that is governed by a set of rules specifying the possible moves for each participant and a set of outcomes for each possible combination of moves." For this reason, "a theory of games promises to apply to almost any social interaction where individuals have some understanding of how the outcome for one is affected not only by his or her own actions but also by the actions of others."[9]

A game specifies the basic rules, but the precise outcomes of interaction between agents shifts depending on a number of variables, much as a literary genre outlines a set of conventions but not the specific arrangement or outcomes of the text. Each game is recognizable as an example of a familiar pattern, but no two iterations of a game are necessarily alike. By shifting game theory's emphasis on social interaction only slightly, we've entered the territory of character development, of plot and narrative sequence, of narrative focus and reliability, of irony. Classic games in the discipline's repertoire bear names indicating an open-ended, playful version of storytelling (or retelling, since many theoretical games are inspired by cultural archetypes): battle of the sexes, prisoner's dilemma, princess and monster.[10]

Historians of game theory have lately looked to its founders' roots in interwar Eastern Europe—von Neumann's experiences as a Jew in Budapest and Morgenstern's background among the economic literati of Vienna—to help explain their rationalist approach to understanding and responding to conflict. The shock and existential threat posed by Nazi occupation, the economic historian Robert Leonard observes, drew the exiled von Neumann toward collaboration with the similarly displaced Morgenstern and eventually inspired von Neumann to apply the field's insights to the wartime intelligence effort.[11] Multi-agent games rehearse genetic imperatives—maximal outcomes might take the shape of survival, wealth accumulation, or reproduction—and the novel is arguably the cultural vehicle best suited to record games that play out historically, even across multiple generations. Game theory has recently animated discussions of literary form, and perhaps it should surprise no one that the two most prominent examples of this scholarly approach center on narratives that interrogate the gendered and racial logic of romantic possibility, property rights, and inheritance. Thus, Michael Suk-Young Chwe reads Jane Austen's characters alongside those found in African American folk tales, and Thadious M. Davis grounds an understanding of Faulkner's characters within the elaborate rules of a chess match.[12]

As in most theoretical games that contemplate romantic relationships, Thurman tends to construct social situations in *The Blacker the Berry* with a particular fixation on similarly aged, gender-balanced groups: a few young men interact with a few young women within a finite social space. In other words, Thurman allows demography and geography to introduce the theme of sexual competition. Following the universally acknowledged truth, young men in the novel compete for the attention of marriage-minded women (and vice versa).

As she's trying to settle into her new life on the University of Southern California campus, Emma Lou encounters "a group of five Negro students, three boys and two girls, standing near a water fountain." Emma Lou is "both excited and perplexed" to meet the group, to find a natural place as the sixth person rounding out three young couples. But she cannot quite figure out how to break the ice: "five people in one bunch all known to one another and all chatting intimately together!—it would seem too much like an intrusion to go bursting into their gathering—too forward and too vulgar." Little does Emma Lou know that the five are talking derisively about her, referring to her alternately as a "pick" (for pickaninny) or as a "Hottentot." The narrator points out that "Emma Lou, of course, knew nothing of this." Instead, "she had gone her way rejoicing" because one of the five, an empathetic coed, returned Emma Lou's sheepish smile.[13] The narrator's knowing intrusion at this important moment may have irked Thurman's critics, but Thurman sacrificed greater subjectivity in the service of dramatic irony, which can only be witnessed from an objective distance; specifically, the narrator highlights what game theorists would label Emma Lou's "imperfect knowledge," her inability to grasp the others' motives. The narrator and reader, by way of contrast, are equipped with "perfect information": we understand that Emma Lou is misguided in her assumption that the five students welcome her presence.

The free-floating, objective narrator gives us a glimpse into the "peculiar" logic—intraracial colorism—governing social dynamics at each of the settings that the novel surveys. Thurman accentuates the influence of social environment on character identity formation by revealing each new locale in *The Blacker the Berry* to be a hermetically sealed and relatively static system, a Petri dish of Negro society. The novel describes Emma Lou's home in Boise as "a semi-white world, totally surrounded by an all-white one," a place with no room for a thoughtful, upwardly mobile black woman. Although she hoped to find Los Angeles filled with "intelligent, broad-minded people of all complexions, intermixing and too occupied otherwise to worry about either their own skin color or the skin color of those around them," Emma Lou instead discovers the USC campus to be an alien, unwelcoming environment: "When she joined the various groups which gathered on the campus lawn between classes, she always felt excluded and out of things because she found herself unable to participate in the general conversation. They talked of things about which she knew nothing, of parties and dances, and of people she did not know."[14] Her small corner of Los Angeles proves as inhospitable as Boise.

And Harlem turns out to be less a Negro Mecca than an anxiety-inducing maze of impenetrable crowds, towering buildings, and stifling rooms. The view from Emma Lou's dank, dingy apartment offers "no privacy . . . , little fresh air, and no natural light after the sun began its downward course." Worse yet, "Fish smells and cabbage smells pervaded the long, dark hallway, swirled into the room when the door was opened, and perfumed one's clothes disagreeably. Moreover, urinal and fecal smells surged upward from the garbage-littered bottom of the court which her window faced."[15] The urban landscape and the social world are for Emma Lou unsolvable riddles, but for Thurman they're a well-appointed laboratory to conduct social experiments. Emma Lou is his primary subject.

We might follow the plot of *The Blacker the Berry* along the lines deployed by game theorists, with a decision tree to track key plot elements and a matrix to record the rewards and penalties of pivotal decisions within the larger plot structure. As these decisions largely revolve around employment opportunities and romantic liaisons, each matrix would be fairly simple and, in a social world skewed by male supremacy and colorism, tend in one direction. Because no true choice is required, this payoff matrix, shown in table 2.1, does not actually exist within traditional game theory.

TABLE 2.1. Game one: heads or tails

	CHOOSE EMMA LOU	CHOOSE ANOTHER
Employer/Suitor Decision	+1, +1	0, +2

Here, the asymmetrical results work against Emma Lou because in a male dominated, colorist society, male suitors or employers choose an individual not just because of her intrinsic worth, but also because of the social capital that she might bring to a relationship (romantic or professional). Thus what might otherwise appear to be a simple yes/no (or heads/tails) dynamic in reality requires an understanding of the unequal value of yes and no for different individuals with varied skin colors. In this example, Emma Lou and a suitor/employer each attain value (+1) from her selection; however, when a suitor or employer chooses another, lighter-skinned woman in her place, he accrues not just the other woman's intrinsic value but also the value attributed to her by society (+2). (In each cell of the table, the first number represents Emma Lou's reward, and the second number represents her suitor's/employer's reward.) For the status-minded suitor or the profit-minded businessman, the choice is a simple one: the coin always lands on tails. Emma Lou is left with nothing. But of course, even in a fictional world the risks and rewards of individual choices rarely tilt so strongly for one person and against another.

Gender balance—the number of men relative to the number of women—complicates matters of the heart. In *The Blacker the Berry,* Emma Lou sets her sights on one suitor at a time, whereas male suitors have multiple romantic options that require more or less emotional commitment on their typically selfish part. The men in Emma Lou's life will take up with her as a sexual partner, and they might even indulge her for a dance or two, but they see little or no reward in more full-fledged romantic involvement. As the novel's character dynamics increase in complexity, we must update the matrix accordingly, as shown in table 2.2.

TABLE 2.2. **Game two: hawk and dove**

	SUITOR CHOOSES COURTSHIP	SUITOR CHOOSES SEX
Emma Lou Chooses Courtship	+2, -1	-1, +1
Emma Lou Chooses Sex	+1, -1	+1, +2

I have scored the payoff matrix as an asymmetrical adaptation of the "hawk-dove" (or "chicken") game, which rewards cooperation or competition across a range of payouts. In this matrix, Emma Lou chooses a row and the suitor chooses a column. (Once again, the first number represents Emma Lou's reward, and the second number represents her suitor's reward.) Emma Lou would most of all like a serious courtship that might possibly lead toward marriage (+2), but she also enjoys sex outside of a serious relationship (+1). When she exposes her emotions by seeking a serious courtship but is used for sex, she feels emotional pain (–1). The suitor has only sex in mind; courtship with Emma Lou is not an option (–1), because social pressures and armchair genetics render the left-hand column a purely theoretical exercise. As the narrator informs us, the novel's characters "want to keep their children and grandchildren from having dark complexions; it was therefore found expedient to exercise caution when it came to mating."[16] The suitor prefers uncomplicated sex with Emma Lou (+2), but he will pursue Emma Lou for sex even when her desire for courtship poses unwanted entanglements (+1).

Because characters in *The Blacker the Berry* do not communicate their desires openly, what is the most rational choice for Emma Lou and her would-be romantic partners? The answer, as the novel reveals in example after frustrating example, is obvious. The best possible outcome for all parties is discreet, emotionally uninvolved sex. But Emma Lou's desire for true love, perhaps even a husband, sometimes renders her irrational. She will go so far in this search as to ignore all evidence to the contrary, to ignore the game represented in this matrix: "It was the way of Emma Lou always to create her worlds within her own mind without taking under consideration the fact that other people and other elements, not contained within herself, would also have to aid in their molding. She had lived to herself for so long . . . that she considered her own imaginative powers omniscient."[17] For this reason, which narrative analysis labels dramatic irony, Emma Lou makes for a very poor game theorist and she sets herself up for regret.

Thurman's seemingly endless supply of disappointment for Emma Lou targets the distorted logic and distorting pressure exerted by early twentieth-century racial discourse. Hostile critics of *The Blacker the Berry* rightly point out that the novel directs cannon fire against colorism even when the situation calls for a marksman's aim. Few care to read a novel as predictable as the matrices shown here reveal. But predictability is precisely Thurman's point: the novel critiques African American society for adopting white America's color prejudice tout court. Unless and until African American society evolves toward a more sophisticated appreciation of individual character, Thurman insists, social outcomes will remain a humdrum matter of skin tone.[18]

The Pathology of Everyday Life

The cold sexual calculus of *The Blacker the Berry* merely annoyed Thurman's aesthetic critics, who would sneer at any narrative that evoked mathematical predictability, but the same indecorous tendencies inflamed his more genteel readers. For characters to apply highly impersonal reasoning to women's virtue smacks of decadence, and it surely signals the Jazz Age's steep moral decline. Such straitlaced concern might also be located in early twentieth-century social thought, including some of the most influential studies of African American social life. Long before Daniel Patrick Moynihan's controversial Department of Labor report *The Negro Family* (1965) exposed a rift between black civil rights leaders and white liberals bent on social engineering, the sometimes strained dynamics of African American families entered into national conversations linking family structures, social conditions, and moral consequences. Indeed, the Moynihan Report's most trumpeted claims about African American family life—that "the deterioration of the Negro family" lies at "the heart of the deterioration of Negro society,"[19] that the dehumanizing effects of slavery and Jim Crow left a lasting negative imprint on family life, particularly (and perhaps ironically) in the urban ghetto—long informed social analysts who helped shape the Harlem Renaissance and who simultaneously created the discipline of African American studies.

The Philadelphia Negro (1899), W. E. B. Du Bois's pathbreaking sociological investigation of life in the Seventh Ward—at the time the largest concentration of African Americans in the nation—makes the disparaging point that the "lax moral habits of the slave régime still show themselves in a large amount of cohabitation without marriage." Du Bois estimated that as many as one in four unions in Philadelphia "slum districts" took place out of wedlock.[20] According to the sociologist E. Franklin Frazier, to take another well-known figure, Emancipation ruptured family structures that had previously been artificially and incompletely glued together by slavery: "Among the demoralized elements in the newly emancipated Negroes promiscuous sexual relationships and frequent changing of spouses became the rule."[21] Some newly freed mothers, Frazier adds, even abandoned their children in search of selfish personal fulfillment. Once uprooted from the rural plantation system and resettled in the big city, the reasoning goes, some behave as though wholly unmoored from moral foundations. Frazier observes:

> What is important in regard to these "tribeless" men and women is that they have become purely individuated and have developed a purely "rational" attitude not only toward the physical environment but also toward men and women. Consequently, we find some of these men maintaining themselves by exploiting women. In some of the bright-light areas of Negro communities in Chicago, Detroit, and New York, it is not unusual to hear these "pimps" boasting of the size of their "stables." Thus, sexual gratification has become entirely divorced from its human meaning and, like the women who supply it, has become a commodity.[22]

In Frazier's highly charged words we see the sociological equivalent of Thurman's coldly calculating, sexually obsessed fictional characters. This is the negative face of urban abstraction. The commoditization of sex might be "rational," but only in the skeptical sense indicated by Frazier's irony-supplying quotation marks. Moynihan's study, which provoked outrage within and beyond civil rights–era Washington, seems sheepishly guarded next to the paternalism of his African American scholarly sources or the exhibitionism of their fictive counterparts.[23]

Well aware that their comments mesh easily with racist stereotypes propagated for centuries, Du Bois and Frazier cautiously temper their observations with notice of mothers and fathers who sacrificed all to provide for their spouses and children, to preserve their families at any cost. Even so, their analyses at times resemble crude melodramas, as we find in Frazier's discussion of African American family life on the post-Emancipation plantation:

> Among a large proportion of Negroes in the plantation South, courtship begins at an early age through mutual attraction and often involves sexual relations. Where sex relations result in pregnancy, the young people may or may not marry. . . . The father of the child may suggest "marriage" because he wants a woman to provide a home for him and he in turn is willing to provide subsistence for his family. The woman's response to his offer of "marriage" depends upon the attitude of her parents or her desire to start a new family. . . . Moreover, even after the men and women have entered "marriage," they may not have a sense of guilt when they have outside affairs.[24]

We find here social investigation via anecdote. Frazier's theatrical discussion of individuals' motives lacks the compelling demographic data that underpin his analysis elsewhere. Unrestrained morality, he reasons, is a simple fact of life within damaged social systems. But Frazier's observations find implicit support in the fact that African American women had outnumbered African American men since the 1840s—dramatically so in the southern "black belt" and in many northern urban centers—and in the fact that the proportion of African American households headed by single women far exceeded the proportion of white households similarly headed by single women.[25] Comparative racial demography, along with an assumption that single-parent households must be somehow dysfunctional, hints at moral decay. Du Bois and Frazier further suggest that the matriarchal structure of many African American families results in a flouting of "traditional" moral values.

Like any number of early twentieth-century intellectuals, African American or otherwise, Du Bois and Frazier advance two gender stereotypes about social behavior predicated on a sexual double standard. First, when the number of unmarried women exceeds the number of eligible bachelors, women are more prone to engage in sex outside of marriage, particularly in anonymous urban settings, far away from the folk community's moral reach; women, it's assumed, use any means necessary, including their sexuality, to compete for a relatively scarce commodity: men. The "disproportion" of the female and male populations in Philadelphia, Du Bois argues, "still indicates an unhealthy condition, and its effects are seen in a large percent of illegitimate births, and an unhealthy tone in much of the social intercourse among the middle class of the Negro population."[26] Second, wherever children are present, an absent father means that a mother must remain an overtly sexual creature within the local marriage marketplace; she competes unnaturally for male attention against her childless counterparts.[27] As Kelly Miller, a Howard University mathematician and sociologist, put it in 1905, "Preponderance of one sex over the other forebodes nothing but evil to society."[28] Moynihan would subsequently be pilloried for labeling latter-day matriarchal societies "pathological."

The ~~Woman~~ Lady Question

Such worries on the part of Du Bois and Frazier and later Moynihan may strike twenty-first-century readers as the quaint concerns of a bygone era, but they provide a rich backdrop for understanding the social pressures of urban life in predominantly African American centers such as Harlem (the "center and symbol of the urban life of the Negro American," according

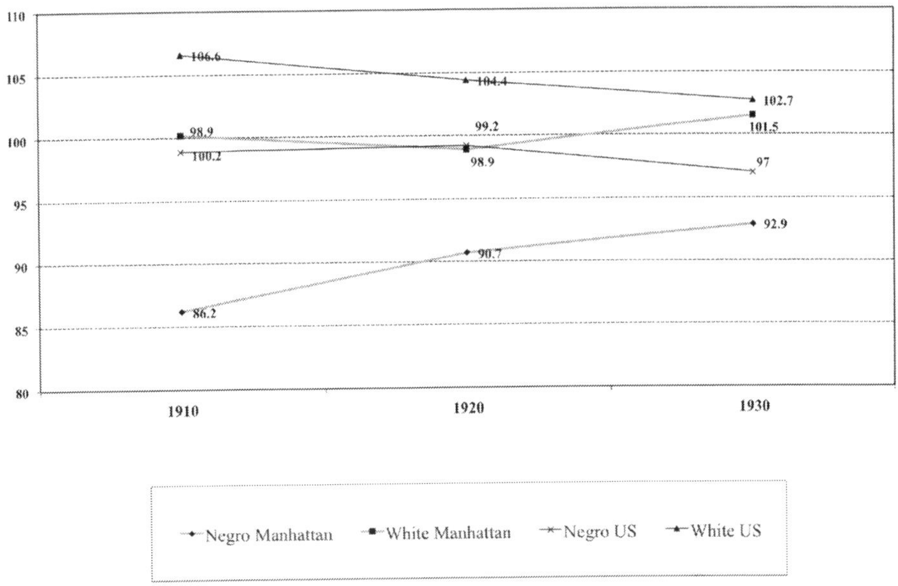

Figure 2.1. Sex ratios (males per 100 females) of Negro and white population for Manhattan and for the United States: 1910–1930. Source: U.S. Census Bureau, Thirteenth Census of the United States, Fourteenth Census of the United States, and Fifteenth Census of the United States.

to Moynihan).[29] A closer look at Harlem Renaissance social organization along gender lines helps us to better understand the real-world conditions animating social scientists and fiction writers alike.[30] As in many urban centers in the United States, females outnumbered males in the African American population in Harlem during the early part of the twentieth century, often by significant—Du Bois would say "unhealthy"—margins.

In 1930, the sex ratio (males per 100 females) in Harlem stood at 96.5, compared to 101.2 for the island of Manhattan, 100.4 for New York City, and 102.5 for the United States as a whole (fig. 2.1), a gender snapshot in keeping with most other large African American population centers. Of the nineteen African American–majority census tracts in Harlem, fifteen also had a majority of females, with sex ratios as low as 85.9. Of the eleven census tracts in Harlem with a population at least three-quarters African American, ten also had a female majority. In contrast, of the nine white-majority census tracts in Harlem, only three had a female majority, and of the three tracts with a population at least three-quarters white, only one had a female majority. In other words, the more African American the

Harlem locale, the more likely it was that females outnumbered males.[31]

As Harlem grew more and more African American over the years, its sex-ratio imbalance demonstrated a persistent racial gap, one that accelerated with time. That is, the white population that remained in Harlem as the century wore on, particularly the dwindling numbers of white immigrants, was increasingly male, whereas the growing African American population was increasingly female (table 2.3). Two trends are particularly striking with respect to the gender shift in early twentieth-century Harlem. First, and most obvious, is the widening sex imbalance among the African American population. In 1920, African American women in Harlem outnumbered African American men by 2,978; in 1930, the African American gender gap grew to 7,683; by 1940, the gender gap exploded to 23,657 (table 2.4). The striking gender imbalance among African Americans living in Harlem can be explained by economic factors that I will discuss shortly; the rate of gender imbalance change reflects the difficulties faced by African American men in a postindustrial economy.

TABLE 2.3. Harlem sex ratios by race and nativity, 1920–1940

	TOTAL	NEGRO	NATIVE WHITE	FOREIGN-BORN WHITE
1920	92.9	92.2	89.9	98.4
1930	96.5	91.6	96.0	124.0
1940	83.4	81.7	86.8	111.0

Source: Based on data supplied by the Minnesota Population Center, National Historical Geographic Information System: Version 2.0. Minneapolis: University of Minnesota, 2011.

TABLE 2.4. Harlem population by sex and race, 1920–1940

	NEGRO MALE	NEGRO FEMALE	WHITE MALE	WHITE FEMALE
1920	35,318	38,296	101,483	109,202
1930	83,731	91,414	46,511	44,141
1940	105,939	129,596	18,394	19,853

Source: Minnesota Population Center, National Historical Geographic Information System: Version 2.0. Minneapolis: University of Minnesota, 2011.

Second, and thus far overlooked within discussions of Harlem social life, is the rapid loss of the foreign-born white population relative to the native-born white population. Foreign-born whites were a much smaller part of the overall white population in 1940 than in 1920 (table 2.5). In a curious subplot to this shift, we must acknowledge a wide fluctuation within the sex ratios for native-born whites in Harlem. In 1920, native-born white women outnumbered native-born white men by 7,104; in 1930 this number dropped to 1,170; and in 1940 the number increased to 1,984. (Because the white population in Harlem was in a steep decline during this time, the shifts were proportionally larger with each decade.) The number of foreign-born white women plummeted faster than any other Harlem subgroup between 1920 and 1940, which meant that the overall white sex ratio evened out over time. In 1920, the white sex ratio in Harlem was 92.9; in 1930 it was 105.4; and in 1940 it was 92.7. In other words, a surplus of foreign-born white men mitigated the exodus of native white men from Harlem. Taken as a whole, these data confirm a social process that might easily be predicted: African Americans who arrived in Harlem during the so-called Great Migration took up low-wage jobs in the manufacturing and service economies that were previously held by recent immigrants.

TABLE 2.5. Harlem white population by sex and nativity, 1920–1940

	NATIVE MALE	NATIVE FEMALE	FOREIGN MALE	FOREIGN FEMALE
1920	29.9%	33.3%	18.3%	18.6%
1930	31.1%	32.4%	20.2%	16.3%
1940	34.2%	39.4%	13.9%	12.5%

Source: Based on data supplied by the Minnesota Population Center, National Historical Geographic Information System: Version 2.0. Minneapolis: University of Minnesota, 2011.

If we expand the scope of our study to include all of New York City, we can locate several distinct areas within Manhattan and the surrounding boroughs where men vastly outnumber women and many more where women outnumber men. Men predominate in those areas dense with recent immigrants to the United States, particularly downtown and the Lower East Side and just across the East River in Brooklyn. These particular census tracts are indicated in the sex-ratio map (fig. 2.2) in white and light gray. Women predominate in Harlem to some degree, and to a greater extent in midtown Manhattan, far Uptown (north of Negro

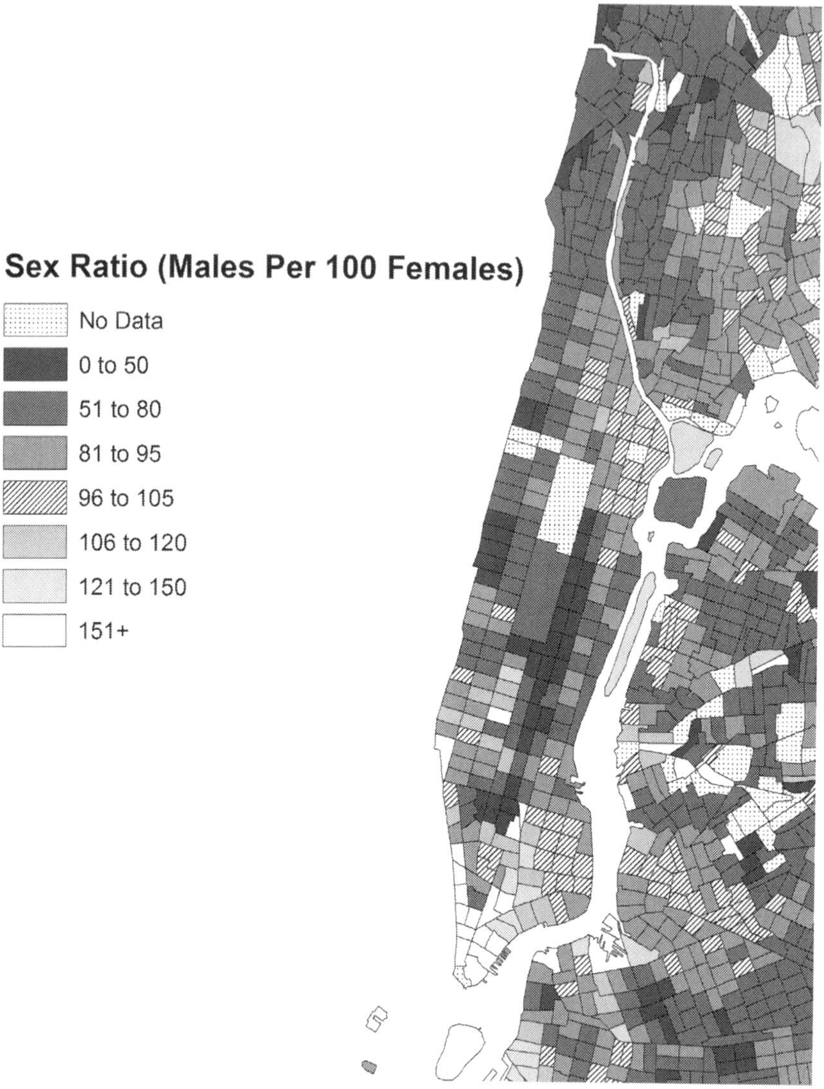

Figure 2.2. New York City sex ratios by census tract, 1930. Data courtesy Minnesota Population Center. National Historical Geographic Information System: Version 2.0. Minneapolis: University of Minnesota, 2011.

Harlem), and in the Bronx. These census tracts are indicated in darker shades of gray and black. Census tracts that are more or less evenly balanced with men and women are indicated with diagonal stripes. (No data are available for a few census tracts and data were not collected for Central Park; these are shown with dots.) In two Upper East Side census tracts adjacent to Central Park, the sex ratio in 1930 was as low as 21.0 (CT 142) and 27.6 (CT 150); this significant proportion of women (83 and 78 percent, respectively) stems from the high concentrations of foreign-born female domestic workers, hotel workers, and sweatshop workers who lived with or alongside New York's "Silk-Stocking District" gentry.

Low sex ratios in New York City in 1930 correlated most strongly with the percentage of foreign-born white females (with a correlation coefficient [*r*] of 0.446 across 3,056 census tracts), confirming that employment opportunities within the postindustrial service economy best explain the city's early twentieth-century social layout.[32] Female immigrants were better positioned than anyone else to climb the economic ladder; their social mobility derives from opportunities in the labor market and the marriage market that were denied to most others on the lower rungs of society. It must be stressed, moreover, that white immigrants had greater latitude to explore distant parts of Manhattan than their nonwhite counterparts, and that ethnic intermarriage has long been more common than racial intermarriage.[33]

It is also worth pointing out that sex ratios in predominately white areas of New York City defied geographic clustering. For example, a Lower East Side census tract with the extremely low sex ratio of 32.0 (CT 63) was contiguous to a census tract with the extremely high sex ratio of 177.8 (CT 57); these individuals might mingle freely during their leisure time in nearby Washington Square Park. In contrast, local instances of gender imbalance were felt more deeply in Harlem than in other parts of the city. As we see in, for example, Jessie Redmon Fauset's *Plum Bun* (1928), social taboos against interracial relationships had profound geosocial effects; the romantic lives of individual African Americans, at least those unwilling or unable to pass as white, were largely confined to a few city blocks in upper Manhattan, the Bronx, and Brooklyn. (Van Cortlandt Park in the Bronx, a slave plantation during the colonial and early national eras, is a rare multiracial, polyethnic retreat in *Plum Bun.*) As a result, social theorists tend to apply the sexual double standard—like Du Bois and Frazier, they interpret gender imbalance as a moral crisis—more stringently to African American enclaves than to more socially mobile white populations.

Among New York City's African American youth entering the age of sexual maturity, courtship, and marriage—that is, young men and women between the ages of 16 and 24—the gender imbalance is even more striking than it is for the overall African American population. The New York City Welfare Council reported a noteworthy snapshot of the city's youth population in 1930, shown in table 2.6. Seen another way, in 1930 the sex ratio for all New York City youth (white and black) was slightly imbalanced at 92.7; for white youth, the sex ratio stood at 93.4, whereas for African American youth the sex ratio stood at 75.4. (The sex ratio among youth belonging to "other races," in sharp contrast, stood at 301.9. The large majority of this number likely consisted of immigrant laborers from Asia.) In other words, if all African American youth in Harlem in 1930 gathered for a dance, for every seventy-five male–female couples on the dance floor, there would be another twenty-five partnerless young women waiting in the wings.[34] A statistical sample taken in 1935 saw a similarly racialized pattern emerge: the sex ratio among white youth in New York City was 93.5, whereas among African American youth it was 68.9.[35]

TABLE 2.6. Population over 16 years of age and under 25 in 1930

COLOR	BOTH SEXES		MALE		FEMALE	
	NUMBER	PERCENTAGE	NUMBER	PERCENTAGE	NUMBER	PERCENTAGE
Total	1,174,398	100.0	564,934	48.1	609,464	51.9
White	1,116,024	100.0	539,230	48.3	576,794	51.7
Negro	56,453	100.0	24,261	43.0	32,192	57.0
Other	1,921	100.0	1,443	75.1	478	24.9

Source: Nettie Pauline McGill and Ellen Nathalie Matthews, *The Youth of New York City* (New York: Macmillan, 1940).

What accounts for the preponderance of females among the African American population of Harlem? Simple economics supplies the most obvious answer: the urban service economy in early twentieth-century New York favored African American women over African American men. Indeed, a preponderance of African American women was an urban phenomenon across the United States; in urban areas, the African American sex ratio in 1930 was 91.3, whereas in rural areas it was 101.7.[36] Although

African American women faced an uphill climb in a labor market governed by tacit segregation and outright racism, they could nevertheless find work as domestics, as laundresses, and as hotel custodians much more easily than African American men could find work as industrial laborers.[37] Recall that in *The Blacker the Berry,* African American women with lighter skin filled the several jobs denied to Emma Lou.

New York City manufacturing was (even then) concentrated in very few neighborhoods, and recent immigrants from eastern and southern Europe performed much of this male-dominated work (table 2.7). According to Frazier, African American men vastly outnumbered African American women in a handful of northern industrial centers (table 2.8), and as a result the number of African American men slightly exceeded the number of African American women in the North overall. As Frazier observes, "In Massachusetts, Rhode Island, Connecticut, New York, and New Jersey, states in which Negro women have found employment, there has been an excess of Negro females." As we have seen, such was the case in Harlem. But at this point Frazier adds an important regional caveat: "However, in the industrial cities of New York, Pennsylvania, Ohio, and Indiana where there has been a demand for the labor of Negro men, there has been an excess of Negro males since 1900."[38] Frazier reasoned that, over a few decades, sex ratios among African American populations in industrial areas would tend to even out as greater employment opportunities presented themselves to both sexes. History, it turns out, proved Frazier wrong in this detail.

TABLE 2.7. **Manhattan population by race, sex, and nativity, 1910–1930**

	1910	1920	1930
Negro Female	32,510	57,221	116,441
Negro Male	28,024	51,912	108,229
White Female Native	589,688	636,746	499,429
White Male Native	572,871	610,080	490,709
White Female Foreign-Born	542,338	453,574	310,287
White Male Foreign-Born	561,681	468,506	331,331

Source: U.S. Census Bureau, Thirteenth Census of the United States, Fourteenth Census of the United States, and Fifteenth Census of the United States.

TABLE 2.8. Negro sex ratios in selected cities, 1910–1930

CITY	CENSUS YEAR		
	1910	1920	1930
Atlanta	81.0	85.8	79.6
Baltimore	85.5	95.4	97.2
Chicago	105.9	104.5	97.5
Detroit	108.3	137.0	107.6
Philadelphia	87.6	100.1	97.6
New York City	85.0	90.3	91.9
Manhattan	86.2	90.7	92.9

Source: U.S. Census Bureau, *Negroes in the United States, 1920–1932* (1935).

Writing in 1983, Marcia Guttentag and Paul F. Secord, the most influential sex-ratio analysts in the field of American social history, observed that "American blacks present us with the most persistent and severest shortage of men in a coherent subcultural group that we have been able to discover during the era of modern censuses." They attribute local sex imbalances to economic migration patterns, and a wider sex imbalance to higher rates of overseas military deployment and to higher rates of mortality among young African American adult males.[39] As table 2.9 shows, the mid-twentieth-century sex-ratio trend among young nonwhites (primarily African Americans) in select U.S. cities stands out as particularly striking.

TABLE 2.9. Sex ratios for nonwhites aged 20–24 in selected cities, 1930–1970

CITY	CENSUS YEAR				
	1930	1940	1950	1960	1970
Atlanta	65	65	74	79	76
Baltimore	87	82	82	79	76
Chicago	79	71	78	73	72
Detroit	87	77	81	69	79
Philadelphia	77	71	74	74	75
New York	76	59	68	73	72
Average Ratio	79	71	76	75	75

Source: Marcia Guttentag and Paul F. Secord, *Too Many Women? The Sex Ratio Question* (Beverly Hills: Sage, 1983).

As the figures in table 2.9 suggest, daily social life in African American enclaves—shopping, dining out, attending church services, strolling busy city streets—would be defined from the start by a preponderance of women. If our imaginary Harlem dance party took place in 1940, nearly half of the young women on hand (41 percent) would be without a partner. In more recent years, sociologists have found that sex-ratio imbalances tend to have a distorting effect on local marriage markets and family structures in both urban and rural settings. Where men outnumber women, families are more likely to follow the pattern widely viewed as "traditional" and "stable": two-parent households with children born in wedlock. Where women outnumber men—or in general where sex ratios tend to be lower—the family structure is more likely to depart from tradition: marriage rates are lower and children are more likely to be born out of wedlock and to live with a single parent.[40] In other words, the culture of family life that Moynihan labeled "pathological" might be better understood in terms of mathematical probability and predictability.

There's a simple logic to the family life described by Du Bois, Frazier, and Moynihan. According to one late twentieth-century study of African American family structures in urban areas, "the difference between 60 and 80 on the sex ratio . . . implied a difference of 10.2 points in the expected percentages of marital births for black women aged 15–19, a difference of 6.8 points in the expected percentage married for black women with children under age 6, and a difference of 4.8 points in the expected percentage of black children residing in husband-wife families."[41] Historically, a relatively balanced distribution of men and women leads to a higher proportion of married couples; what's more, because of women's relatively limited avenues for economic independence, where men outnumber women, women still tend to choose marriage over the uncertainties of single life in an inhospitable workplace. In other words, gender imbalance historically skews family structures in only one direction.

If we assume a stable influence throughout the century, the sex-ratio figures for 1930 mentioned earlier would predict many thousands of Harlem families headed by a single mother. A late 1930s survey conducted by the New York City Welfare Council adds credence to the hypothesis: out of 202 randomly sampled African American youth, 39.1 percent had no father at home, compared to 17.1 percent of white youth.[42] And because imbalanced African American sex ratios are historically a function of limited job opportunities with wide regional variation for men and women, "pathological" family structures are an American—not strictly an African American—problem. Socially disruptive family life is an economic problem, not a moral one. As Thurman implies quite strongly in *The Blacker the Berry,* Emma Lou's personal and professional challenges are mutually reinforcing and wholly beyond the scope of African American cultural adjustment. What's needed, Thurman's exhibitionist propaganda speculates, is a radical reordering of American racial attitudes *and* workplace opportunities.

Imaginative Social Engineering

Let's extend the consideration of gendered social patterns in early twentieth-century Harlem and in the wider U.S. context, particularly with a view to how gender dynamics might shape the literature about the Harlem experience. Deborah McDowell's provisional observation about African American women's novels up to the Harlem Renaissance—that they "are all unified by their common concern with the question of black women's struggle for self-realization, wholeness, and autonomy in a racist and sexist society fundamentally antagonistic to individualism and the ideal of autonomy for women and blacks"—gains added dimension when viewed against the specifics of gendered social organization and against the backdrop of contemporaneous social commentary attentive to the now-clichéd, but still truly important, "mystical, holy trinity" (to borrow McDowell's phrase) of race, class, and gender.[43]

As we have seen, the value-neutral modernity of urban population density was often, and in some cases still is, measured against the negatively valued modernity of female sexual independence. What's more, the imbalanced sex ratio in Harlem and elsewhere meant that courtship rituals leading to marriage—the meat and potatoes of many a novel's plot—might be figured in terms supplied by game theorists, in terms of an internally logical competition over scarce resources. As early as 1899, Charles W. Chesnutt, in the short story "A Matter of Principle," explored the marriage market among Blue Vein mulatto elites: the narrator points out that "the supply of eligible men" often runs short because eligible young mulatto women "would not marry black men, and except in rare instances white men would not marry them."[44]

Representations of marriage as a highly competitive (and sometimes full-contact) sport is particularly likely in novels set in modern urban centers with discrete geographic boundaries: their narratives typically deploy a finite number of individuated characters who are meant to represent the seemingly infinite array of urban social types.[45] Cultural analysis might benefit by asking questions at the heart of game theory because the same questions routinely inform the urban novel and at times the poem and short story of urban life. These questions include: How can one make rational personal choices when the outcomes of personal choice depend upon the choices of others? What, in other words, counts as "rational" in a given situation?[46] Does cooperation, aggression, or a combination of the two best serve individual and social needs? Is it possible to define "morality" independent from rapidly evolving, context-specific rules of behavior, independent from (for example) class pressures?

Harlem Renaissance writers occasionally take up these questions directly, as the journalist and educator Elise Johnson McDougald does in "The Task of Negro Womanhood," an essay in Alain Locke's anthology *The New Negro* (1925). Anticipating the revisionist work of feminist scholars, who have made the essay well known since the late 1970s, McDougald offers that "the Negro woman does not maintain any moral standard which may be assigned chiefly to qualities of race, any more than a white woman does," and adds, "Sex irregularities are not a matter of race, but of socio-economic conditions." Regardless of their racial identity, McDougald insists, women yield to a sexual logic imposed by their social class: "Her emotional and sex life is a reflex of her economic station."[47] When economic opportunity is diminished, she asserts, lax sexual morals inevitably follow. McDougald repeatedly deflects questions of sex and race for her social reformist readership—and *The New Negro*'s original readers certainly had social reform in mind—and instead maneuvers toward questions of economic self-preservation, toward social facts that might be improved on rather than apparently immutable facets of social identity. In this sense, McDougald's analysis of African American social life far outstrips Thurman's in terms of complexity and generosity.

More often, Harlem Renaissance writers take up similar questions by deploying motifs common in novels of city life, motifs investigating questions of personal choice and social gain, but with an added layer of racial analysis. Novelists routinely figure social competition in terms of animal appetites and the gratification of bodily needs; the Harlem Renaissance took up the motif and superimposed onto it the provocative notion of cultural primitivism. Writing about competition among Harlem women for Harlem men, Claude McKay, in *Home to Harlem* (1928), offers a striking comparison: "A jungle atmosphere pervaded the room, and, like shameless wild animals hungry for raw meat, the females savagely searched the eyes of the males."[48] McKay's female characters, at least in this instance, see no reason to abide by unnatural inhibitions; nothing at the Myrtle Avenue apartment party holds them back. (Technically, the competition rages in Brooklyn, home to one of New York City's greatest concentrations of African Americans outside Harlem at the time.) Characters who cannot or refuse to acknowledge their animal instincts, who repress their sexuality—such as Joanna Marshall in Jessie Redmon Fauset's *There Is Confusion* (1924) and Helga Crane in Nella Larsen's *Quicksand* (1928)—often find themselves alienated from Harlem society and shut off from personal fulfillment.

I would argue that Joanna and Helga repress their "authentic" desires because they bear such tremendous weight as racial and gender exemplars, because for better and (mostly) for worse they *are* Negro Womanhood, much as Fauset was in Harlem Renaissance cultural discourse.[49] To succumb to base, "primitive" urges, no matter how natural, would be a betrayal of the uplift cause, a betrayal of the middle-class moral code. For an iconoclast such as Zora Neale Hurston, questions of gentility and appropriate sexual behavior, of primitivism and sexual appetite, offer an opportunity for humor and social commentary. Significantly, Hurston addressed these issues not in her better-known, seemingly apolitical agrarian novels, but rather in her urban short fiction, most of it only recently recovered into the Hurston canon.[50]

In her well-known "Story in Harlem Slang" (1942), originally published in the *American Mercury,* Hurston represents a comical contest between two "pimps" over the attention of a young, unnamed, working-class Harlemite. (Ironically, "pimp" in the short story refers to men who trade sexual favors for food and money; an *American Mercury* footnote reveals that the "Harlem pimp is a man whose amatory talents are for sale to any woman who will support him . . . ; in this sense, he is actually a male prostitute.") The short story's narrator observes that she "was a girl and [the pimps] both remembered that it was Wednesday afternoon. All of the domestics off for the afternoon with their pay in their pockets. Some of them bound to be hungry for love. That meant a dinner, a shot of scrap-iron [cheap liquor], maybe room rent and a reefer or two" for an enterprising pimp.[51] With this raunchy scenario in place, Hurston turns the tables on Harlem demographics: the two men, Jelly and Sweet Back, are accustomed to impressing (and swindling) the large numbers of young women who are "hungry for love," but because in this instance the men outnumber the lone woman, it is the men who must compete for a scarce resource. She plays along with their flirting, even encourages it—that is, until the men reveal that they're penniless.

The story's humor derives partly from Jelly's and Sweet Back's ineptitude, and partly from the woman's creative rejection of their advances: "You skillets is trying to promote a meal on me," she says, "But it'll never happen, brother. You barking up the wrong tree. I wouldn't give you air if you was stopped up in a jug. I'm not putting out a thing. I'm just like the cemetery—I'm not putting out, I'm taking in! Dig?"[52] The woman's mastery of language requires first a mastery of Harlem's gendered social dynamics as well as an understanding of her tactical advantage in this situation. Her rejection of their spectacularly incompetent advances has nothing to do with race, and everything to do with her relative financial freedom.

Fifteen years earlier, Hurston took up a similar theme but deployed a more over-the-top approach in "Monkey Junk: A Satire on Modern Divorce" (1927), published in the *Pittsburgh Courier,* one of the era's leading African American newspapers. The short story derives its humor largely from the awkward juxtaposition of pseudo-biblical cadences and mock-sacred jargon (with numbered verses, liberal sprinklings of "thous" and "verilys," and a psalmic concluding "Selah") alongside contemporary slang and references to modern cultural practices. It's a reference to one of these modern practices—a bank checking account—that underscores the more serious social issue under investigation:

> 1. And it came to pass in those days that one dwelt in the land of the Harlemites who thought that he knew all the law and the prophets.
>
> 2. Also when he arose in the morning and at noonday his mouth flew open and he said, "Verily, I am a wise guy. I knoweth all about women." . . .
>
> 6. And in that same year a maiden gazeth upon his checkbook and she coveted it.
>
> 7. Then became she coy and sweet with flattery and he swalloweth the bait.[53]

The checkbook, an invention of nineteenth-century banking, functions in Hurston's short story as a symbol of gendered access to capital in the twentieth-century American family, in which husband and wife exist on an uneven financial footing. In "Monkey Junk," the unnamed wife cynically exchanges sexual favors for money, first with her husband and later with a host of suitors. (The narrator even makes a pseudo-biblical game out of euphemisms for an adulterer and for adultery: "13. Then did his pearl of great price form the acquaintance of many men and they prospered her.") When the cuckolded husband threatens to leave her, the wife raises the stakes, but with an intriguing caveat: "19. But she answered him with much gall, 'Thou canst not do better than to go—but see that thou leave behind thee many signed checks.' "[54] Even in the 1920s, the woman cannot access her husband's bank account directly; from a purely financial standpoint, she is wholly his dependent.

Neither of the primary characters in "Monkey Junk" elicits much sympathy. Glenda R. Carpio and Werner Sollors, who rescued the short story from obscurity, observe that "the cheating wife is no feminist hero," and "her greenhorn husband is no male exemplar."[55] (Divorced twice, Hurston tended to depict marriage in fiction as a sordid, violent institution.) This much is clear, though: the wife easily outmaneuvers her country bumpkin husband and, with the exception of her clever young divorce lawyer, she has her way with all the other men whom she encounters.

The attorney, Miles Paige—the name also belongs to a real-life Pullman porter turned Columbia law student and New York magistrate—does his part, spouting forth an impressive list of clichés: "'When in the course of human events, Romeo, Romeo, wherefore art thou and how come what for?' And many other sayings of exceeding wiseness," Paige tells the judge and jury during the divorce proceedings. But it's the wife's elaborate performance that truly steals the courtroom show. Much like Lorelei Lee in Anita Loos's *Gentlemen Prefer Blondes* (1925), Hurston's wife appraises her circumstances in the courtroom and summons her wits or her feminine charms ("she turned soulful eyes about her and all men yearned to fight for her") as the situation calls for. Her performance pays off when the judge orders alimony in the sum of "an hundred shekels per month"; the former husband returns to his native Alabama in defeat.[56] The other men in the short story—judge, jury, and even Miles Paige—aid and abet the legally sanctioned redistribution of wealth.

Hurston's narratives are counterfactual in the sense that they deviate from the larger pattern of gender imbalance in Harlem, where interactions between multiple women and a lone man would be more likely, at least statistically, than what occurs in her fictive world. I label this approach to representing Harlem society "imaginative social engineering," a phrase that applies to all creative writing to some extent but most aptly to scenarios contrived to force readers into taking a fresh look at social reality. Such texts tend towards realism, even if they present unlikely "facts." Hurston sharply contrasts the social facts of "Story in Harlem Slang" with the fantastical boasting of Jelly and Sweet Back, who claim to have virtual harems of wealthy, light-skinned women at their beck and call. In "Monkey Junk," fact and fancy grate together in the humorous juxtaposition of insider slang and biblical cadences.

Hurston's short stories isolate incidents that highlight gender imbalance and turn the tables on gendered power dynamics. She thus develops a more serious point amid all the humor, the same point that McDougald advanced with a perfectly straight face: given ample opportunity for economic self-reliance and social independence, women's behavior evolves in ways that render moot questions of sexual morality. Hurston takes up James Weldon Johnson's notion (in his preface to *The Book of American*

Negro Poetry [1922]) that the "national mental attitude toward the race" is of great importance—opinions matter—but corrects his naive assumption that "actual conditions" play little role in determining social outcomes.[57] Actual conditions matter, Hurston declares, and these might be improved by fiction that confronts mental attitudes. Hurston's short stories insist that the conditions driving their humorous scenarios need not exist; like all emancipatory discourses, they envision a future in which they are no longer necessary. Imaginative social engineers such as Hurston thus believe in the capacity of cultural work to reshape social reality—not unlike social reformers, including social realist writers, but without their necessary focus on degrading conditions facing the poor and working classes, and without the sentimentality that degradation sometimes compels. In this sense Hurston and Thurman extend the social reform project to settings typically excluded from social realist literature and visual art.[58]

The Blacker the Berry similarly points toward more intriguing explorations of rational choices within strictly defined social dynamics. The novel complicates America's one-drop rule and further underscores a preoccupation with the social performance of racial identity by inserting a character, Arline Strange, who is easily recognized as a stand-in for Lenore Ulric, a well-known Broadway and film performer. Ulric gained notoriety among the Harlem intelligentsia when she played the title role of a prostitute in *Lulu Belle* in blackface.[59] The novel's character reveals that racial identity, even skin tone, is a matter of public performance with subtle gradations of "authenticity" that hugely depend on the specific performative context.

Even more intriguingly, the social groups studied in *The Blacker the Berry* aren't uniformly heterosocial. Looking to upgrade her shabby and smelly Harlem apartment, Emma Lou encounters "*Miss* Carrington" (original emphasis), a potential landlady who makes a clumsy pass at Emma Lou on a "damask-covered divan." Says Carrington to Emma Lou: "Don't worry any more, dearie, I'll take care of you from now on. . . . We call this the 'Old Maid's Home.' We have parties among ourselves, and just have a grand time. Talk about fun!"[60] Even though Emma Lou hastily departs the decadent cliché without taking the apartment, the novel nevertheless offers the hint of a lesbian alternative to the social dynamics that so plague her existence, an alternative less bound by the economic and sexual logics of intraracial colorism.[61] The rules that govern the predictable payoff matrices I outlined earlier do not apply to Old Maids.

Thurman's Harlem Renaissance roman-à-clef, *Infants of the Spring* (1932), explores this latter possibility of a liberating homosocial environment in much greater depth. The novel thus complicates game theory by casting into question the reigning heterosexist assumptions built into scenarios like those that dominate *The Blacker the Berry. Infants* introduces young male characters in ratios and circumstances that strongly suggest homosexual tension, and in fact the novel openly explores homosexual attraction in the character of Paul Arbian, modeled on the openly gay writer and artist Richard Bruce Nugent, or R.B.N. ("Ar-bi-an"). In sharp contrast to the novel's relatively successful homosexual relationships, the heterosexual couples in *Infants* face insurmountable negative pressures because they rashly cross the restrictive boundaries of race or class. Stephen, for instance, is a white Columbia University graduate student from Denmark whose dalliances with the light-skinned African American woman Aline and the dark-skinned African American woman Janet end in drunken violence. The affair between the working-class African American man Bull and the middle-class African American woman Lucille crashes to an end in violence and an aborted pregnancy.

These cutting-edge, cross-racial or cross-class heterosexual relationships, doomed by the light of day, nevertheless thrive under cover of darkness. *Infants* shows us a "Donation Party" that lures New Yorkers to the bohemian outpost dubbed Niggeratti Manor for an exchange of kitchen staples and merriment: "The lights in the basement had been dimmed, and the reveling dancers cast grotesque shadows on the heavily tapestried walls. Color lines had been completely eradicated. Whites and blacks clung passionately together as if trying to effect a permanent merger. Liquor, jazz music, and close physical contact had achieved what decades of propaganda had advocated with little success." The novel's protagonist, an African American novelist named Raymond (who very closely resembles Thurman), reflects during this climactic moment in *Infants,* "This . . . is the Negro renaissance, and this is about all the whole damn thing is going to amount to."[62] Until U.S. society evolves beyond its "peculiar conflicts," Thurman's fiction asserts, Americans are destined to repeat the pattern of botched personal relationships and social turmoil rehearsed in *The Blacker the Berry* and *Infants of the Spring*. Until then, radical alternatives to prevailing social forces will amount to little more than fleeting, inconsequential scenes in decadent fiction.

Nearly one century later, Raymond's prophetic vision has come closer to fruition: during the twentieth century, the rate of black–white intermarriage rose from less than 0.05 percent in 1900 to 1.8 percent in 2000. Although still quite low, these percentages represent a thirtyfold increase in the number of married black–white couples. Our first "black" president of the United States is an immediate product of one such union during the 1960s. The number of persons in a black–white marriage or in a Latino–non-Latino marriage grew from 900,000 in 1970 to 4,900,000 in 2000; the rate of intermarriage among all racial groups stood at about 6 percent in 2000.[63]

And these figures come nowhere near to representing the total number of interracial couples—married or unmarried, gay or straight—who go about their lives with little care about color lines. Their children already wonder what all the fuss was once about. Americans of all racial and ethnic backgrounds no longer find themselves bound by racial demography, at least not to the degree faced by men and women during the Harlem Renaissance. Locales marked by imbalanced sex ratios still exist, to be sure, but one's blackness or whiteness no longer has the powerful amplifying effect that once plagued the Emma Lou Morgans of the world. Even so, for as long as we measure and analyze rates of racial intermarriage—for as long as the act strikes us as measurable—we will not inhabit the chimerical postracial society. The next chapter investigates some of the cultural baggage that accompanies the notion that individuals might pursue romance and marriage across racial lines.

3
Harlem Diversity
Nations within a Nation

The "Colorist Collage"

My understanding of Harlem Renaissance texts takes a strong cue from Romare Bearden's hyperkinetic collages. More often than not, Bearden's collages depict individual figures with a simple, monochromatic color scheme; even when this is the case, however, Bearden populates his collages so densely and with such variety that the eye cannot easily settle on a single figure but instead whirls quickly from figure to differently colored figure. In his famous tableau *The Block* (1971), for example, Bearden arranges photographic cut-outs, colored paper, ink, and paint to represent a rich variety of Harlem types. A census count of *The Block* would reveal dozens of individuals representing almost as many social classes and life callings. Just as important, to be "black" in a Bearden collage is to be one of a rainbow of colors. The effect can be kaleidoscopic.

Rachel Farebrother reads Nella Larsen's *Quicksand* (1928) in similar fashion: the novel presents "a vision of African Americans as a kaleidoscope of racial types."[1] At its core, *Quicksand* is a novel about visual art and artistry, with a central character, the Danish painter Axel Olsen, driving much of the plot once it moves to Denmark. But the novel is also about the visual artistry of Beardenesque character description, necessarily so because its protagonist, Helga Crane, is a mulatta who is not welcomed by her dead mother's Danish family and who is not at home among the African American society that her father's background consigned her to.[2] Being neither one nor the other, Helga slides along a continuum between whiteness and blackness.

And so the novel gives us a wide and entertaining range of modifiers to describe skin color: a character might be "saffron-hued" or "lemon-colored" or "coffee-colored" or more simply "tan" or "brown" or "black" or "yellow." Much as a train conductor fleeces Helga for a Chicago-bound sleeper car berth, charging her extra because he knows that she's African American, the narrator subjects individual characters "to a keen, appraising look" to assign them a skin color and by extension a racial identity.[3] Ann E. Hostetler is thus entirely correct to label *Quicksand* "a meditation on color," one that "advances a thematics of race."[4] The two concepts, one objectively real but difficult to pin down (color), the other abstract but felt everywhere (race), constitute each other in Larsen's novel.

Perhaps because Helga is surrounded by her dormitory room's small luxuries as the novel opens, *Quicksand*'s narrator initially describes her skin as a precious object, "like yellow satin." The racial gaze in the novel is more obviously sexualized whenever one of Helga's potential suitors takes her into view. Each time Helga encounters the striving African American educator Robert Anderson, she is "conscious of the man's steady gaze"; his "prominent gray eyes [are] fixed upon her, studying her, appraising her." Not only does Olsen select a garish wardrobe for Helga so that he might paint a lurid, primitive portrait of her, he also looks "intently at her for what seemed to her an incredibly rude length of time from under his heavy drooping lids" when they first meet. Even after Olsen's clumsy marriage proposal in his Copenhagen studio, Helga has "a stripped, naked feeling under his direct glance." A character plucked right out of a fin de siècle Decadent text, Olsen functions almost as an allegorical figure in the novel: with his insatiable desire to "picture" Helga as (in her opinion of the portrait) "some disgusting sensual creature," Olsen stands in for a white consumer's fantasy about what it means to be Negro in the modern Western world, a world thoroughly exhausted with itself and in need of sexual rejuvenation.[5] Olsen's selfish decadence reveals the ugly, distorting underbelly of Negro primitivism.

But there is one moment in *Quicksand* that suggests, however fleetingly, a means by which Helga might escape the social and psychological quagmire that she struggles through. In a much-discussed Harlem cabaret scene, which occurs on the eve of Helga's journey to Denmark, the novel's narrator, a voice filtered almost exclusively through Helga's consciousness, highlights the club dancers "ambling lazily to a crooning melody, or violently twisting their bodies, like whirling leaves, to a sudden streaming rhythm, or shaking themselves ecstatically to a thumping of unseen tomtoms." The language used here might easily be confused for the stereotypically primitivist rhetoric of Larsen's friend and supporter Carl Van Vechten, or her less intimate acquaintance Claude McKay, but instead we realize that the ordinarily prim and reserved Helga is supplying the ideas behind the words: "a shameful certainty that not only had she been in the jungle, but that she had enjoyed it, began to taunt her."[6] The crowd that ordinarily fills Helga with distaste or dread and the Negro race that the crowd represents emerge at this jazz-fueled moment as objects of aesthetic wonder, much more evocative than the expensive knickknacks and finery that normally occupy so much of Helga's attention.

As the jazz music penetrates Helga's consciousness, the "crowd [becomes] a swirling mass" and her blurred view a revelation:

> For the hundredth time she marveled at the gradations within this oppressed race of hers. A dozen shades slid by. There was sooty black, shiny black, taupe, mahogany, bronze, copper, gold, orange, yellow, peach, ivory, pinky white, pastry white. There was yellow hair, brown hair, black

> hair; straight hair, straightened hair, curly hair, crinkly hair, wooly hair. She saw black eyes in white faces, brown eyes in yellow faces, gray eyes in brown faces, blue eyes in tan faces. Africa, Europe, perhaps with a pinch of Asia, in a fantastic motley of ugliness and beauty, semi-barbaric, sophisticated, exotic, were here.[7]

The scene unfolds as an art-inflected version of the polyethnic melting pot that progressive Americans at this moment held up as a utopian alternative to the nativist crazy quilt. No obvious visual logic explains the sequences of skin colors, hair colors, hair textures, and eye and face colors; instead, sound patterns more than anything else explain the progression of each list. The lists reenact the rhythmic pulse of the jazz that fills the surrounding air.

But Helga cannot remain in this state of synesthetic euphoria for very long, and she's therefore "blind to its charm, purposely aloof and a little contemptuous," the narrator tells us in a rare moment of nonfocalized detachment; Helga soon loses "interest in the moving mosaic" of the crowd.[8] (Larsen appears to be punning at this point on the similar sounds and etymologies of "music" and "mosaic.") If my identification of a "colorist collage" such as this one is inspired by Bearden's modernist experiments with visual media and visual space—and by Marjorie Perloff's reminder that "in French, collage is also idiomatic for an 'illicit' sexual union, two unrelated 'items,' being pasted or stuck together"—then Larsen's "moving mosaic" represents an updated, paradoxical, even modernist version of the ancient visual art form.[9]

In her perceptive study of this cabaret crowd scene, Mary Esteve notes the similarities between the description of the swirling crowd and the earthy quicksand of the novel's title. Despite the stereotypical rhetoric (invoking jungles and tom-toms) and despite the title's dangerous referent (quicksand), immersion in the cabaret crowd represents transcendent possibility: in Esteve's words, "In contact with this moving mosaic, Helga simultaneously explodes out of it."[10] The crowd's ecstasy is also Helga's for a while. Jazz music and the visually diverse crowd that it draws to the cabaret thus function as the modern and genuinely liberating alternative to Helga's short-term and wholly unsuccessful conversion to the African American church at the novel's end.[11] The cabaret crowd signals Helga's true calling, her best way out of the quagmire, if only she were capable of listening, if only she fully appreciated the diversity within her own race.

In 1928, Larsen won the second-place bronze medal for literature awarded by the William E. Harmon Foundation; she was edged out by McKay, whose *Home to Harlem,* which won the gold medal, appeared to mixed and sometimes scandalized reviews that year. The protagonist of *Home to Harlem,* the easygoing, working-class Jake Brown, stands almost as Helga Crane's polar opposite: where she is uptight, he is carefree; where she obsesses over Orientalist fashion details, he is most comfortable in his loose-fitting English suit; where she is prudish, he is unabashedly sexual. Among the only things they share in common is their tendency to quick flight and rootless wandering. That, and their obsession with skin color.

Technically speaking, I should say the third-person narrator's obsession with skin color, but for most of the novel the narrator hovers closely around Jake and the narration clearly reveals Jake's conscious (and less conscious) thoughts.[12] To read *Home to Harlem* is to encounter dozens of characters, almost all of them described in terms of their skin color and little else. In addition to black and white and brown and yellow, we encounter characters who are "ebony," "golden-brown," "coffee-colored," "putty-skinned," "potato-yellow," "dull-black," "crust-yellow," "yellow-skinned," "spade," "chocolate-to-the-bone," "lemon-colored," "paper-brown," "chocolate," "burnt-cork black," "potato-skinned," "light-brown," "high-brown," "straw-colored," "yellow-cream," "bronze," "dark-brown," "leather-brown," "chestnut brown," "light-yellow," "coffee-skinned," "rich-brown," "chestnut," "chocolate-complexioned," "teasing-brown," "near white," "fair brown," "dim brown," "clear brown," "copper," "mahogany," "gleaming anthracite," "red-brown," "cocoa-brown," "lacquer black," and "cream." Skin colors substitute for proper names in *Home to Harlem;* minor characters are known not as "Claude" or "Mr. McKay" in the novel, but as "crust-yellow girl" or "cocoa-brown youth."[13] In this context, even Jake's surname—Brown—feels like a heavy-handed identity label.

Home to Harlem exerts a heavy hand in celebration of African American diversity at the same time that it insists on a stable African American identity. Much to the chagrin of its critics, the novel often ties African American identity to a vulgar form of cultural primitivism. In one of the novel's many cabaret scenes, and one of its many colorist collages, the narrator exclaims: "It was a scene of blazing color. Soft, barbaric, burning, savage, clashing, planless colors—all rioting together in wonderful harmony. There is no human sight so rich as an assembly of Negroes ranging from lacquer black through brown to cream, decked out in their ceremonial finery."[14] Whether they want to or not, the Negroes of *Home to Harlem* live up to Axel Olsen's stereotype of the race: they relish vivid color, spontaneous emotional outbursts, and perhaps most of all, jazz music. Elsewhere I have discussed how *Home to Harlem* deploys back-to-the-jungle jazz rhetoric not only to flout convention, but also to provide a modernist inquiry into the nature of literary representation.[15] The same might be said of McKay's use of the colorist collage.

Whenever *Home to Harlem* depicts jazz music or a colorist collage, the narrator relies heavily on ellipses, as though mere language valiantly strains to represent an idea (jazz, intraracial diversity) but ultimately and gladly admits defeat. At the Brooklyn apartment of Gin-head Susy, the narrator ponders the notion that "civilization had brought strikingly exotic types into Susy's race." With this, the narrator describes still another colorist collage, which trails off with a final ellipsis mark: "Ancient black life rooted upon its base with all its fascinating new layers of brown, low-brown, high-brown, nut-brown, lemon, maroon, olive, mauve, gold. Yellow balancing between black and white. Black reaching out beyond yellow. Almost-white on the brink of a change. Sucked back down into the current of black by the terribly sweet rhythm of black blood. . . ."[16] In the same way that the novel represents jazz music, we find here a jettisoning of grammar rules, a leveling of syntactic hierarchies, and an impressionistic synesthesia, such that the visual experience (color diversity) is depicted in terms of sound and taste ("sweet rhythm"). *Home to Harlem* screams its artifice at moments such as this one, suggesting that any realist attempt to represent intraracial diversity is doomed to dazzling failure.

Given the Census Bureau's obsession with blood fraction racial identities (mulatto, quadroon, octoroon, and so on) during the late nineteenth and early twentieth centuries, it is interesting to consider the proliferation of passing narratives, many of which take up the colorist collage in some form, at this same time. The period after *Plessy v. Ferguson* (1896) marks a parallel moment, when the machinery of U.S. law and bureaucracy insists on the absoluteness of a black/white binary racial system. Werner Sollors's comprehensive, thirty-four-page "Chronology of Interracial Literature," which begins in the fifth century BCE, includes thirteen pages spanning the Reconstruction era through the Harlem Renaissance, and fully seven pages spanning the 1910s through the 1930s.[17] That is, a mere thirty years in the 2,500-year chronology of interracial literature occupies fully 21 percent of its timeline. The literary attention to passing and interracial romance confirms that American writers understood national identity to be at a crossroads.

Given Charles W. Chesnutt's and James Weldon Johnson's prominent roles in the early days of what we now call African American fiction, the theme of mulatto identity and passing played a central part in the budding discourse. Before long, Robert Browning and Alexander Pushkin were claimed as "Negro" or, almost as often, as "octoroon" (in the case of Browning) and "quadroon" (in the case of Pushkin) writers; Alexandre Dumas is still often held up as the foremost "Negro" or "quadroon" writer of the nineteenth century. As the concept of a Negro Renaissance emerged in the early 1900s and gained a foothold in the 1920s,[18] discussions of "Negro literature" routinely addressed fiction (and even some poetry) that expressly develops mulatto characters and themes of interracial passing.

For strategic reasons, though, the Harlem Renaissance solidified around the consolidation of a singular "Negro" identity. The novelist and NAACP officer Walter White—considered by George S. Schuyler to be "one of the whitest white men ever to have an octoroon for a grandfather"—explains why this is so in his essay "The Paradox of Color," in Alain Locke's *New Negro* anthology (1925).[19] White illustrates the paradox with an anecdote, in which he and his wife, Gladys, wish to join Paul and Essie Robeson for a late-night dinner after Paul's successful performance in *The Emperor Jones* (1920), the Eugene O'Neill play then running at the Provincetown Playhouse in Greenwich Village. Not wishing to risk the indignity of being rebuffed at a downtown restaurant, the foursome instead travels seven miles uptown to dine in Harlem, where they're sure to be warmly received.

The color paradox lies in the solidarity forged out of race prejudice: where White might easily pass as white and enter any restaurant without a second thought, he and the millions of other light-skinned African Americans identify with darker folks, even though these may be complete strangers. "Negroes of the United States have been welded into a homogeneity of thought and a commonness of purpose in combating a common foe" in race prejudice, he writes. The solidarity "applies to that large element of colored people whose skins are lighter who realize that their cause is common with that of all Negroes regardless of color."[20]

Much as Benedict Anderson identifies the cultural foundations that allow total strangers to imagine themselves as part of the same nation, so too does White identify the cultural and legal conditions that compel individuals to embrace an abstract African American identity. Although, as tables 3.1 and 3.2 show, the 1920 census counted 1.7 million mulattoes in the United States and nearly 27,000 in New York City alone (residing primarily in Harlem), most, according to White, would assume kinship with the 8.8 million "blacks" who made up the bulk of the African American population.

TABLE 3.1. U.S. black/mulatto/Negro population, 1900–1940

	1900	1910	1920	1930	1940
Black	unreported	7,777,077	8,802,577	N/A	N/A
Mulatto	unreported	2,050,686	1,660,554	N/A	N/A
Total Negro	8,833,994	9,827,763	10,463,131	11,891,143	12,865,518

Sources: U.S. Census Bureau, Twelfth Census of the United States, Thirteenth Census of the United States, Fourteenth Census of the United States, Fifteenth Census of the United States, Sixteenth Census of the United States.

TABLE 3.2. New York State black/mulatto/Negro population, 1900–1940

	1900	1910	1920	1930	1940
Black	unreported	103,583	171,507	N/A	N/A
Mulatto	unreported	30,608	26,976	N/A	N/A
Total Negro	99,232	134,191	198,483	412,814	571,221

Sources: U.S. Census Bureau, Twelfth Census of the United States, Thirteenth Census of the United States, Fourteenth Census of the United States, Fifteenth Census of the United States, Sixteenth Census of the United States.

It's Transnation Time

The Great Migration led to a profound redistribution of the African American population, bringing the number of northern African Americans more into line with the number of African Americans living in the South and forever changing the wider American understanding of African American social and cultural identity. This conceptual model, though, assumes a fairly homogenous group of dislocated southerners planting roots in the North. While the majority of northern African Americans at this time had southern roots, a significant portion, particularly within the Harlem enclave, traced their origins elsewhere than the South. In one of his contributions to *The New Negro* in 1925, James Weldon Johnson remarked that "Harlem's lure . . . reached down to every island of the Carib Sea and penetrated even into Africa."[21] Since then, a number of creative writers and cultural critics have stressed what we would now call the transnational or Pan-African character of the Harlem enclave; few, though, have provided anything beyond anecdotal evidence for their observations. In contrast, social historians tend to offer Harlem as the prime example of the Great Migration, sometimes throwing in references to Spanish Harlem as an afterthought. Here I wish to address not only the racialization of Harlem, but also its internationalization.

There's no shortage of celebrations of African American diversity—cultural, social, linguistic—in Harlem Renaissance literature and cultural history. The landmark Federal Writers Project study *The Negro in New York,* completed in 1930 but not published until 1967, offers an early and fairly representative example. The contributors to the volume write of the wide array of nationalities that contributed to Afro-diaspora diversity in early twentieth-century Harlem—as they put it, "voluntary Negro immigration" at this time "brought a worldliness to Harlem early in its career"—and they provide separate discussions of Harlem's Haitian, French colonial, Puerto Rican, and British West Indian populations.[22] Similarly, the Jamaican politician and journalist W. A. Domingo observes in *The New Negro* that "colored people of Spanish, French, Dutch, Arabian, Danish, Portuguese, British and native African ancestry meet and move together" in Harlem.[23] We might also look to the creative work of, for example,

Rudolph Fisher, Zora Neale Hurston, and Claude McKay for similar celebrations of cultural pluralism in Harlem, and for nuanced critiques of its pitfalls and of the hypocrisies of American cultural life.

Who, then, called Harlem home during the renaissance that now bears its name? How did the machinery of the state identify them? If they were part of a Great Migration, where did they come from? If we consider a longitudinal snapshot of race in Harlem, the results are strikingly clear from the Census Bureau's perspective, in which "Negro" identity trumps other varieties of Afro-diaspora heritage: as the century progressed, Harlem became strikingly more African American. In the 28 census tracts that make up Harlem, the overall population fluctuated slightly between 1920 and 1940, but the proportion of the Harlem population identified as Negro grew rapidly, from 73,614 (25.9 percent) in 1920 to 175,145 (65.6 percent) in 1930 and 235,535 (85.8 percent) in 1940. In central Harlem (Metropolitan Statistical Area M8B), the Negro population grew from 64 percent in 1920 to 95 percent in 1930. In census tract 230, located at the geographic heart of the neighborhood (eight city blocks between 138th and 142nd Streets and between Lenox and 8th Avenues) the proportion of the population identified as Negro grew from 88.5 percent in 1920 to 99.4 percent in 1930 and 1940. In 1920, Negroes were a majority of the population in seven Harlem census tracts; in 1930 this number rose to nineteen tracts (fig. 3.1), and in 1940 to twenty-four tracts. In other words, as midcentury approached, residential segregation ensured that Harlem was unmistakably "black."

It is not surprising that in census tracts with a significant jump in the Negro population there is also a significant decline in the numbers of whites, including foreign-born whites. To return to the example of census tract 230, the foreign-born white population dropped from 4.4 percent in 1920 to 0.3 percent in 1930 and to 0.1 percent in 1940. The U.S.-born white population in this census tract dropped from 7 percent to 0.2 percent then to 0.5 percent over the same period. (The number of U.S.-born whites here is a function of the number of immigrants; the native group includes second-generation children of immigrants.) Throughout Harlem, white residents—in particular, foreign-born whites—were displaced by Negro transplants (table 3.3). (Foreign-born white women accounted for 13.7 percent of the Harlem population in 1920; by 1940, this number dwindled to 1.7 percent.) By 1930, the number of whites in this and many other Harlem census tracts is miniscule: during that year, census tract 230 was home to 42 foreign-born whites, 49 U.S.-born whites, and 15,783 Negroes. Nativist outcry is significantly complicated by social facts: how is it possible to lay blame for urban problems at the feet of immigrants when so much social change in cities is being driven by an influx of African Americans? At the same time, the popularly held belief encapsulated in Rudolph Fisher's essay title, "The Caucasian Storms Harlem," seems overstated given the extent of Harlem's social transformation.

TABLE 3.3. **Harlem population by race and nativity, 1920–1940**

	TOTAL	NATIVE WHITE	FOREIGN-BORN WHITE	NEGRO
1920	284,598	46.7%	27.3%	25.9%
1930	266,806	21.6%	12.4%	65.6%
1940	274,378	10.3%	3.7%	85.8%

Source: Minnesota Population Center, National Historical Geographic Information System: Version 2.0. Minneapolis: University of Minnesota, 2011.

For a variety of reasons, figures about large-scale social trends in Harlem can be misleading, or at best incomplete. Before 1910, it's difficult to gain much geographic precision from Census Bureau data because the census tracts that allow for pinpoint geospatial analysis did not yet exist.[24] More important, the data reported by the Census Bureau fell into five mutually exclusive racial/national identity options: 1) native white of native parentage; 2) native white of foreign or mixed parentage; 3) foreign-born white; 4) Negro; or 5) other race. According to the Census Bureau's state report for New York in 1910, "Classification according to nativity and parentage is scarcely necessary for the other [nonwhite] races, since nearly all negroes and Indians are native born of native parentage, and nearly all Chinese and Japanese are either foreign born or of foreign parentage."[25] Writing in 1939, Ira Reid, an Atlanta University sociologist and the leading authority on Negro immigration during the first half of the twentieth century, observed that "statistical data on the Negro foreign-born and immigrant populations are scattered, diverse, and, from the viewpoint of validity, almost

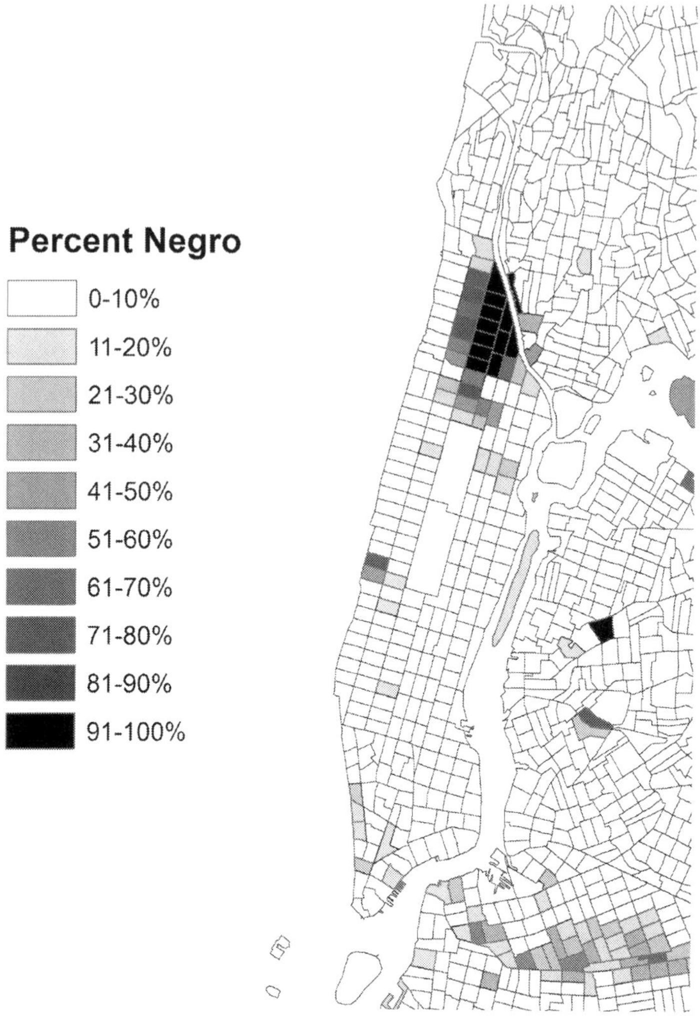

Figure 3.1. New York City percent Negro by census tract, 1930. Data courtesy Minnesota Population Center. National Historical Geographic Information System: Version 2.0. Minneapolis: University of Minnesota, 2011.

non-existent."[26] The census schedules allowed for much more detailed data collection, but in its reporting the Census Bureau assumed that Negro status and nativity cancelled each other out: one was simply "Negro," not a native or foreign-born Negro. For the overall U.S. black population, the assumption is a fairly safe one, but in places such as Miami, Boston, and New York City the assumption misses the mark spectacularly.

This is not to say that we have no data about the nativity of blacks living in Harlem or elsewhere, and in fact we can make relatively safe inferences based on data collected by the Bureau of Immigration and Naturalization, which was transferred from the Treasury Department to the now-defunct Commerce and Labor Department in 1903, and later based on data released by the Census Bureau.[27] We know, for example, how many Afro-diaspora immigrants entered or departed the United States in any given year beginning in 1899. Rather than specify the country of origin for Afro-diaspora immigrants, and rather than allow immigrants to self-report their racial identity, the Census Bureau lumped together all such persons into the catchall category "African, black."

The bureau reported immigrants' area of last residence in broad geographic terms—"British North America" or "Central America" or "West Indies"—but the numbers yield little of interest except in the aggregate. For instance, between 1900 and 1924 the number of black immigrants to the United States climbed steadily, so that in 1924 alone the net gain (arrivals minus departures) in the "African, black" immigrant population was 10,794. The exclusionist Immigration Act of 1924 reversed the trend, so that in 1925 the net loss was 303. The numbers slowly crept up into positive territory until 1932, when the Great Depression led to a steady loss of foreign-born blacks. The most significant such year was 1933, when 84 black immigrants entered the United States and 1,058 departed, for a net loss of 974.

Beginning in 1930, the Census Bureau began reporting more detailed figures for "Country of Birth of the Foreign-born Population . . . by Color or Race," and in 1935 it compiled data from the previous censuses in a manner that took into account Negro nativity. (The bureau subtracted the number of Mexicans from the foreign-born "colored" population to derive its number of foreign-born Negroes for 1930, the only year in which "Mexican" was a racial category on census schedules.) This set of data, which looks back as far as the 1920 census, demonstrates that a significant part of the population growth among the total Negro population in the early part of the century, including its rapid northern expansion felt as a Great Migration, derived from an explosion in the number of Negro immigrants.

In 1910 there were 40,339 foreign-born Negroes in the United States, and in 1920 this number increased to 73,803, a gain of 83 percent (table 3.4). Large numbers of Negroes from Puerto Rico and the U.S. Virgin Islands, not counted among these foreign-born figures, also lived in the United States.[28] By contrast, the Negro native-born population grew by 6.1 percent and the white foreign-born population grew by just 0.9 percent during this same decade. (The percentage increase within the Negro foreign-born population was even greater in the preceding decade; see fig. 3.2.) According to Reid, a majority of all foreign-born Negroes lived in and around New York City at this time, and the bulk of these lived in the Harlem enclave.

TABLE 3.4. Native and foreign-born Negro U.S. population and white foreign-born U.S. population, 1900–1930*

	1900	1910	1920	1930
Negro native	8,813,994	9,787,424	10,389,328	11,797,523
Negro foreign-born	20,336	40,339	73,803	98,620
White foreign-born	10,213,817	13,134,312	13,255,394	13,366,407

**Excludes Negroes born in U.S. protectorates (e.g., Puerto Rico, U.S. Virgin Islands).*

Source: U.S. Census Bureau, *Negroes in the United States, 1920–1932* (1935).

For a variety of reasons—economic, political, and legal—the overwhelming majority of foreign-born Negroes emigrated to the United States from somewhere in the Americas, and three-fourths were from the West Indies. Travel from the West Indies to the United States was relatively simple, not only because of geographic proximity but also because of the legacy of America's imperial efforts there and because of the era's exclusionist regime of immigration laws. Owing to recent U.S. military intervention and the political pressures exerted by transnational corporations and American agribusiness, U.S. protectorates and independent nations in the Western hemisphere (such as Cuba, the Dominican Republic, Haiti, and Mexico) were non-quota countries; the citizens of these nations, black or white, could travel freely to the United States, even under the strict post-1924 immigration regime.[29] Travel from the British West Indies (including Jamaica, Trinidad, the Bahamas, and Barbados) was governed by the liberal national origin quotas reserved for British subjects. The Emergency

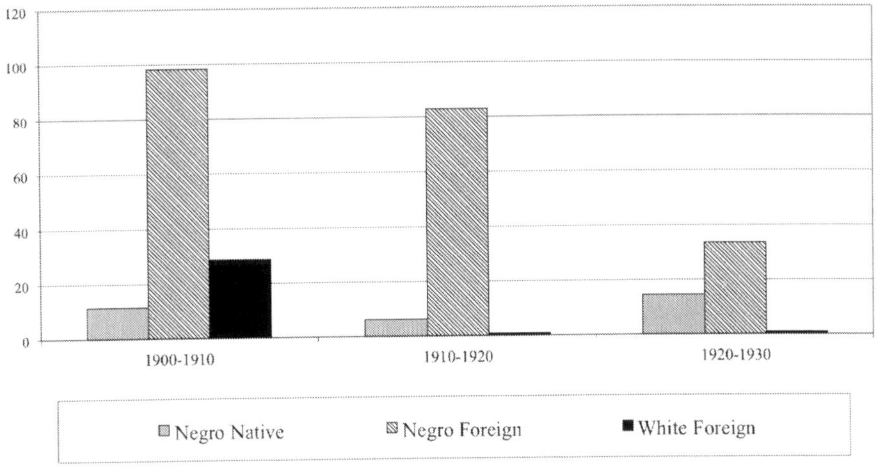

Figure 3.2. Percentage increase of native and foreign-born Negro population and white foreign-born U.S. population, 1900–1930.

Quota Act of 1921 set the national origin quota at 1910 population ratios; the Immigration Act of 1924 set the national origin quota at 1890 ratios. This restrictive quota system, meant to increase the proportion of "desirable" immigrants from western and northern Europe, remained in place until 1952.

In this respect, the changing face of Harlem during its renaissance reflected very directly the imperial projects of turn-of-the-century America and Great Britain as well as the liberalization of Western hemispheric trade amid the commercial turbulence of World War I. As table 3.5 shows, in 1930 only 4.7 percent of foreign-born Negroes were from Europe; 5.9 percent were from Canada, 3.2 percent from South America, 2.7 percent from Central America, and a scant 1.0 percent (986 individuals) from Africa. In sharp contrast, the largely white, overall foreign-born population was mostly (82.7 percent) European in origin.

As we see in table 3.5 and figure 3.3, the Great Migration left its mark on Harlem society, but not to the extent commonly believed; more accurately, the Great Migration was only partly southern in origin. During the heyday of the renaissance, New York City was home to almost half as many foreign-born Negroes (mostly West Indian in origin) as southern-born Negroes. In 1930, just over five out of ten U.S.-born Negroes (55.2 percent) in Manhattan, most of whom lived in Harlem (table 3.6), were born outside of New York State, and almost all of these were born in just four southern states: Virginia (16.5 percent of Manhattan Negroes), South Carolina (12.9 percent), North Carolina (8.5 percent), and Georgia (7.8 percent). By way of contrast, Chicago in 1930 drew much of its Negro population from Mississippi (16.4 percent), Tennessee (10.0 percent), and Alabama (9.1 percent). Here I wish to underscore a crucial sociohistorical detail that tends to be overlooked in discussions of the Great Migration within Harlem Renaissance scholarship: roughly two out of ten Manhattan Negroes were foreign-born—about the same as the number of Negroes native to New York State, and more than the number of Negroes born in any individual southern state. As a phenomenon experienced over time, the southern presence in Harlem actually diminished during the course of the renaissance, whereas the foreign presence increased rapidly at first and then held steady at the outset of the Great Depression.

TABLE 3.5. Country of birth of foreign-born U.S. Negroes

COUNTRY OF ORIGIN	1920	%	1930	%
Canada	5,651	7.7	5,817	5.9
Newfoundland	6	0.0	9	0.0
Cuba	1,934	2.6	2,362	2.4
Other West Indies	50,488	68.4	72,138	73.1
Mexico	3,123	4.2	915	0.9
Central America	816	1.1	2,662	2.7
South America	1,668	2.3	3,191	3.2
Europe	3,996	5.4	4,632	4.7
Asia	27	0.0	44	0.0
Africa	556	0.8	986	1.0
Australia	107	0.1	81	0.1
Azores	206	0.3	177	0.2
Other Atlantic Islands	5,143	7.0	5,411	5.5
Pacific Islands	40	0.1	95	0.1
Born at sea or not specified	44	0.1	99	0.1
Total	73,803	-	98,620	-

Source: U.S. Census Bureau, *Negroes in the United States, 1920–1932* (1935).

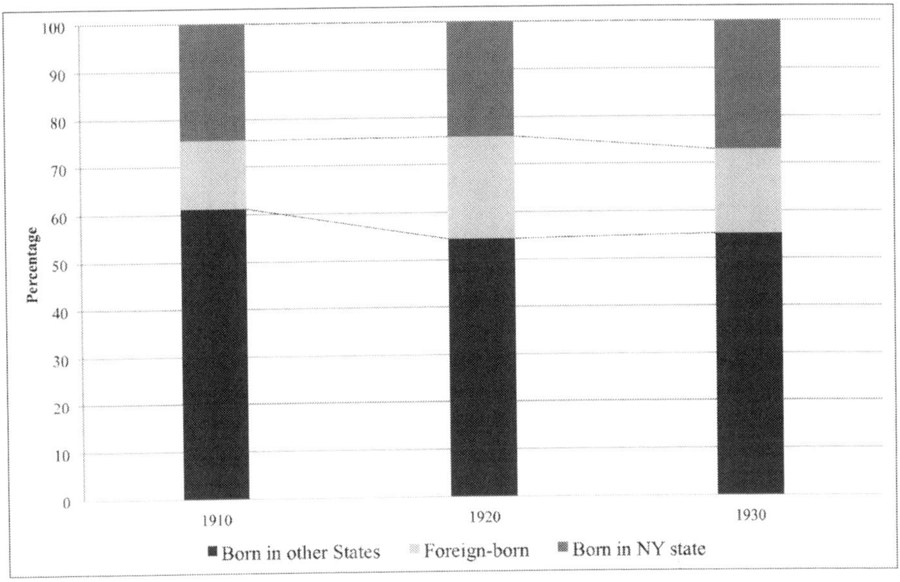

Figure 3.3. Percentage of Manhattan Negroes by nativity, 1900–1930.

TABLE 3.6. Negro nativity in Manhattan and New York City, 1900–1930

	1910	1920	1930
MANHATTAN			
% born outside New York	61.1	54.5	55.2
% foreign-born	14.4	21.4	17.7
NEW YORK CITY			
% born outside New York	56.9	51.3	53.8
% foreign-born	12.8	20.0	16.7

Source: U.S. Census Bureau, *Negroes in the United States, 1920–1932* (1935).

The precise numbers of foreign-born Negroes who emigrated from a specific location to New York are unknown, but we can arrive at a fairly close estimate based on the ratios found in the overall U.S. population of foreign-born Negroes. (Because in 1930 a majority [55.5 percent] of foreign-born U.S. Negroes lived in New York City, with nearly half [40.4 percent] in the Manhattan borough alone, the likelihood of major distortions is small. Significantly, these figures do not include Negroes from

Puerto Rico or the U.S. Virgin Islands; they were classified as native-born.) Using this ratio and the number of foreign-born Negroes known to live in New York City, we can then assume that in 1930 there were roughly 40,025 Negroes of West Indian origin in New York City, with about 29,118 in Manhattan alone. By themselves, these transplanted West Indians would constitute a fairly large metropolis in their homelands. For instance, the Jamaican census of 1943 reported a Kingston population of just 110,083.[30] We can similarly estimate that 2,350 Negroes from Canada called Harlem home, along with 956 from Cuba, 1,872 from Europe, 398 from Africa, and 1,275 from South America. Table 3.7 provides a longer list of foreign-born Negro population estimates.

TABLE 3.7. **Estimated population of foreign-born Negroes in Manhattan and New York City, 1930**

COUNTRY OF ORIGIN	%	MANHATTAN EST.	NEW YORK CITY EST.
[Reference Population]	-	[39,833]	[54,754]
Canada	5.9	2,350	3,230
Cuba	2.4	956	1,314
Other West Indies	73.1	29,118	40,025
Mexico	0.9	358	493
Central America	2.7	1,075	1,478
South America	3.2	1,275	1,752
Europe	4.7	1,872	2,573
Africa	1.0	398	548
Other Atlantic Islands	5.5	2,191	3,011

Although I can point to some logic in these estimates of the countries of origin for Harlem's foreign-born Negro population, we must recall that throughout most of the twentieth century the Census Bureau relied on art as well as science when tracking the number of Negroes in the population. To determine an individual's nationality, census enumerators were instructed in 1930 to ask a series of questions to determine the precise location of her or his birth (with special care given to those born in a European nation that experienced a shift in geopolitical boundaries following World War I). The individual's race, on the other hand, was a matter strictly left to an enumerator's presumably visual interpretation. This combination of strict scrutiny and lax demography yielded some difficult to fathom results.

Take the example of the six U.S. Negroes who in 1920 were reported by the Census Bureau to have been born in China. By 1930, this Census Bureau number dwindled down to a single Negro born in China. According to the census instructions to enumerators for that year, such a person would be a logical impossibility: Negro and Chinese racial identities cancelled each other out in a strict either/or fashion. But of course, according to modern state apparatuses, with their awkward legacy of identity labels that predate the modern nation-state, to be Chinese is to possess a nationality as well as a racial heritage. Seen as a purely practical matter, this Negro from China raises a number of vexing questions. There have been, to be sure, significant Afro-Chinese communities in the Caribbean, particularly in Cuba; even the U.S. South witnessed the emergence of an Afro-Chinese identity in the early twentieth century.[31]

But if one were both black and Chinese, gaining entry into the United States and achieving a livelihood would be far easier by "passing" as a Negro citizen of a quota or non-quota country. Recall that, for the purposes of the Bureau of Immigration, any Negro who landed on U.S. shores was regarded simply as "African, black"; not to continue in this relatively safe bureaucratic space makes little sense in light of the rigid Asian exclusion laws in place since the 1880s. (Because Chinese immigrants were ineligible for U.S. citizenship, their admission to the United States was technically prohibited at the time.) Seen through a more theoretical lens, to be a Negro born in China who then immigrated to the United States is a Du Boisian problem not of double, but of triple or even quadruple consciousness. Was this theoretical conundrum, though, a product of the bureaucracy itself? An enumerator filling out the 1930 census schedule would come across the "color or race" question (column 12) before coming across the "place of birth" question (column 17). If an enumerator identified an individual as Negro, would he later change the identification if the individual subsequently claimed China as a birthplace? If the person counted understood that he was being identified as Negro, what would compel him to report his country of origin as China? We can imagine this scenario unfolding in countless peculiar ways.

Racial Safety Valve

In *The Autobiography of an Ex-Colored Man* (1912), James Weldon Johnson explores an existential crisis born of deeply sociocultural, rather than merely bureaucratic, dilemmas. The Ex-Colored Man, the novel's unnamed narrator, grabs the reader's attention with his early promise to "divulg[e] the great secret of [his] life"—a professional career and family situation made possible by his passing as white—but the bulk of the novel is given over to the clinical analysis of white society, black society, and the blurry color line that separates the two. A central chapter in the novel, which traces the Ex-Colored Man's fortunes in Jacksonville, Florida, tenders the most elaborate sociological analysis in a narrative preoccupied with sociology. Pondering the deforming influence of the "race question" on white America, the Ex-Colored Man observes that "the condition of whites [is] more to be deplored than that of the blacks. Here, a truly great people, a people that produced a majority of the great historic Americans from Washington to Lincoln [is] now forced to use up its energies in a conflict as lamentable as it is violent."[32] Race prejudice, the Ex-Colored Man concludes, shackles American progress by steering the nation's collective energy, white and black, toward needless strife. This passage immediately follows—strategically, I'm convinced—a brief description of the narrator's Florida landlord, a Cuban exile who introduces the Ex-Colored Man to the cigar-rolling trade.

The landlord, a "light colored Cuban" with racially ambiguous "Spanish eyes," excels in rolling always-precise cigars, but his trade serves a more noble purpose:

> We drifted along in conversation until my companion struck the subject nearest his heart, the independence of Cuba. He was an exile from the island, and a prominent member of the Jacksonville *Junta*. Every week sums of money were collected from *juntas* all over the country. This money

> went to buy arms and ammunition for the insurgents. As the man sat there nervously smoking his long, "green" cigar, and telling me of the Gomezes, both the white one and the black one, of Maceo and Bandera, he grew positively eloquent.[33]

Larger-than-life figures from Cuba's recent past, Máximo Gómez, Juan Gualberto Gómez, and Antonio Maceo embody the revolutionary zeal and the self-sacrifice of George Washington and Abraham Lincoln. Just as important, they represent for this Cuban exile, who is married to a "fine looking, stout, brown-skinned" American woman, a biracial—or, within the Cuban racial caste system, multiracial—effort to rid the island of imperial Spanish influence.[34] Antonio Maceo was the mixed-race son of an Afro-Cuban mother and a Venezuelan father; known as the "bronze titan" (*titán de bronce*), Maceo played a key role in the Ten Years' War (1868–1878) and the subsequent Cuban War of Independence (1895–1898), for which he gave his life in 1896. Juan Gualberto Gómez, the "black one," was the son of African slaves; he emerged as the leading voice for Afro-Cuban rights during the long struggle for independence, and he was closely allied with Cuba's most important icon of resistance, José Martí. Together with Martí, these revolutionaries envisioned and helped to forge a Cuba free of racial divisions.[35]

Long overlooked within Harlem Renaissance scholarship, in the twenty-first century Johnson's diverse connections to Latin America have come under scrutiny as an important intervention prying open the black/white binary that governs racial discourse in a U.S. context. In a 2010 discussion of Johnson's career as a U.S. diplomat stationed as a consul in Latin America, Brian Russell Roberts explores the constraints and opportunities presented to Johnson in Puerto Cabello, Venezuela, where he wrote the *Autobiography*, and later in Corinto, Nicaragua; Roberts also highlights the multiple forms of "strategic indirection," the language of intentionally vague diplomacy or racially inauthentic hypocrisy, in the *Autobiography* and in American racial discourse. By offering language that parallels diplomatic rhetoric, Roberts observes, "the novel seeks to disrupt the essentialist interpretive approaches that have racialized readings of strategic indirection as either hypocrisy or diplomacy."[36]

More immediately relevant to the particular episode that I have in mind, Amanda M. Page remarks that "Johnson uses the rhetoric of the Cuban war of independence as a way to present an interracial alternative to the Jim Crow South"; the postcolonial Cuban republic thus serves as a shining example of a society that extends its freedoms beyond a creole elite.[37] Seen in this light, we might reconfigure the narrator's Washington–Lincoln historical axis to include the possibility of a reference to Booker T. Washington among the foundational "great historic" figures; the Ex-Colored Man, we might recall, concludes his narrative by announcing that Booker T. Washington, among others, has "the eternal principles of right" on his side.[38] It's also important to consider that the narrator presumably knew, as Johnson certainly did, that Juan Gualberto Gómez sent his son, Juan Eusebio, to study under Washington at the Tuskegee Institute.[39]

As Roberts and Page demonstrate, Johnson's invocation of Latin American independence is both historically myopic and evasive of his own diplomatic complicity with U.S. imperial conquest in the region. Even so, as a rhetorical gesture, the description of a nurturing Afro-Cuban community in the heart of the American South presents a geographic and theoretical alternative to the novel's not-so-rigid North/South and black/white binaries. The Ex-Colored Man offers a rose-tinted, multiracial version—and a deeply nostalgic version—of Johnson's childhood home in Jacksonville: the Ex-Colored Man has risen in the ranks at the multiracial, multilingual cigar factory owing to his well-honed manual dexterity and to his quick and easy grasp of the Spanish language; he belongs to a literary society and frequents church festivals and fetes at the city's many fine homes; he goes to the Pablo Beach seaside resort with his factory friends; and he even falls "in love with a young school teacher and [begins] to have dreams of matrimonial bliss."[40]

This placid moment in Jacksonville history, sometime between Johnson's birth there in 1871 and the novel's publication in 1912, witnessed the city's transformation from a small, Negro-majority town with a substantial foreign-born population to a bustling, white-majority city with a smaller proportion of foreign-born residents. The census of 1870 records

6,912 Jacksonville residents, 57.7 percent Negro and 6.2 percent foreign-born; in 1910, there were 57,699 Jacksonville residents, 50.8 percent Negro and 4.7 percent foreign-born. Johnson would recall in his autobiography, *Along This Way* (1933), that Jacksonville "had a Cuban population of several thousand."[41] By 1920, Jacksonville had 91,558 residents; 54.6 percent were white, 45.3 percent were Negro, and 4.5 percent were foreign-born.

The Ex-Colored Man offers, as he puts it, "the observations [he] made in Jacksonville as seen through the light of after years."[42] Viewed from this perspective, it hardly makes sense to offer too sociological an explanation for the narrator's experiences there; however, the Ex-Colored Man immediately adds that his observations "apply generally to every Southern community," and he goes on to relate an elaborate theory of Negro society's threefold strata (the desperate class, the servant class, and the "well to-do and educated" class), along with an equally elaborate analysis of the four universally recognized Negro contributions to world culture (Uncle Remus stories, Jubilee songs, ragtime, and the cakewalk). For Johnson, social and cultural analyses go hand in hand, even within the pages of a novel.[43]

The U.S. sociohistorical context, it almost goes without saying, overrides the fluid, multiracial options suggested by Johnson's short-lived ideal of an Afro-Cuban society in Jacksonville—but not entirely. Similar, more localized alternatives find their way into Harlem Renaissance literature in the form of an Afro-Latino motif: representations of the effort to pass not as "white," but specifically as "Spanish" or just as often "Cuban." The device might be understood as the metonymic attainment of whiteness: because the Spanish have achieved the status of "white" despite the nation's complex racial heritage, even an obviously "Moorish" Spaniard partakes of Spanish whiteness; because a Cuban mulatto has more in common with a *criollo* (a Latin American of European stock) than with a European or an aboriginal native, something of the *criollo*'s whiteness transfers to the mulatto, both in terms of proximity within the Cuban racial caste system and in terms of social mobility.

Transplanted into a Jim Crow environment, a Cuban mulatto's social mobility has a direct impact on his literal mobility,[44] as we see once again in the example of Johnson. He recounts in *Along This Way* a train trip from Jacksonville to New York in which he enters the men's car to smoke a cigar, only to find that he's being "scrutinized more carefully than politely" by the handful of men there. One turns out to be an official from the Savannah-based railroad; another is the official's son, just returned from Cuba after serving as an officer in the Spanish-American War:

> The silence was broken by the young man just back from Cuba, who said, "Dad, there's a genuine Panama hat." The elder man looked over intently at the hat I was wearing. Without saying anything, I took it off and passed it to him for closer inspection. Panama hats were then rare in the United States. The hat was passed round and examined with expressions of admiration; it was a very good one. When it reached the young man he noticed the Havana-stamped lining and said to me, *"¿Habla Vd. español?" "Sí, señor,"* I answered. Thereupon he and I exchanged several commonplace phrases in Spanish; but in a short while his knowledge of the language was exhausted, and general conversation in English was resumed. I said little except in answer to some questions the preacher asked me about conditions in Cuba, where I had not yet been but concerning which I had a good deal of information. . . . The railroad official went into his bag and brought out his private flask of whisky, from which each of us, including the preacher, took several samples, all drinking out of the same glass. Before we reached Savannah a bond of mellow friendship had been established. My newly made friends got off at Savannah, and I went to bed repeating to myself: In such situations any kind of Negro will do; provided he is not one who is an American citizen.[45]

I quote from this episode at length for the same reason that Johnson recreates the scene in substantial detail: passing narratives necessarily dramatize social encounters fraught with danger for the person passing and rich with insider evidence about both sides of the color line.

Johnson lingers over the minutiae of the examination of the Panama hat and the bilingual conversation to emphasize his precarious situation among unreconstructed southerners and to demonstrate his caginess throughout the ordeal. Johnson quotes a snippet of Spanish conversation to reveal that the young southerner treats his fellow passenger with the respect, indicated by the formal Spanish *usted,* that an older black man might take for granted in Latin America but that a Negro would never expect to encounter in the South. Johnson strongly insinuates that he willfully lies about hailing from an island that he's never even visited. And he emphasizes the shared drink to underscore the hypocrisy not so much of the preacher as of Johnson's other new friends, who willingly fraternize with someone assumed to be Afro-Cuban even though they would never share a glass with an American Negro.

To acknowledge Johnson as Cuban rather than as Negro functions for these archetypal southerners as a kind of racial safety valve: they allow themselves freedoms to associate with a black man in ways denied them by the demands of their southern way of life. The categories—Cuban, Negro—must remain separate in their minds for the charade to play out appropriately. Cubanism is thus divorced from blackness by being non-Negro. For Johnson to reveal his nationality by speaking too gregariously, even though the situation calls for it, would be to call his fellow passengers' bluff and to bring an unceremonious end to the "mellow friendship." Johnson peacefully coexists as a Cuban; as a Negro, social roles would impose a rigid, racist hierarchy, breaking up the fun. To function smoothly in a rigidly racist framework, American society created such opportunities for light-skinned Negroes not to be black, if only temporarily and individually.[46] We can never know with certainty how many times people such as Johnson took advantage of similar scenarios, but we can quickly highlight a few such moments in Harlem Renaissance fiction.

When Irene Redfield, the protagonist of Nella Larsen's *Passing* (1929), first encounters, but does not yet recognize, her girlhood friend Clare Kendry at a Chicago hotel dining room, she wonders if this woman will identify her as a Negro passing for white. "Absurd! Impossible!" Irene's thoughts begin. "White people were so stupid about such things for all that they usually asserted that they were able to tell; and by the most ridiculous means, finger-nails, palms of hands, shapes of ears, teeth, and other equally silly rot. They always took her for an Italian, a Spaniard, a Mexican, or a gypsy." Within the American racial scheme of things, any number of "Latin" origins occasionally stand in for non-blackness, and therefore authenticate a non-Negro, or white, existence.[47]

By the same token, Anthony Cross, a central character in Jessie Redmon

Fauset's *Plum Bun* (1928), claims to be a Spaniard who gave up his original name, Cruz, for the anglicized, more racially symbolic alternative, all so that he can better assimilate into mainstream U.S. society. (The Spanish name "Cruz" shares the religious symbolism of the English "Cross.") At least, that's the version of his story that Anthony shares with strangers and casual acquaintances. With the novel's protagonist, his beloved Angela Murray, Anthony reveals, tragically late, that he is in fact the son of a Georgia-born Negro sailor and a Brazilian mother "with the blood of many races in her veins." As Valerie Popp observes, Latin America is for Fauset "an imaginative play zone" that is simultaneously exotic and an extension of southern geography, where American social relations might be imaginatively reconceived in liberating ways.[48] Anthony brings his "Spanish" identity to New York, where he fits in semi-comfortably with his freethinking fellow artists, who wouldn't think to question his whiteness. To the extent that Anthony doesn't fit in, characters such as Angela, who is also passing as white, presume that financial difficulties or perhaps a violent past prevent his full immersion into the American mainstream. Never do others suppose that it's the "black blood that was in [Anthony's] veins" that prevents his full assimilation and that stands in the way of his romance with Angela, whom he mistakenly believes to be white.[49]

John Hall, Anthony's seafaring Negro father, returned to Georgia to claim his inheritance after marrying the Brazilian woman, Maria Cruz, only to have his land and his life taken from him by scheming, jealous southerners. Fauset's novel redirects the tragic mulatto plot device to explore the movement of capital across national boundaries at the same time that it considers the role of geography in establishing social identity. Anthony and Angela are able to "cross" national borders in a manner that is more or less complicated depending on their willingness to "cross" racial identity boundaries and to pass as white. Their freedom of movement thus has everything to do with yet another crossing: the interracial relationships that would yield indeterminate racial phenotypes, that would produce in the case of Angela a "creamy complexion and . . . soft cloudy, chestnut hair" or in the case of Anthony a "sallow" appearance.[50]

A focus on intraracial color gradation challenges the Great Migration paradigm, with its emphasis on southern origins, at least in theory. Rhetorically, a rainbow-colored African American population unveils the South's history of racialized sexual violence; there can be no single font of racially pure African American identity in the South, or for that matter anywhere else, if so much of the African American population springs from miscegenation. Geopolitically, intraracial color diversity points to transnational alternatives for understanding racial identity, including the elaborate racial caste options found immediately south of the U.S. border. Maria Cruz, for example, would have been legally defined as Negro in the United States, but these days she would likely be classified as *branco* [white] by the Brazilian Institute of Geography and Statistics (IBGE), which administers the nation's decennial census.[51] It's important to note, however, that the category *branco* does not carry with it an ideal of racial purity; as the sociologist Stanley R. Bailey reveals, "a Brazilian *branco* may be considered non-*branco* by a third party using the U.S. notion of whiteness as a universal yardstick for measuring racial classification." Maria Cruz's fellow Brazilians might less formally identify her by one of more than one hundred color terms recorded by the IBGE when they asked in 1976 how individuals identified themselves by color or race: she might be known as *morena clara* [light brown] or *castanha* [chestnut] or *mista* [mixed], to list but a few of the more popular unofficial racial designations.[52]

Speaking as a practical matter, the racial identity options are less fluid, more clear-cut for a Maria Cruz or an Anthony Cross taking part in the Great Migration. Although the Census Bureau reported (as we saw earlier in table 3.5) some 3,191 South American–born Negroes in the United States in 1930 (it did not specify the number of immigrants from Brazil until 1960), Anthony Cross would have been counted among the 30,655 South American–born whites identified that year. (Because the Census Bureau in 1930 included "Mexican" among its racial categories, it also reported 278 South American–born Mexicans. Humorously confusing examples such as this are all too easy to come by in historical census documents.)

In citing these figures, my point is quite simple: an individual such as Anthony Cross, or even Anthony Cruz, would have been rare enough to be exotic, to capture the attention of the Greenwich Village art scene, but not unheard of in New York society. His skin color would have been quickly and easily understood as falling squarely into the white side of the white/black divide. Indeed, Anthony Cross would have been part of the steady, white background against which a black Great Migration was cast into sharp relief; his whiteness would help to crystallize and consolidate an African American literature responsive to a difficult social environment, an environment that led scholars and lay audiences alike to interpret the Great Migration as a key element in the formation of African American racial solidarity. The next chapter explores how and why this transregional racial cohesion came to be.

4
Harlem Modernity
Inventing the New Negro

Great and Greater Migrations

In 1920, Emmett Jay Scott, in his Carnegie Endowment–sponsored *Negro Migration during the War,* cemented the still fresh idea that a Great Migration of African Americans from the rural South to the urban North altered the course of American society. Scott, a civic leader, adviser to Booker T. Washington, and Howard University administrator, argued that "within the brief period of three years following the outbreak of the great war in Europe, more than four hundred thousand negroes moved north. In extent this movement is without parallel in American history, for it swept on thousands of the blacks from remote regions of the South, and spread from Florida to the western limits of Texas." True to his political ties and his academic career path, Scott tends not to editorialize or otherwise pass judgment on the demographic trends that he highlights; he merely points to "problems," both in the North and in the South, created or exacerbated by the sudden population shift.[1]

The next year, speaking before a Birmingham, Alabama, audience of over a hundred thousand, U.S. president Warren G. Harding remarked, "The World War brought us to full recognition that the race problem is national rather than merely sectional. While there are no authentic statistics, it is common knowledge that the World War was marked by a great negro migration from the Southern into the Northern states, where the negroes were attracted by the demand for labor and the higher wages offered in the North and West. The movement had been slowly underway for decades. But in the World War . . . it was greatly accelerated and has subsequently continued at only a slightly reduced rate."[2] Harding was nothing if not political in the speech, which navigates a narrow path meant to retain the electoral support of unlikely Republican Party bedfellows: recently enfranchised black voters and white voters wary of social integration.

Harding was reacting not only to the immense social change represented by the grand-scale redistribution of the African American population from one region to another, but also to the socially cataclysmic force of interracial romance and miscegenation. The president's immediate inspiration was W. E. B. Du Bois's *Crisis* essay "The Social Equality of Whites and Blacks," published in November 1920, which argued for the legality and morality of interracial marriage; Harding, according to *New York Times* coverage of the speech, was "contemplating a new policy with respect to the negro in the South which would make it clear that the [Republican] party would not countenance any claim on the part of the negro to social equality with whites."[3]

As these widely reviewed (in the case of Scott) or widely reported (in the case of Harding) examples suggest, by the early 1920s, the initial moments of the Harlem Renaissance, most Americans believed that the internal migration of African Americans from the rural South to the urban North had, for better or for worse, redrawn the American social landscape. The tectonic social shift required all Americans to rethink the political, social, and cultural roles of the African American in U.S. life.

Here I wish to explore questions relevant to the notion that a Great Migration fundamentally altered the American experience. How did the idea of a great migration enter early twentieth-century racial discourse? And how did the idea transform academic and cultural disciplines—from history to anthropology to sociology to visual art—leading up to the moment when African American studies came into existence? Several foundational motifs in African American culture and cultural studies, including the linking of Afro-diaspora experiences with the biblical Exodus and the many varieties of Afro-centric cultural nationalism, depend on or dovetail with the myriad sources, academic and otherwise, of great migration discourse. Intellectuals as far apart as Du Bois and Marcus Garvey were guided by the rhetorical and actual promise of mass racial migration. Writers as far-flung as the much-traveled Nella Larsen and Jean Toomer broached the idea of a racial homeland that might or might not be relocated across a continent or across the Atlantic. The result was and remains a rich chorus of possibilities that has been exploited to meet a number of cultural, intellectual, political, and even economic interests. At the outset, this much is certain: our contemporary understanding of the Harlem Renaissance relies heavily on the Great Migration as an interpretive lens through which we view twentieth-century society and culture. Indeed, the institutionalization of great migration discourse helped transform our understanding of the cosmopolitan, polyglot Negro Renaissance into the anglophone, domestic Harlem Renaissance.

Great migration references first appear in the mid-nineteenth century, in the budding field of ethnology, which sought to explain the geographic basis for human variety. Typically, ethnologists conveyed the "greatness" of early human mass movements by emphasizing the existential challenges of drought and famine and intertribal warfare. Such forced shifts in the human population had far-reaching racial implications. The comparative methods that inform great migration discourse in ethnology (and later anthropology) worked their way into related fields of knowledge. In taxonomy and evolutionary biology, great migrations help to account for speciation across diverse environments, as well as structural and phylogenetic similarities within closely related species. In plant and animal paleontology and zoology, great migrations explain evolution-hastening shifts of populations across vast swaths of territory, including species dispersal that takes place over generations and even across multiple centuries.[4] Human paleontologists sometimes refer to the earliest expansions of *Homo sapiens* out of Africa—a series of tribal wanderings that began roughly eighty thousand years ago—as a great migration. We now understand that, as a result of this process, non-African natives share up to 4 percent of their DNA with extinct Neanderthals, who roamed Europe and Asia alongside early humans until thirty thousand years ago.[5]

The notion that migration in more modern times might take place on a scale that deserves the modifier "great" similarly presupposes consequences on an epic, nation-building or nation-changing scale. (In a related way, we use the labels "Great War" and "World War" interchangeably.) In the fields of ethnography and archeology, the "great migration" designation identifies mass movement occasioned by the survival instinct; it defines prehistoric or ancient imperial conquest, tragic flight from invading hordes, or the desperate search for food in times of insufferable famine. Linguists might explain structural similarities between seemingly disparate languages in great migration terms. The very idea of an Indo-European (or Aryan) source of European languages and cultures, a product of early nineteenth-century comparative philology, presumes change over time and dispersal across space. References to the Jewish exodus as a great migration are also commonplace from the nineteenth century forward. The Puritan upheaval during the early modern era occasioned plentiful great migration references during the nineteenth and early twentieth centuries; one example might be found in Madison Grant's nativist screed, *The Conquest of a Continent* (1933), which identifies "the arrival of Governor Winthrop's fleet in Massachusetts Bay in 1630" as "the first great migration" from England to the New World.[6]

By extending these patterns figuratively, it's possible to address the movement of large numbers of African Americans using the exact same terms and to imply similarly nation-building and nation-changing consequences. If the first mass migration of Africans to the United States—the Middle Passage—required American society's refusal to admit a subject people into the body politic, great migration discourse presents an occasion to broach the possibility, however belatedly, of full political and social inclusion. As African Americans relocate across the Mason-Dixon Line and adapt to the pitfalls and opportunities presented by life in the North, they evolve as a society and at the same time redefine lived experience for all northerners, black *and* white. To the extent that assimilation to the northern experience is possible, the Great Migration reveals what is universal across all Americans. To the extent that African Americans remain outside the mainstream of American life in northern locales underscores the irresolvable particulars of a racially divided society.

The earliest reference to a Great Migration in the sense understood within African American studies—the mass movement of rural southern African Americans to the industrial North during the early twentieth century—appears to have been by E. Dana Durand, U.S. Census Bureau director from 1910 to 1913. Trained as an economist at Cornell University, Durand oversaw the Thirteenth Census in 1910, and on January 7, 1913, at the National Museum, he read a paper on "Race Statistics of the Last Census" before the Anthropological Society of Washington. "There has been no great migration of negroes out of the South," Durand observed, "nearly nine-tenths of the total number being still found in that section."[7] Durand has in mind great migration analysis because the relative rates of growth among diverse populations allow him to consider racial existential outlooks in both the North and the South.

Five years later, the Census Bureau published *Negro Population, 1790–1915* (1918), a hefty compilation of data recording population growth and population drift "in response to the universal gravity pull of complex economic and social forces." Because its data predate World War I, the study is equally occupied with westward as with northward Negro migration. In 1910, the last census prior to the study's publication—the census that provided Durand with his "great migration of negroes" data—nearly 9 million Negroes (fully 89 percent of the total Negro population) still resided in the South; this contrasts with nearly 21 million whites (or 25 percent of the total white population) who lived in the South. Out of a total northern population of nearly 56 million, only 1 million were Negro in 1910.[8] The Great Migration was only just under way and, as Durand reported, was not yet reflected statistically.

If we extend our analysis to 1930, however, the dramatic population shift that commanded the attention of Scott and Harding—its greatness—comes into much sharper focus. Let us consider Negro population growth in six states north of the Mason-Dixon Line, shown in table 4.1. In terms of raw population numbers, the shifts represented are striking: they equal the addition to each state of a new town or small city in the span of a decade. Each of these six states added the equivalent of a mid-sized city between 1920 and 1930. But relative to the still-large Negro population in the South, the northern population trend appears less significant. In 1910, the five states with the greatest number of Negroes were (in order) Georgia, Mississippi, Alabama, South Carolina, and Louisiana; Pennsylvania ranked fourteenth and New York ranked seventeenth. By 1930, these remained largely the same—Georgia, Mississippi, Alabama, North Carolina, and Texas—and Pennsylvania and New York rose to twelfth and thirteenth, respectively. It is more important to consider the relative rates of Negro population growth for each state and for the U.S. overall; here we see a much more dramatic picture emerge, as is shown in table 4.2.

TABLE 4.1. Negro population in selected northern states

STATE	1900	1910	1920	1930
Illinois	85,078	109,049	182,274	328,972
Michigan	15,816	17,115	60,082	169,453
New Jersey	69,844	89,760	117,132	208,828
New York	99,232	134,191	198,483	412,814
Ohio	96,901	111,452	186,187	309,304
Pennsylvania	156,845	193,919	284,568	431,257

Sources: U.S. Census Bureau, Twelfth Census of the United States, Thirteenth Census of the United States, Fourteenth Census of the United States, and Fifteenth Census of the United States.

TABLE 4.2. Percentage increase of Negro population for selected northern states, of U.S. Negro population, and of U.S. total population (all races)

	1900–1910	1910–1920	1920–1930
Illinois	28.2	67.1	80.5
Michigan	8.2	251.0	182.0
New Jersey	28.5	30.5	78.3
New York	35.2	47.9	108.0
Ohio	15.0	67.1	66.1
Pennsylvania	23.6	46.7	51.5
U.S. Negro	11.2	6.5	13.6
U.S. Total	21.0	14.9	16.1

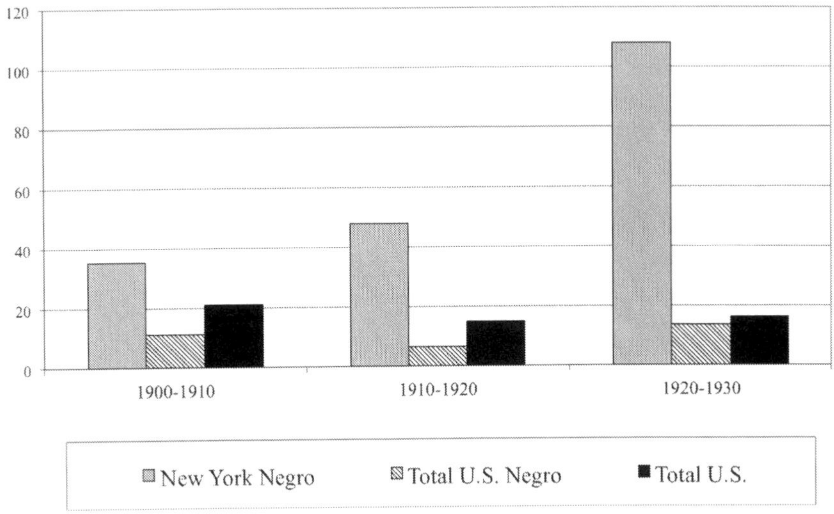

Figure 4.1. Percentage increase of New York Negro population, total U.S. Negro population, and U.S. total population (all races), 1900–1930.

As these figures reveal, the Negro population in northern states, particularly the heavily industrialized states, grew at a clip that far exceeded overall U.S. population growth, and surpassed by even wider margins the relatively flat growth of the overall U.S. Negro population. Because Negro population growth relied mostly on a surplus of births over deaths, without the additional boost of new immigrants (with a few localized exceptions), its rate of growth has lagged behind the overall U.S. population growth rate since the end of the transatlantic slave trade.

The visual snapshot of the Negro population growth rate for New York State shown in figure 4.1 showcases the explosiveness of the population shift. The Negro population in New York State expanded from 1900 to 1930 by some 313,582 persons, a 316.0 percent rate of increase. In stark contrast, the Negro population in Georgia, the state with the largest Negro population during these three decades, grew by only 39,088 persons (from 1,035,037 to 1,071,125 Negroes), just a 3.8 percent rate of increase. Georgia actually lost Negro population (135,240 persons) between 1920 and 1930.

The Great Migration was thus experienced across all parts of the nation, even if only negatively. The slow Negro growth rate in Georgia would be felt as a sharp decline by Negro civic leaders, who would worry about a loss of southern political influence, and by white farmers, who would worry about a "loss" of available labor. Two southern states, Mississippi and South Carolina, evolved from Negro-majority populations to white-majority populations between 1920 and 1940. By the middle of the 1910s, references to an ongoing Great Migration of southern Negroes were increasingly common in the popular press, a trend that rapidly escalated with the onset of World War I and the abundant Great Migration scholarship that quickly followed.[9] The U.S. Department of Labor viewed the "great migratory stream of Negro wage earners" as a wartime national security concern, and in 1917 initiated a study of the impact of this population shift on southern and northern industry.[10]

Questions of *who* made the trek from South to North were most often answered in broad sociological terms of *why* they made the trek, of push and pull factors prompting a decision to migrate. When the historian Carter G. Woodson, one of the founding fathers of African American studies, took up the issue in *A Century of Negro Migration* (1918), he carefully distinguished between the causes of migration during the eras of slavery and Reconstruction and the causes of a World War I–era "exodus" "in such large numbers as to overshadow in its results all other movements of the kind." Woodson relied on previously published interviews to identify now-familiar sociopolitical causes (including "*bulldozing*, terrorism, maltreatment and what not of persecution," "injustice in the courts, unrest, lack of privileges, denial of the right to vote, bad treatment, oppression, segregation or lynching") and economic causes (including "to find employment, to secure better wages, better school facilities, and better opportunities to toil upward").[11]

Most social historians today would agree with Scott's assessment that "the economic motive stands among the foremost reasons for the decision of the group to leave the South," particularly once World War I severely curtailed immigration from Europe, which in turn increased northern industry's demand for African American labor.[12] An important catalyst for the Great Migration, most observers suggest, was the invasion of the Mexican boll weevil, which decimated southern cotton crops as early as 1892, just ahead of the Panic of 1893. Crop damage caused by the boll weevil amplified the destruction generated by the inevitable floods along the Mississippi River Valley, where the greatest concentrations of African Americans lived.

If Harlem Renaissance artistic production was a "cultural nationalism of the parlor," as David Levering Lewis puts it,[13] then the Great Migration was understood at the time as the civil rights movement of demographic change. That is, many believed that the economic and social pressures exerted by the mass movement of African Americans would reshape U.S. politics and society, potentially in ways that would improve the status of African Americans, particularly in the South. If enough African Americans departed the South, the thinking went, scarcity of labor there might push wages upward; given sufficient labor market pressures, southern elites might induce poor whites to end their violent resistance to African American progress. Some expressed the naive hope that dwindling numbers of African Americans in the South might relieve southern whites of their paranoid fears of African American domination and thus reduce the tendency toward lynching and other forms of racial terrorism.[14]

Depictions of the South during this time of mass migration were most likely to invoke a figure with deep roots in African American culture: exodus, arguably the single most potent trope serving African American "typological ethnogenesis," to borrow a phrase from Werner Sollors.[15] The powerful symbolism of an escape from bondage to salvation in a land of milk and honey, as Albert J. Raboteau observes, simultaneously questions traditional American historiography and reaffirms the Afro-diaspora mission: "From the earliest days of colonization, white Christians had represented their journey across the Atlantic to America as the exodus of a New Israel from the bondage of Egypt into the Promised Land. . . . For black Christians, the imagery was reversed: the Middle Passage had brought them to Egypt land, where they suffered bondage under a new Pharaoh. White Christians saw themselves as the New Israel; slaves identified themselves as the Old." The story of the biblical Exodus thus "functioned as an archetypal myth for the slaves," offering divine meaning to this-worldly suffering. "It would be hard to exaggerate the intensity of [slaves'] identification with the children of Israel," Raboteau concludes—an identification that spans the more recent past as well, lending resonance to thinkers as diverse as Martin Luther King Jr. and Bob Marley in the latter half of the twentieth century.[16]

African American writers typically called on the structural similarities between Israelite and African slavery so that the former oppression prefigures a later, American suffering. As a result, latter-day exoduses pay little attention to the migratory wandering at the heart of the biblical Exodus. Harlem Renaissance retellings of the exodus story, much like antecedents written by Frances E. W. Harper and Paul Laurence Dunbar, tend not to touch on Israelite dislocation and resettlement. In his *God's Trombones: Seven Negro Sermons in Verse* (1927), for example, James Weldon Johnson records a sermon, "Let My People Go," that places the Moses story in the voice of a southern Negro preacher who is much more interested in juxtaposing Old Pharaoh's vengeful pride against the Hebrew God's cosmic reckoning than he is in describing the movement of millions of Israelite men, women, and children (beginning in Exodus 12). The journey of the Hebrews to the Red Sea occupies a mere seven lines in a poem that extends to more than two hundred lines. As with all of the sermons, Johnson's preacher concludes by addressing his flock, this time as "All you sons of the Pharaoh"; nothing in the poem, however, signals a correspondence to the Great Migration from South to North.[17]

Zora Neale Hurston provides the most thoroughly staged reference to the biblical Exodus in her *Moses, Man of the Mountain* (1939), a novel that hints in its descriptions of the Nile river valley and the land of Canaan at an association with the southern agrarian experience. And the novel's intertextual wanderings, in particular its use of southern dialect, open up still more possibilities for an American allegory, even as they muddle the reading experience.[18] But the novel's plot hews too closely to its biblical source to suggest a correspondence between the Israelite and the African American great migrations.

For Hurston and Johnson, the cues linking Israelite bondage and African American suffering are chiefly linguistic, such that Negro dialect and southern colloquialisms signal Hebrew identity. Consider how Hurston's Moses slips into southern colloquialisms as he rallies the Israelites just before bringing the Red Sea crashing down on Pharaoh's army:

> As the chariots drew near the panic grew in Israel. They committed every kind of folly and showed their inside weakness. Then Moses showed his power again. He turned his back on the Egyptian horde and spoke to his people. Spoke to them in their own dialect as one of them.

> "Stand still!" he commanded in a sterner voice than they had ever heard before. "Stand still, every last one of you and stop that screaming and yelling. You haven't got a thing to be scared of. That ain't nobody but Pharaoh and his army and we done beat them too many times before. Don't get so excited about nothing!"[19]

Throughout the novel, Moses struggles with an Egyptian upbringing that distances him from the much folksier Israelites, who simultaneously covet and distrust all things Egyptian, from the food to the clothing to the manners. It's Moses's sincere effort to acquire and deploy "Hebrew"—despite his biblically inspired "stammering tongue" (Exodus 4:10)—that wins him the loyalty of the Israelites and victory over the Pharaoh. Similarly, Johnson's Moses protests, "Lord, you know I'm slow of tongue"—nevertheless, Moses speaks with the same sure cadences as both the Pharaoh and the God of Israel.[20] Moses commands his people as much with his voice as with his rod.

The best known and most influential example of exodus symbolism applied to the African American experience—and specifically to the Great Migration—develops the Israelite–Negro analogy visually. Jacob Lawrence's powerful *The Migration of the Negro* (1941), a post-renaissance reevaluation of African American history, treats the causes and the consequences of the Great Migration in a series of sixty tempera-on-hardboard-panel paintings, and references to the biblical Exodus replicate visually the historical framework that Lawrence supplies in textual captions for each panel.[21] Lawrence understood his life as deeply connected to both the Great Migration and the Harlem Renaissance, and for obvious reasons: he was born in Atlantic City, New Jersey, in 1917 as his parents were relocating from South Carolina to Virginia; the family—Jacob and his mother and siblings—finally settled in Harlem in 1930. At the Harlem branch of the New York Public Library, the teenaged Lawrence received art instruction from the painter Charles Alston, who introduced him to Alain Locke. Lawrence would also find a mentor in Claude McKay, who like the young painter counted himself a member of the multimedia Studio 306 Workshop (so named because Alston's studio was located at 306 West 141st Street). Lawrence and McKay lived in the same 125th

Street apartment building shortly after Lawrence achieved national acclaim when *Fortune* magazine reproduced twenty-six panels (with an accompanying essay by Locke) in November 1941 and with his December 1941 showing of the entire Migration Series.

The Migration Series melds powerful visual images with an accompanying textual narrative to record the history of the Great Migration. In keeping with the style that Lawrence would adapt throughout his career, the paintings in the Migration Series are composed of simple geometric shapes superimposed one over another. The lines sharply cut across the plane of the panels, which allows space to function symbolically by clearly separating representatives of distinct social identities. Lawrence's colors—painted one by one on all sixty panels, resulting in a limited and self-referencing palette—tend to be vibrant earth tones evenly applied over individual shapes rather than subtly gradated in chiaroscuro fashion. The technical approach, coupled with the use of hand-mixed tempera paints (a centuries-old process most closely associated with Italian painting, including examples that Lawrence studied at the Metropolitan Museum of Art), creates a unique blend of ancient and modern, a visual style that Lawrence described as "dynamic cubism."[22]

The subject matter depicted in the Migration Series is quickly summarized by a few of the panel captions that Lawrence wrote before he ever began to paint:

> 1. During the World War there was a great migration North by Southern Negroes.
>
> 2. The World War had caused a great shortage in Northern industry and also citizens of foreign countries were returning home.
>
> 8. They did not always leave because they were promised work in the North. Many of them left because of Southern conditions, one of them being great floods that ruined the crops, and therefore they were unable to make a living where they were.
>
> 9. Another great ravager of the crops was the boll weevil.
>
> 14. Among the social conditions that existed which was partly the cause of the migration was the injustice done to the Negroes in the courts.
>
> 15. Another cause was lynching. It was found that where there had been a

> lynching, the people who were reluctant to leave at first left immediately after this.
>
> 34. The Negro press was also influential in urging the people to leave the South.
>
> 44. Living conditions were better in the North.
>
> 47. As well as finding better housing conditions in the North, the migrants found very poor housing conditions in the North. They were forced into overcrowded and dilapidated tenement houses.

As these few captions suggest and as Lawrence scholars correctly point out, the painter studiously engaged Great Migration history, including Scott's and Woodson's analyses, while conducting background research for the project in the Harlem branch of the New York Public Library. When he applied for a Rosenwald Fund grant to complete the Migration Series, Lawrence borrowed six of Scott's chapter titles for his project outline.[23] The cultural historian Christopher Capozzola makes the important case that the Migration Series must be understood not simply as historically informed, but also as an intervention into Great Migration historiography: these captions further indicate that Lawrence took up Great Migration history with a critical eye; rather than merely celebrate the movement, he underscores the more sinister aspects of relocation to the North.[24]

The visual symbolism of the Migration Series is significantly informed by Locke's wish to bring African antiquity into conversation with American modernity. One panel—"24. Child labor and a lack of education was one of the other reasons for people wishing to leave their homes"—is done in the style of an Egyptian relief, with hunched-over children dressed in loincloths and carrying woven baskets filled, presumably, with cotton. Another panel—"13. Due to the South's losing so much of its labor, the crops were left to dry and spoil"—depicts a sun bearing down on the fallow earth with hard-edged, golden rays; the style is reminiscent of ancient Egyptian sacral art, with a nod as well to the plagues of the biblical Exodus.

Lawrence's exodus symbolism is especially noteworthy in two panels that cross-reference each other and thus call for side-by-side consideration.

Panel 54—"One of the main forms of social and recreational activities in which the migrants indulged occurred in the church"—shows an African American congregation in sharp relief against the backdrop of a pseudo-triptych mural. The painting-within-a-painting depicts a single blue cross atop Calvary hill on the left-hand panel. The right-hand panel shows a shrouded woman hunched over in prayer; her blue shawl, according to Christian iconography, indicates that this woman is the Virgin Mary (whose pose interestingly mirrors the praying African American woman in the foreground). In the center panel we find a longhaired, bearded man in an orange-red and white robe. Given the other two panels, this clearly represents Christ. But Lawrence's Christ firmly grips a long, straight staff in his left hand. Images of the Good Shepherd routinely depict Christ holding a staff, but this is almost always curved on one end so that stray sheep might be brought back gently into the fold. The straight staff in Lawrence's painting is instead a loud visual echo of the rod of Moses, which some Christian commentators view as a prefiguration of the Good Shepherd's staff. The effect of Lawrence's typological symbolism is to cast Christ in the role of Moses and the African American church congregation in the role of the wandering children of Israel.

The same potently symbolic staff reappears three panels later: "57. The female worker was also one of the last groups to leave the South" (fig. 4.2). The panel depicts a solitary African American washerwoman as she tackles the laundry with a long, orange-red stirring stick. Like the Christ figure in panel 54, she wears a long white robe and faces the viewer directly; however, her head is humbly bowed and covered in a white scarf or shawl in the manner of the nearby panel's Virgin Mary. The laundry—jigsaw pieces of orange and green and yellow and black paint—floats atop a tremendous brown vat (or an even larger body of water); behind the woman are hung large sheets or rugs done in the same colors. It's a very short stretch from the historical "facts" of the painting to identifying the washerwoman as a twentieth-century, female Moses parting the Red Sea as the Tribes of Israel symbolically encamp behind her. That Lawrence previously painted a series about Harriet Tubman, the "Black Moses" of nineteenth-century American history, further indicates that Lawrence understood African American migration as a latter-day exodus.

Figure 4.2. Jacob Lawrence, *The Migration of the Negro,* no. 57: "The female worker was also one of the last groups to leave the South," 1941.

In the Migration Series we see the culmination of a century of great migration discourse. Lawrence's paintings are simultaneously rooted in the individual experience and easily identifiable by art historians as "crafting a vast and epic history."[25] The washerwoman, to retain the example for a moment longer, represents both the everyday trials of a southern laborer and a larger-than-life figure leading her people from bondage into the Promised Land. Lawrence knew countless such individuals—including his mother, who performed domestic work to earn a living—and his Migration Series elevates their commonplace acts into heroic feats of nation building. Here, then, we have a cultural nationalism of the art gallery, an imaginative intervention into a larger conversation about the past and future status of African Americans in the wider society. The motto of the Migration Series might well be *E pluribus unum,* for in its narrative arc we see regionally distinct environments and customs forged into a singular racial experience.

In a Bluer Vein

In his moralistic short story "The Wife of His Youth" (1899), Charles W. Chesnutt refers in a tongue-in-cheek way to the biblical Exodus, linking turn-of-the-century mulatto elitism with Israelite spiritual wandering.[26] At an early moment in the story, the third-person narrator, whose perspective relies heavily on a focus that hovers near the principal character, the upward-striving mulatto Mr. Ryder, shares these thoughts about the so-called Blue Veins, a "little society of colored persons" organized "to establish and maintain correct social standards among a people whose social condition presented almost unlimited room for improvement": "There were those who had been known to assail it violently as a glaring example of the very prejudice from which the colored race had suffered most; and later, when such critics had succeeded in getting on the inside, they had been heard to maintain with zeal and earnestness that the society was a lifeboat, an anchor, a bulwark and a shield,—a pillar of cloud by day and of fire by night, to guide their people through the social wilderness."[27] In tracking the Blue Vein members' search for an appropriate metaphor, the narrator finally settles on the biblical one (the supernatural pillar depicted in Exodus 13:21) that undermines the more traditional linking of Israelite servitude with African American suffering. Here, the Children of Israel prefigure neither U.S. slaves nor their post-Emancipation progeny, but rather a small, elitist, and colorist faction—light-skinned mulattos—whose Blue Vein Society distances them from darker African Americans.

If we extend the analogy, the Egyptian dessert prefigures not so much an actual, physical space, but instead the "wilderness" of a Jim Crow society, along with its "one-drop rule" system of legal apartheid, that denies Blue Veins the special privileges to which they feel entitled. Most important, the metaphorical Egyptians remain difficult to pin down: Are they white America? This hardly fits the analogy, for Ryder prefers (in a clear echo of Census Bureau rhetoric) the mulattoes' "absorption by the white race" over "extinction in the black."[28] In his would-be fiancée, the light-skinned Mrs. Molly Dixon, Ryder sees an opportunity "to further the upward process of absorption he had been wishing and waiting for." Ryder's dwelling upon mulatto "extinction" in the black race, a "backward step" in his view, signals that black America may indeed be the metaphorical Egyptians required of the larger analogy.[29] Leave it to Chesnutt, however, to keep the analogy wholly unstable: the South, where the freeborn Ryder scarcely escaped being fraudulently sold into bondage, also represents a kind of Egypt. That Mrs. Dixon shares her name with an imaginary line distinguishing North from South adds yet another dimension to the biblically inspired analogy.

References to the Blue Vein Society in American literary history provide evidence not only that questions of racial purity (or impurity) occupied much thought among U.S. writers,[30] but also that such questions were often addressed in terms of membership within exclusive, sometimes genealogical, societies. The Blue Vein Society, according to the many versions of the legend, was a group of mulatto elites who socialized and strategized for mutual benefit in various centers of African American life—precisely where depends on who is telling the tale.[31]

Chesnutt's fictional Blue Veins can be found in "a certain Northern city"; Chesnutt scholars are quick to point out that Cleveland served as the likely source of inspiration for the group.[32] (Chesnutt's "A Matter of

Principle" [1899] locates the Blue Vein Society in "Groveland.") In "The Blue Vein Club" (1902), the poet Katherine Davis Chapman Tillman placed the eponymous club in "Darktown," a fitting location for the farcical, verse send-up of mulatto pretensions and unscrupulous hair-straightening hucksters. The Harlem Renaissance troublemaker Wallace Thurman put his fictional "blue vein circle" in, of all places, Boise, Idaho, where there were so few Negroes to begin with "that there wasn't much cream to skim off." Despite their varying locations, what unites these examples is their fixation on genealogical societies that emphasize physical appearance rather than birth or baptismal records as the criterion for membership. A person's skin color is her or his proof. As Thurman's mordant narrator tells us, the "blue vein circle" was "so named because all of its members were fair-skinned enough for their blood to be seen pulsing purple through the veins of their wrists."[33]

Of course, it's important to take these blue vein references with a healthy dose of salt. Chesnutt's narrator expresses views in every respect antithetical to the political agenda that the author espoused throughout his life. Ryder's notions of racial absorption and racial extinction more closely resemble the paranoid, eugenicist rhetoric of those whom Chesnutt battled throughout his career as a civil rights advocate and activist. By the poignant end of "The Wife of His Youth," even Ryder's calloused Blue Veins understand that the man must reunite with his dark-skinned former wife.

Although she favored religious uplift over satire, Tillman's poem reads like a tongue-in-cheek, Jim Crow–era premonition of Dr. Seuss and his more famous Sneetches; its lyric voice makes light of racialized discourse in general ("Down in Darktown there is trouble / Of a most peculiar kind") and in particular of the "beauty" and hair care products that made people like the Harlem mogul C. J. Walker a wealthy woman:

> Miss Dare she did the straightening
>   For a neat five dollar bill.
> There were all in all one hundred
>   Swallowed Miss Dare's Blue Vein pill.[34]

In a mere five quatrains, Tillman takes on unprincipled businesswomen who profit from Blue Vein pretension and the rubes who serve as willing victims.

Bernard W. Bell highlights Thurman (along with Rudolph Fisher and George S. Schuyler) as one of the exemplars of "satiric realism" during the Harlem Renaissance, and Bell singles out Thurman's preference for "dramatic irony" over "ridicule" to provide distance between himself and his protagonist, the dark-skinned Emma Lou Morgan.[35] As we might expect, though, there is ridicule aplenty when it comes to Thurman's treatment of the blue veins: "In their veins was some of the best blood of the South," his narrator expounds, underscoring the sexually violent foundations of mulatto identity. Indeed, he goes on to categorize intraracial color hierarchy as a continuation of slavery's caste system: the blue veins "were closely akin to the only true aristocrats of the United States. Even the slave masters had been aware of and acknowledged in some measure their superiority. Having some of Marse George's blood in their veins set them apart from ordinary Negroes at birth." Ironically, the narrator reports that such light-skinned "mulattoes as a rule were not ordered to work in the fields beneath the broiling sun at the urge of a Simon Legree lash"; they were instead "saved and trained to be ladies' maids and butlers," the very same demeaning domestic labor that Emma Lou finds beneath her station.[36]

The blue vein designation clearly leverages its association with the "blue blood" metaphor—in each of the cases cited above, the two phrases are virtually interchangeable—but its appeal within late nineteenth- and early twentieth-century racial discourse derives as well from ongoing discussions about the value of sunlight for the human body and a history of pseudoscientific ideas related to skin color. Racialized blue vein references emerge at the tail end of the Victorian era's close association of female beauty with pale skin, poetically registered in metaphors involving alabaster, ivory, porcelain, and so forth. It's not uncommon to see depictions of blue veins showing through a desired person's breast, temple, or forehead in popular nineteenth-century poetry and prose.[37] Coupled with pseudoscientific theories about the opacity of African skin,[38] it is easy to understand why the blue vein motif might serve colorist hierarchies in the post-Reconstruction United States.

By the time we reach Thurman's novel, however, references to a literal blue vein test, of the sort that Emma Lou's grandmother applied to her favored social circle, must be understood as woefully out-of-date, as antithetical to the trends that made suntanning a fashion craze by the end of the Roaring Twenties. The cultural historian Kerry Segrave notes, "Suntanning as an activity spread rapidly through all parts of society in the 1920s, driven by an enormous number of articles about the sun as a healer. . . . Articles on the fashion of tanning in the 1920s and 1930s began to stress that a tan made a person look better, appear healthier, and become more attractive to the opposite sex."[39] One study of *Harper's* and *Vogue* magazines pinpoints the U.S. arrival of the fashionable suntan to a specific few months, noting that "a marked cultural shift favoring tanning occurred during the period 1927 to 1928," with a simultaneous decline in the fashion prominence of skin bleaching agents and sun-blocking apparel. In June 1928, one *Vogue* article went so far as to celebrate beaches "black with the recumbent figures of the new sun-worshippers"; the following June, *Harper's* opined that "if you haven't a tanned look about you, you aren't part of the rage of the moment."[40]

Not only was blue vein-ism no longer fashionable by the late 1920s, it was medically out of date as well. By this point, the therapeutic value of ultraviolet light, extensively studied since the late nineteenth century, was widely known throughout Europe and the United States: in 1903, the same year that the Icelandic physician Niels Finsen won the Nobel Prize for medicine for his use of light therapy to treat infectious disease, the first heliotherapy clinic opened in Switzerland; by 1923, *Vogue* featured its first advertisement for a sunlamp designed for home use.[41] Even F. Scott Fitzgerald (in *The Beautiful and the Damned*) and D. H. Lawrence (in "Sun") extolled the health and fashion virtues of a suntan in 1922 and 1926, respectively. Blue vein discourse, a sharp rise in melanoma and other forms of skin cancer notwithstanding, had met its match.

Or at least that's what George S. Schuyler hoped. Like Tillman's poem, Schuyler's Harlem Renaissance science fiction satire, *Black No More* (1931), aims its venom at those who exploit American racial attitudes for personal financial gain. When Dr. Junius Crookman develops a technology that miraculously transforms even the blackest Negro into a the lily-whitest Caucasian—the secret apparently lies in "electrical nutrition and glandular control"—he forces all who make a living on or near the color line, from civil rights crusaders to dyed-in-the-wool white supremacists, to scramble so that they might somehow remain relevant in a land where everyone ends up passing for something else.[42] If anyone can be white, then whiteness no longer guarantees social advantage. As Werner Sollors notes, "Schuyler's fictional scheme is to take genealogical definitions of race to the point at which no 'white' person in America could be sure of 'racial purity' any more." Racial purity is revealed in the novel to be a fiction, an absurd fantasy.[43]

Throughout Schuyler's romp through America's near future—the novel is subtitled *Being an Account of the Strange and Wonderful Workings of Science in the Land of the Free, A.D. 1933–1940*—the protagonist, Matthew Fisher, né Max Disher, a one-time struggling Negro insurance salesman and eventual Grand Exalted Giraw of the white supremacist Knights of Nordica, exploits America's obsession with racial boundaries for personal gain. Fisher makes his fortune steering the white supremacist movement to political prominence, and he finds personal fulfillment when he marries Helen Givens, the daughter of the Imperial Grand Wizard of the Knights of Nordica. (Years before, Helen had rebuffed the advances of the Negro Max Disher.) Indeed, Fisher's two triumphs are closely intertwined: he very nearly manages to get his racist father-in-law elected to the White House.

Blacks-turned-white can escape their former lives in *Black No More,* but they can't escape genetics, which means that Fisher's son with Helen turns out "very, very dark." Fisher's redemption, if one can call it that, takes two forms. First, an extensive genealogical study carried out in the interest of white supremacy reveals that most Americans are in fact of mixed-race background. This includes Helen's white supremacist family, who take responsibility for the baby's darkness. Second, the Black-No-More scheme has proven so popular that virtually no Negroes remain in America, and in fact "extreme whiteness" stemming from the process is seen as "evidence of the possession of Negro blood." A peculiar version of Tillman's scenario unfolds: "Those of the upper class began to look around for ways to get darker. It became the fashion for them to spend hours at the seashore basking naked in the sunshine and then to dash back, heavily bronzed, to their homes, and, preening themselves in their dusky skins, lord it over their paler, and thus less fortunate, associates. Beauty shops began to sell face powders named *Poudre Nègre, Poudre le Egyptienne* and *L'Afrique*."[44]

The novel comes to a close with Dr. Crookman, by then one of the very few characters *not* to undergo his race-defying process, looking through his newspaper and finding a "photograph of Americans arrayed in the latest abbreviated bathing suits on the sands at Cannes."[45] Among the Riviera jet set working on their suntans: Matthew and Helen Fisher, along with their "dusky" little boy, Matthew Crookman Fisher.

The "Racial Blazon"

Taken to its next, logical position, Crookman's bemused interest in the baby's "dusky" appearance—no doubt partly obscured by the daily newspaper's cheap print quality—looks more like the concentrated interest in skin-tone gradations expressed by Chesnutt's narrator. We are told, for example, that, although Ryder "was not as white as some of the Blue Veins, his appearance was such as to confer distinction upon them. His features were of a refined type, his hair was almost straight; he was always neatly dressed; his manners were irreproachable, and his morals above suspicion." It is worth noting here that Ryder's appearance, in particular his whiteness or blackness, can only be judged in relation to others. Some Blue Veins are whiter, including most obviously Molly Dixon: "She possessed many attractive qualities. She was much younger than he; in fact, he was old enough to have been her father, though no one knew exactly how old he was. She was whiter than he, and better educated."[46] Within the irony-laden logic of "The Wife of His Youth," characters are judged first and foremost by the whiteness of their skin, which serves as a visual proxy for their more abstract worth, for their "manners" and "morals."

From such equivalences, poets (most famously Petrarch) give us a widely reproduced figure of speech, the blazon. The poetic blazon derives from the verbal description of arms, a heraldic practice that signifies inherent moral worth and differential identity by means of the verbal representation of armorial bearings (or coats of arms).[47] The heraldic blazon concentrates its formulaic verbal attention on the shield, which functioned as a blank canvas onto which hereditary devices might be superimposed. For example, Arthur's three crowns against a blue background (*azure three crowns*) contrasts with Lancelot's three red bands against a silver background (*argent three bends gules*). The blazon, in heraldry as in poetry, thus signals visual difference, moral worth, and an exalted lineage simultaneously; it functions as the antique, genealogically precise alternative to the modern colorist collage.

Chesnutt's late nineteenth-century version of the blazon interrogates and ultimately dismisses the visual and verbal logic of the literary device. Most obviously, the story distorts the connection between visual signifier (in this case, relative whiteness) and moral worth: 'Liza Jane, because of her unwavering loyalty to her distant husband over many decades, embodies the story's moral center; hers is the model to which the other characters, sometimes grudgingly, aspire. Chesnutt drives home a larger point—that visual beauty and inherent worth do not correlate—with his unflattering description of the fiercely loyal 'Liza Jane: "And she was very black,—so black that her toothless gums, revealed when she opened her mouth to speak, were not red, but blue."[48]

Ryder encounters 'Liza Jane precisely at the moment that he is meandering through numerous poetic blazons by his favored poet, Tennyson, in search of an appropriate banquet toast, one that matches Molly Dixon's fair form and "buxom build."[49] Finally, Ryder settles on Tennyson's blazon of Guinevere (in his "Sir Lancelot and Queen Guinevere" [1872]), which emphasizes the queen's "dainty finger-tips" and her "perfect lips." Considered in this light, 'Liza Jane's blazon is the very definition of the grotesque: the repulsive deformation of a familiar form. Ryder's final acceptance of his long-lost wife signals that he has come to value her not for her visual appearance, and certainly not because of her lineage, but for a devotion that exceeds even the promise of more immediate social rewards. 'Liza Jane's loyalty, unlike that of Guinevere, wins over even the most upward-striving Blue Vein.[50]

The Harlem Renaissance intelligentsia treated Chesnutt as a traditionalist; he was, after all, a key part of the tradition that they were claiming for their own. (In *The New Negro,* Alain Locke counts Chesnutt among the "pioneers and path-breakers" in Negro fiction.)[51] But Chesnutt's updated version of the blazon reads more like the "deformation of mastery" paradigm that Houston Baker identifies as central to an avant-garde African American modernism.[52] The tendency to "deform" the blazon continues and accelerates in both the poetry and the prose of the Harlem Renaissance, which gives us frequent versions of the same figure. I label this device the "racial blazon": a catalog of a woman's (and occasionally a man's) racialized physical features. Sometimes writers deploy the racial blazon playfully, as we see in Gwendolyn Bennett's "To a Dark Girl" and Jessie Redmon Fauset's "Touché," both published in Countee Cullen's *Caroling Dusk* anthology (1927). More often, the racial blazon, as in the example of Chesnutt, allows writers to consider important questions in the history of American culture and society in addition to reworking and updating familiar literary terrain.

Perhaps the most deformed and chilling version of the racial blazon is Jean Toomer's "Portrait in Georgia":

> Hair—braided chestnut,
>   coiled like a lyncher's rope,
> Eyes—fagots,
> Lips—old scars, or the first red blisters,
> Breath—the last sweet scent of cane,
> And her slim body, white as the ash
>   of black flesh after flame.[53]

Possibly because of its stark imagism, "Portrait in Georgia" initially found its way into the inaugural issue of the avant-garde *Modern Review* as one of three "Georgia Portraits." When Toomer later republished the poem in his groundbreaking *Cane* (1923), it appeared alongside the impressionistic "Blood-Burning Moon," a short story about a lynching prompted by an interracial love triangle. The pairing suggests that southern history etches a painful narrative even onto an imagist poem. By superimposing the implements and outcomes of racialized violence (rope, fagots, scars, ash) onto the more traditional female figure (hair, eyes, lips, body), Toomer's racial blazon entwines the Petrarchan sexual gaze with a modern American racial gaze, an unsettling combination that has not been lost on Toomer scholars.[54] The two objectifying systems produce each other within the construct of the poem, such that "Portrait in Georgia," as Walter Benn Michaels observes, functions as a myth of racial origins, in which desire produces racial difference and racial difference produces desire in an endless and tragically violent cycle: "What begins as a narrative of the attempt to preserve racial difference turns out to be a narrative of the origins of racial difference, a narrative in which white bodies are depicted as the consequence of violence against black bodies."[55]

With "Portrait in Georgia," Toomer rejuvenated an antique literary conceit and insisted on its inherent modernity within the unforgiving social context of the U.S. South. The poem's formal modernism—most obviously its perversely detached, imagist tone, one that anticipates Abel Meerpol's better-known "Strange Fruit" (1936)—resembles Ezra Pound's call in "A Few Don'ts by an Imagiste" for verse that follows "the way of the scientists rather than the way of an advertising agent for a new soap."[56] The poem's haunting detachment also resembles, not coincidentally, any number of pseudoscientific means to determine racial identity that proliferated in the nineteenth and twentieth centuries, the era when negative social pressures occasioned widespread racial passing. Some of these methods rely on an "objective" measure of skin color, whether the measuring instrument is a brown paper bag or a children's top mounted with a color wheel.[57] Werner Sollors demonstrates the existence of an entire genre of texts, mostly fictional, that take up the "fingernail motif": narratives in which a person's fingernails are read as signs of her or his whiteness or blackness. And as we have already seen in the example of Chesnutt, among many others, the visibility of blue veins beneath a person's skin signals her or his suitable lightness of complexion. What we have in the racial blazon, then, is an effort to resist by clever transformation a wider cultural pattern in which individual body parts are scrutinized as evidence not just of social worth, but also of placement within an unforgiving legal hierarchy.

Chesnutt, a light-skinned attorney whose resume included a highly successful court stenography business, knew well the practical legal effects of the racial gaze. In his *Independent* essay "What Is a White Man?" (1889), Chesnutt took up the antebellum and Jim Crow courtroom's disenfranchising attitudes and practices regarding persons of color. He cites at considerable length two South Carolina court decisions that define who counts as "white" liberally, relative to other southern states, and dissociatively, as a citizen granted legal rights denied to a "Negro" or a "mulatto":

> But the state which, for several reasons, one might expect to have the strictest laws in regard to the relations of the races, has really the loosest. Two extracts from decisions of the Supreme Court of South Carolina will make clear the law of that state in regard to the color line.
>
> "The definition of the term mulatto, as understood in this state, seems to be vague, signifying generally a person of mixed white or European and Negro parentage, in whatever proportions the blood of the two races may be mingled in the individual. But it is not invariably applicable to every admixture of African blood with the European, nor is one having all the features of a white to be ranked with the degraded class designated by the laws of this state as persons of color, because of some remote taint of the Negro race. The line of distinction, however, is not ascertained by any rule of law. . . . Juries would probably be justified in holding a person to be white in whom the admixture of African blood did not exceed the proportion of one-eighth. But it is in all cases a question for the jury, to be determined by them upon the evidence of features and complexion afforded by inspection, the evidence of reputation as to parentage, and the evidence of the rank and station in society occupied by the party. The only rule which can be laid down by the courts is that where there is a distinct and visible admixture of Negro blood, the individual is to be denominated a mulatto or person of color."
>
> In a later case the court held:
>
> "The question whether persons are colored or white, where color or feature are doubtful, is for the jury to decide by reputation, by reception into society, and by their exercise of the privileges of the white man, as well as by admixture of blood."[58]

Chesnutt goes on to surmise the cause for South Carolina's malleable definition of whiteness: perhaps, because at the time African Americans outnumbered whites in South Carolina, its society was quick to add to its numbers of fully enfranchised, upwardly mobile white citizens.[59] Not to embrace a liberal understanding of whiteness, we can only presume, would stifle South Carolina's economic progress; what's more, stricter definitions of whiteness would penalize families with long histories among South Carolina's social elite.

The two cases that Chesnutt quotes here—*State v. Davis* (1831) and *State v. Hannah* (1831)—involved defendants who attempted, somewhat paradoxically, to use the state's racial laws to secure their liberty. Typically, individuals were punished for being "Negro" and, say, carrying a firearm or crossing a jurisdictional boundary without permission. In *Davis* and *Hannah,* the defendants instead attempted to take advantage of their "mulatto" status: each case indicted a woman under the South Carolina bastardy act of 1795, a statute that applied only to "white" women; illegitimacy was simply assumed in nonwhite relationships. In addition, only "white" persons could serve as witnesses in a trial in South Carolina. The defense claimed that the women could not be compelled to the witness stand, nor should they even be indicted, because they were "mulatto" rather than "white."

Because the trial judge, Josiah J. Evans (later a U.S. senator), charged both juries to consider the defendants "white," the juries returned guilty verdicts. Evans instructed the *Davis* jury "that a mulatto was the offspring of parents, one of whom was white, and the other black," and that he was therefore "disposed to think that where the white blood predominated, the disqualification ought not to attach."[60] In a state such as Michigan, which attached whiteness to an individual even more liberally than South Carolina, Evans would have been correct in his notion that a "predomination" of one racial background or another determined a subject's legal status, but not so in the Palmetto State. More important, in keeping with the traditions of American jurisprudence, the South Carolina court of appeals (which functioned as a supreme court, but was not so named until 1868) vacated the trial judge's instructions and affirmed the jury's central role in determining the facts, including a defendant's racial identity, of the case.

Citing *State v. Davis,* the legal historian Ariela J. Gross argues that "judges in the nineteenth-century South repeatedly held that the determination of an individual's race was 'a question very proper for a jury,' because the jury represented the sense of the community; race was something commonsensical—something *we know when we see it.*" She adds that "witnesses in the courtroom reinforced the notion of race as common sense by invoking the idea that there was an ineffable quality making someone white that any Southerner could discern—and, likewise, that a drop of African blood would make itself known."[61] A jury could affix a racial identity label based on "the evidence of features and complexion afforded by inspection," including, presumably, such measures as the blue vein test, the fingernail test, the brown paper bag test—perhaps even the color-wheel top test.

What's fascinating about this controversy is not so much the relative weight of the judge or the jury in establishing the facts of a case, but rather the logic by which Judge Evans reached his decision versus the logic implied by the South Carolina court of appeals. In his ruling, Evans, despite some hemming and hawing, was thinking about race as a mathematical certainty: he had in mind the *Code Noir* of France and the elaborate racial classification systems of Louisiana and Latin America. In those contexts, one need only count the various ancestors (white + Negro = mulatto; mulatto + quadroon = white) to determine a person's legal status. Justice William Harper, writing for the court of appeals, understood racial identity as emerging from an elaborate speech act, with social location and a range of other variables, including physical appearance, contributing to a subject's racial identity.

Four years later, in *State v. Cantey* (1835), Justice Harper reaffirmed his earlier view when he wrote, in a passage much discussed by legal historians:

> We cannot say what admixture will make a colored person. The condition is not to be determined solely by visible mixture but by reputation and it may be proper, that a man of worth should have the rank of a white man, while a vagabond of the same degree of blood should be confined to the

> inferior caste. It is hardly necessary to say that a slave cannot be a white man. We wish it to be understood that this matter is regarded as settled. I think it to be regretted that the question was made in the present case, it is doing unnecessary violence to the feelings of persons of much worth and respectability.[62]

Here we find just one among many social constructionist approaches to racial identity to emerge from a nineteenth-century southern courtroom.[63] South Carolina would maintain this relatively smooth path to "whiteness" until its post-Reconstruction constitution of 1895, which codified a blood fraction legal definition of racial identity like that found elsewhere in the South.

In the context of a society that literally judges its subjects by the color of their skin, it stands to reason that a literature would emerge to question and even challenge quite explicitly the logic on which legal and other day-to-day decisions are based. Chesnutt did so himself in his novel *The House behind the Cedars* (1900), which includes this piece of advice from Archibald Straight, a white judge in North Carolina, to the protagonist John Walden, a young mulatto who wishes to become an attorney:

> As he kept on looking at the boy, who began at length to grow somewhat embarrassed under this keen scrutiny, the judge's mind reverted to certain laws and judicial decisions that he had looked up once or twice in his lifetime. Even the law, the instrument by which tyranny riveted the chains upon its victims, had revolted now and then against the senseless and unnatural prejudice by which a race ascribing its superiority to right of blood permitted a mere suspicion of servile blood to outweigh a vast preponderance of its own. . . . "You have the somewhat unusual privilege, it seems, of choosing between two races, and if you are a lad of spirit, as I think you are, it will not take you long to make your choice. As you have all the features of a white man, you would, at least in South Carolina, have simply to assume the place and exercise the privileges of a white man. You might, of course, do the same thing anywhere, as long as no one knew your origin. But the matter has been adjudicated there in several cases, and on the whole I think South Carolina is the place for you. They're more liberal there, perhaps because they have many more blacks than whites, and would like to lessen the disproportion."[64]

Walden possesses "his [white] father's patrician features and his mother's Indian hair, and no external sign to mark him off from the white boys on the street," and thus he might easily blend into antebellum South Carolina's white society. Judge Straight arrives at his advice by way of comparison; he notices that a young lad from the town's social elite "was sallow, with amorphous features, thin shanks, and stooping shoulders." Walden, in contrast, is "straight, shapely, and well-grown."[65] Walden's "straightness," Judge Straight surmises, tells the story of his whiteness—it testifies to his racial pedigree and his moral worth; indeed, Walden's physical features reveal that he is descended from an old friend of the judge.

Chesnutt's keen interest in the legal framework of "blackness" or "Negro" identity marks his fiction as a painfully obvious example of "African American literature" in the sense deployed by Kenneth W. Warren; that is, Chesnutt's approach to fiction belies his debt, if we can call it that, to a regime of racial apartheid.[66] The coherence of Chesnutt's literary work (and arguably his entire career) derives, as Warren puts it, from a "social world defined by the system of Jim Crow segregation"; this work "was an imaginative response not merely to the lived reality but also to the legal fact of segregation."[67] A similar interest in how physical appearance determines legal rights and social mobility similarly informs many of the now-classic narratives of the Harlem Renaissance, several of which develop the colorist collage motif. When judicial and bureaucratic discretion during the era of slavery and Reconstruction gave way to the more clear-cut black/white binary in the post-*Plessy* years, African American writers responded with a literature that insisted on intraracial color diversity and simultaneously on African American racial solidarity. As we will see in the final chapter, Harlem during the renaissance was the epicenter of this delicate balancing act.

5
Harlem Geography
Race and the Spatial Imagination

Harlem Modernity, Harlem Geography

One way of locating the modernity of the Harlem Renaissance is to identify an *annus mirabilis* for the movement, much as writers and scholars have done for "modernism" as a cultural concept. (And so Virginia Woolf, D. H. Lawrence, and Harry Levin give us, respectively, 1910, 1915, and 1922.) But the space of Harlem, its geography and social landscape, plays as large role in defining the movement's modernity. David Levering Lewis begins his important study of the Harlem Renaissance with the Fifteenth New York Regiment's triumphant homecoming parade; the specific date (February 17, 1919) matters less than the Fifth Avenue route taken by the so-called Harlem Hellfighters.[1] Nathan Irvin Huggins expands on the familiar theme in Jazz Age cultural history: in addition to the Fifteenth Regiment's return from overseas, Huggins identifies James Weldon Johnson's return to Harlem in 1914, W. E. B. Du Bois's and Marcus Garvey's moves to New York in the 1920s, and Boni and Liveright's publication of *The New Negro* anthology, expanded from the *Survey Graphic*'s Harlem number, in 1925.

More recent analyses may be more nuanced in their appraisal of key turning points in Harlem Renaissance cultural history, but they also tend to situate cultural emergence squarely in a single year—most often 1925—and in a single upper Manhattan neighborhood: Harlem. Houston A. Baker, to take one important example, privileges the aesthetic "deformation of mastery," the gradual emergence of folk idioms into a posture of subtle subversion vis-à-vis mainstream U.S. culture, in his provocative discussion of the movement. Baker nevertheless identifies the social reformist *New Negro* anthology as the "first fully modern figuration of a nation predicated upon mass energies."[2] George Hutchinson provides an exhaustive investigation of the interracial dynamics underpinning the 1920s literary marketplace, that is, the national and (to a lesser extent) international institutions that mediate between writers and the reading public. Even so, the 1925 publication of *The New Negro* functions in Hutchinson's comprehensive analysis as the central moment in a complex "staging" of the Harlem Renaissance.

Harlem Renaissance intellectuals themselves often looked to 1925 and the publication of *The New Negro* as signal moments in the life of the fledgling movement. They also highlighted the publication of Jean Toomer's *Cane* in 1923 or the publication of Jessie Redmon Fauset's *There Is Confusion* a year later. It's worth noting that these early fictional examples are set not in Harlem, but in the rural South, Washington, D.C., and Philadelphia; even so, as Boni and Liveright imprints, the books were closely associated with New York City and its Jazz Age flair. Harlem entered African American writing on a large scale only after the *Survey Graphic* Harlem number grew into *The New Negro*. James de Jongh's "Checklist of Black Harlem in Poetry" begins in 1922 with Helene Johnson's "Sonnet to a Negro in Harlem." If we omit Toomer, de Jongh's extensive "Checklist of Black Harlem in Novels" begins in 1925 with the publication of Rudolph Fisher's short story "The City of Refuge."[3]

Fisher's *Atlantic Monthly* short story, the first published during his tragically brief career, views Harlem's modernity through the eyes of a transplanted southerner. King Solomon Gillis has fled rural North Carolina after fatally shooting a white man and finds refuge, at least temporarily, among the hustle and bustle of the big city. Gillis is a latter-day Rip Van Winkle, transplanted not just in space but also in time. Fisher's fiction returns habitually to a handful of Harlem's distinctly urban spaces: subway trains, high-rises, airshafts, elevators, automobiles, and cabarets. Each of these modern spaces furnishes visual evidence of speed or urban density or both, and in "The City of Refuge" Fisher deploys their vertical spacing symbolically, as in the opening scene: "Confronted suddenly by the daylight, King Solomon Gillis stood dazed and blinking. The railroad station, the long, white-walled corridor, the impassable slot-machine, the terrifying subway train—he felt as if he had been caught up in the jaws of a steam-shovel, jammed together with other helpless lumps of dirt, swept blindly along for a time, and at last abruptly dumped. . . . Jonah emerging from the whale."[4] Traditional interpretations of the story of Jonah and the whale—concerning obedience to God, concerning the nature of miracles, concerning divine mercy—do not readily apply to Fisher's text. The biblical reference here relies more on physical similarities between the "great fish" of the Old Testament and a modern subway station—large size, murky interior, a character disgorged—than on any resemblance between Gillis and Jonah (or Gillis's namesake, King Solomon). Nor do the respective plights of Gillis and Jonah lend themselves to comparison.[5] In the quick-paced story, Gillis's deliverance is only fleeting; his ultimate capture by the police finally severs the character's connection to a biblical source.

Along with the visual symbolism of vertical spaces, Fisher in "The City of Refuge" indicates Harlem's modernity by putting on show the visual diversity of its inhabitants, who span a rainbow of colors and a vast range of sizes and shapes. We find in this short story the earliest example of a Harlem-centered colorist collage:

> Gillis set down his tan cardboard extension case and wiped his black, shining brow. Then slowly, spreadingly, he grinned at what he saw: Negroes at every turn; up and down Lenox Avenue, up and down 135th Street; big, lanky Negroes, short, squat Negroes; black ones, brown ones, yellow ones;

> men standing idle on the curb, women, bundle-laden, trudging reluctantly homeward, children rattle-trapping about the sidewalks; here and there a white face drifting along, but Negroes predominantly, overwhelmingly everywhere. There was assuredly no doubt of his whereabouts. This was Negro Harlem.[6]

As we have already seen, the literature of black Harlem abounds with similar descriptions of Harlemites' visual diversity, so much so that it's fair to call the colorist collage a modernist literary motif. Many of the examples that de Jongh lists contain a set piece devoted to capturing Harlem's social diversity in visual shorthand form. Like a writer displaying her Futurism by describing an airplane in flight, or evincing his Americanism by describing a boxing match or baseball game, a New Negro writer could signal newness and Negro-ness by describing the rich and colorful blur of Harlem society in constant motion, by staging a colorist collage. Stereotypes make little sense in the modern crowd.

Ethnicity and the Metropolitan Matrix

Given its size and standing in U.S. social and cultural history, New York City understandably serves as a (if not *the*) preeminent model of the modern city's emergence during the nineteenth century. As the historians Edwin G. Burrows and Mike Wallace point out, New York during this time grew into "a place of ever-increasing potency in global affairs, and as the United States evolved from colony to empire, the city migrated from the edge to the center of the world."[7] I wish to suggest here that an important reason for New York's emergence as a hub of commerce and culture is the city's geography—not so much its natural landscape, although easy shipping access clearly played a major role, but rather the artificial landscape forced on the island by human hands.

Specifically, the gridiron street pattern (or urban grid) for which Manhattan is famous helped shape decades of urban planning in the nineteenth and into the twentieth century and made New York City a template for future urban development in other locales. Although the urban grid had earlier examples in Philadelphia, New Orleans, and Savannah—

indeed, the grid pattern dates to classical antiquity in Asia and Europe—the example of Manhattan, "the great entrepôt for the continent" and "the apotheosis of the gridiron" according to the city planning scholar John W. Reps, furnished the paradigm for late nineteenth-century urban planning in the Midwest and West.[8] The urban grid subsequently shaped the contours of twentieth-century race studies; the grid gave geospatial evidence of Harlem's racial destiny.

To gain a better sense of the radical transformation of New York City brought to life by the urban grid pattern, one need only compare maps of colonial New Amsterdam / New Haarlem with maps of twentieth-century Manhattan.[9] During its brief seventeenth-century history, New Amsterdam expanded with little apparent design into a somewhat awkward assembly of geographic landmarks: a fort, several shipping kills (inlets), a few dozen oblong farm tracts, public grazing lands, several dozen small commercial and residential buildings, and a handful of larger public buildings, all interspersed with oddly angled streets (most prominently Broad Way) that followed old Indian trails or paths marked by grazing animals. Although New Haarlem was not incorporated until 1658, the area's boweries (farms) were first depicted on the Manatus Map (1639), a Dutch colonial document (which survives only in later copies) depicting New Amsterdam and its environs. New Haarlem first entered cartographic history with the Nicolls Map (c. 1665), a document likely commissioned by its namesake, Richard Nicolls, the first governor of colonial New York. The Manatus and Nicolls maps portray an irregularly laid-out town (New Amsterdam / New York) at the southern end of a Manhattan Island dominated by hills and woods.

By the middle of the eighteenth century, new commercial and residential development gave lower Manhattan its recognizably modern form. The areas just north of present-day City Hall Park were designed during the late colonial and early national eras in an urban grid pattern or, rather, multiple neighborhood grids set at competing angles. Some lands were held privately, and the urban grid allowed for the most efficient and thus most profitable subdivision and improvement; other lands were confiscated from loyalists after the Revolutionary War, allowing for unfettered

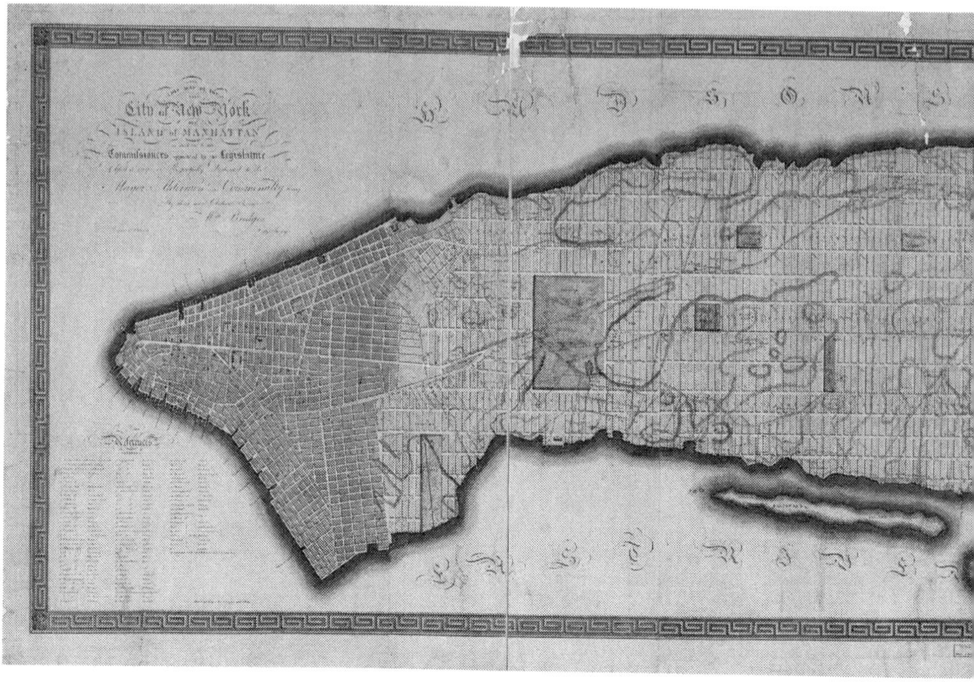

Figure 5.1. "Map of the City of New York and Island of Manhattan as laid out by the Commissioners appointed by the Legislature April 3d 1807," from *The Iconography of Manhattan Island,* 1920.

city planning.[10] Such early urban grid development is recorded in late eighteenth- and early nineteenth-century maps such as the Maerschalck Plan (1755), the Taylor-Roberts Plan (1797), and the Mangin-Goerck Plan (1803). Each of these examples of urban planning (rather than simple mapping) records with some measure of accuracy the future shape of lower Manhattan, but none of them anticipates the right-angled audacity of Manhattan's future development, set on its course by the Commissioners' Plan of 1811 (fig. 5.1).

The Commissioners' Plan represents the most important development in the history of Manhattan geography.[11] This document, created by a state-appointed commission and granted the full weight of law by the New York state legislature, extends a right-angle urban grid for 155 blocks, with twelve avenues running north–south, all the way to Harlem; odd-angled Broadway remained one of the few (and easily the most famous) geographic legacies of the Dutch colonial era. Most hills standing in the way of progress would be leveled; most ponds and streams would be filled. As the Commissioners'

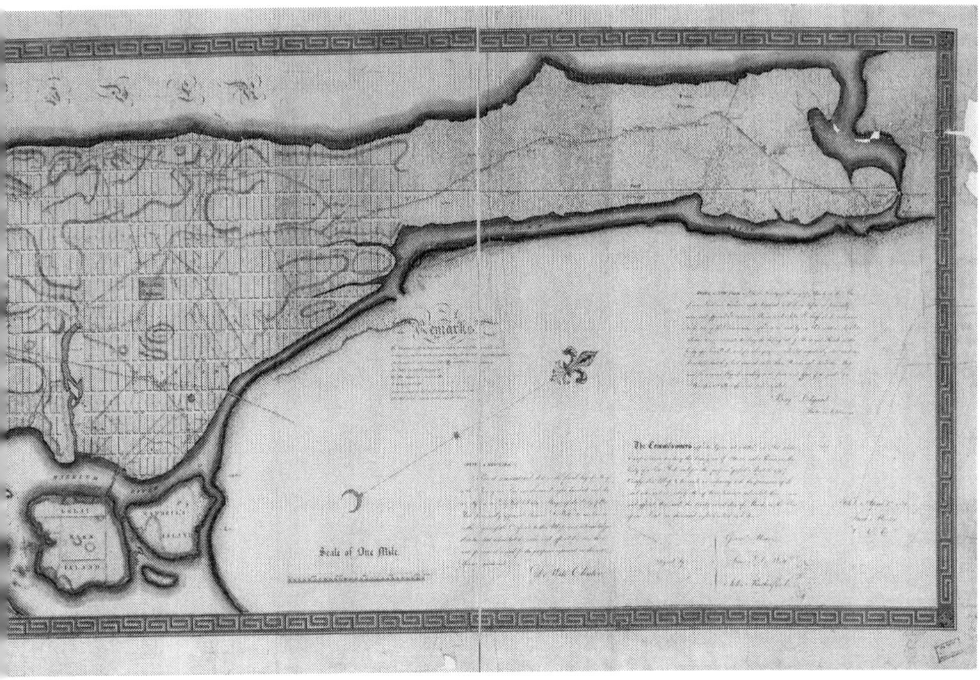

Plan was subsequently realized in actual development, numerous changes occurred, most obviously the incorporation of Central Park during the 1850s. Still, the Commissioners' Plan resembles today's Manhattan much more closely than it does Manhattan as it stood in 1811.

In his monumental *The Culture of Cities* (1938), Lewis Mumford, a long-time New York City resident, argues that Manhattan's urban grid signals the failure of civilization on multiple levels. First, the urban grid represents the unprofessional, even anti-intellectual, abdication of serious engagement with design: "An office boy can figure out the number of square feet involved in a street opening, or in a sale; and a lawyer's clerk can write a description of the necessary deed of sale, merely by copying a standard document. With a T-square and a triangle, finally, the municipal engineer, without the slightest training as either an architect or a sociologist, could 'plan' a metropolis. The neatness of the mechanical drawing, as in the plan of 1811 for New York, would obscure the extent of the eventual civic folly." Second, the urban grid's apparent efficiency of design often masks unintended wastefulness of time and resources, with engineers building streets that "swept through swamps, embraced dump-heaps, accepted piles of slag and waste, climbed cliffs, and ended up a quarter of a mile below the low water mark," and with citizens facing "daily economic loss, measurable in tons of coal and gallons of gasoline wasted, to say nothing of undoing the major esthetic possibilities of a hill-site that is intelligently platted." Third, the urban grid results in a large number of privately owned parcels, each destined for a unique and highly individualized fate. Large-scale, strategic urban planning in such an environment proves difficult and sometimes prohibitively expensive. Fourth, rather than order city growth, the urban grid encourages blind speculation and shortsighted sprawl: "Each lot, being uniform in shape, became a unit, like a coin, capable of ready appraisal and exchange. . . . Being conceived as a purely physical agglomeration of buildings, the town planned on rectangular lines could sprawl in any direction, limited only by gross physical obstacles and the means of transportation." Fifth, and perhaps most important, the urban grid surrenders topography to geometry, nature to artifice, and humanism to instrumentalism, meaning "that the abstract figure determines the social contents: the institutions of the community no longer generate the plan and modify it in accordance with the special needs of living."[12] In short, the urban grid fails Mumford's tests of reason, aesthetics, and ethics.

As his discussion of the urban grid pattern reveals, Mumford betrays considerable ambivalence about the connection between city geography and modern civilization. On the one hand, cities represent the triumph of civilization; together with "language itself, [the city] remains man's greatest work of art."[13] On the other hand, city design often ransoms human welfare to merely political or merely economic interests. (Mumford's larger critique of hyperrationality in city design is a thinly veiled attack against European fascism.) Much of the tone and some of the substance of Mumford's critique overlaps with the influential work of the German historian—and unwitting source of fascist inspiration—Oswald Spengler, whose *The Decline of the West* (1918–1922) tackles the question of the "soul of the city," where modern design sacrifices organic culture to decadent civilization. Spengler cites as a prime example of civilization's decline "that artificial, mathematical, utterly land-alien product of pure intellectual satisfaction, . . . the city of the city architect. In all Civilizations alike, these cities aim at the chessboard form, which is the symbol of soullessness." Like many others, Spengler specifically identifies American urban planning as the culmination of centuries of hyperrational city design, and he further sees "the rise of New York to the position of world-city during the Civil War . . . [as] the most pregnant event of the nineteenth century."[14] For their own quite different reasons, the state commissioners behind the Plan of 1811 would likely agree.

The commissioners' "chessboard form" met with the approval of Le Corbusier, the paragon of architectural modernism, because within the urban grid "your mind is free instead of being given over every minute to the complicated game imposed on it by the puzzle of European cities." The man whose work is synonymous with the International Style labeled the "grille of streets" found in New York the "American layout" because modern U.S. city planners rediscovered in the urban grid an efficient and, paradoxically, organic relationship between citizen and cityscape:

> Manhattan, in New York, is a granite rock more than twelve miles long and two miles wide, between the Hudson River and the East River. In length it is laid out in nine parallel avenues; across, in nearly two hundred streets parallel to each other and at right angles to the avenues. The avenue in the middle, Fifth Avenue, serves as a spinal column for this gigantic sole. On one side it is west, on the other east. The first street is at the south, on the ocean side, the last is at the north, on the land side. Everything is ordered accordingly. You have to go to 135 East 42nd Street? Everything is determined with a Euclidean clearness. 42nd Street? You are at your hotel on 55th Street; you go to Fifth Avenue, go down thirteen streets. East? You turn left. 135? You walk to number 135. Thus you know instantly whether to walk, whether to take a taxi, or whether to catch the bus on the avenue or use the subway. I say that it is an immense and beneficent freedom for the mind. It will be said that I am stopping over an anatomical detail of the city and that I attach a great deal of importance to it. This is not an anatomical detail, but the outstanding and essential biological structure of the city.[15]

Le Corbusier, who once proposed, in all seriousness, razing central Paris and constructing in its place a vast network of interlocking skyscrapers, is known for embracing a machine age aesthetic that most regard as at odds with "organic" principles of design.[16] But in Manhattan's urban grid Le Corbusier witnessed a "clear checkerboard" on which millions of New Yorkers "act simply and easily," with all governed by the same set of quickly learned rules.[17] The urban grid allows even newly arrived immigrants, be they from eastern Europe or from the deep South, to take quick stock of their present location and to plot an appropriate course to where they would like to go. Every street is a passage from one place to the next; every corner is an orienting landmark for the lost or a way station for the weary.

Defenders of the Commissioners' Plan found that it had several advantages over the previous regime of asymmetrical urban planning and street design; most obviously, it served the commercial needs of a burgeoning metropolis. Mumford puts it more cynically: "The rectangular street and block system, projectable indefinitely toward the horizon, was the universal expression of capitalistic fantasies."[18] The needs of the capitalist and the needs of the transplant to New York are remarkably similar: simple and transparent negotiation, quick and easy exchange. The urban grid also allows for an interchangeable understanding of how individuals relate in social space: one pawn (or one queen) has just as much freedom of movement as another. The urban grid further allows the geographic imagination to extend to infinity, like a never-ending chessboard; social forces that operate in Manhattan might also be identified far beyond the horizon, in Chicago or Los Angeles. But on the chessboard of Manhattan, different rules apply depending on whether the pieces involved are black or white.

In part because of its informal boundaries within a larger urban environment, in the period since the 1920s Harlem has emerged as a part-for-whole version of the urban ghetto experience, with counterparts in Chicago's South Side or South Central Los Angeles. Even Le Corbusier's example of a stroll through the city streets defies his ultramodern idealism: most hotels near the intersection of 55th Street and Fifth Avenue—perhaps he had in mind the St. Regis, built by John Jacob Astor IV on that very corner—did not accept African American guests during the

1930s. (Midtown hotels were the site of the city's budding convention industry, attracting visitors from all parts of the nation.) And the Chrysler Building (at 135 E. 42nd Street) would not be the likely destination of an African American in Depression-era New York.[19]

Harlem's ability "to mean," to signal urban blackness geospatially, creates meaning as well for the rest of Manhattan. In his short story "High Yaller" (1925), Fisher explores the dangers of being black in white Manhattan: reflecting on Harlem's shifting boundaries, the protagonist, a real estate agent named Jay Martin, recalls "the time when his father, a pioneer preacher, had been forever warning him never to cross Lenox Avenue and never to go beyond 135th Street; a time when no Negroes lived on or near Seventh Avenue and when it would have been almost suicidal for one to appear unarmed on Irish Eighth."[20] Indeed, "Harlem" would be meaningless in the absence of "downtown" or the "Lower East Side"; "Spanish Harlem" requires us to specify "black Harlem." As Harlem Renaissance scholars well know, the neighborhood's differential identity has been recorded verbally for generations; in the following pages I would like to consider how difference also finds its way into our visual understanding of Harlem geography.

The Black Image in the White Map, or the One-Dot Rule

Maps not only encode a mapmaker's understanding of physical geography; they also generate a culture's differential understanding of itself and in relation to its other. The rise of the modern, bureaucratic nation-state since the late eighteenth century required precisely measured boundaries on the part of geographers, and precisely registered boundaries on the part of cartographers. Benedict Anderson's instructive points about the role of maps in constructing national identity—that maps helped legitimize colonial transfers of power by constructing geospatial genealogies, and that maps created the notion of geopolitical space as a readily identifiable visual logo—suggest additional state apparatuses (census bureaus, halls of records, border guards, passports and visas, electoral privileges) that confer or deny citizenship and its attendant social and economic benefits. Maps are the bureaucratic ideal in visual shorthand form. Early European cartographers went so far as to advocate a purist and potentially nativist approach to map coloring during this formative period: according to the geographic historian Ulla Ehrensvärd, eighteenth- and nineteenth-century cartographers stressed that map colors "should serve only the informative purpose of emphasizing the administrative, religious, ethnic, and other divisions of a country."[21] Subnational bureaucratic labels require a taxonomy of social identity and difference, the type of system formalized somewhat awkwardly in the United States by the Census Bureau during the nineteenth and twentieth centuries.

By the time of the Harlem Renaissance, maps had been deployed in national identity formation for two centuries, and in social analysis for at least six decades. The socially transformative run-up to the Jazz Age was a particularly important time in the formation of a sophisticated map-reading public. Jacob Riis's muckraking *How the Other Half Lives* (1890) described how an imaginary map of New York City, "colored to designate nationalities, would show more stripes than on the skin of a zebra, and more colors than any rainbow."[22] For Riis, as for most of his contemporaries, the Manhattan urban grid reinforced the notion that neighborhoods and even individual city blocks were segregated according to race and ethnicity.

Maps became a crucial tool in the Harlem Renaissance's understanding of American social patterns generally, and of urban growth and decay, along with residential segregation within a Harlem context more specifically. The Harlem Renaissance produced its own maps, to be sure, along with varied notions of geographic self-understanding, and these are best understood against the backdrop of two overlapping strains in early twentieth-century cultural and political thought: nativism and eugenics. These exclusionist, exclusivist devices—both undergirded by emergent scientific or pseudoscientific methods—required an acute fear of individual difference as well as a paranoid understanding of the social consequences of difference (conceived primarily in racial or ethnic terms). Although maps lack the blunt hate informing the racist caricatures proliferating in turn-of-the-century newspapers and magazines, maps never-

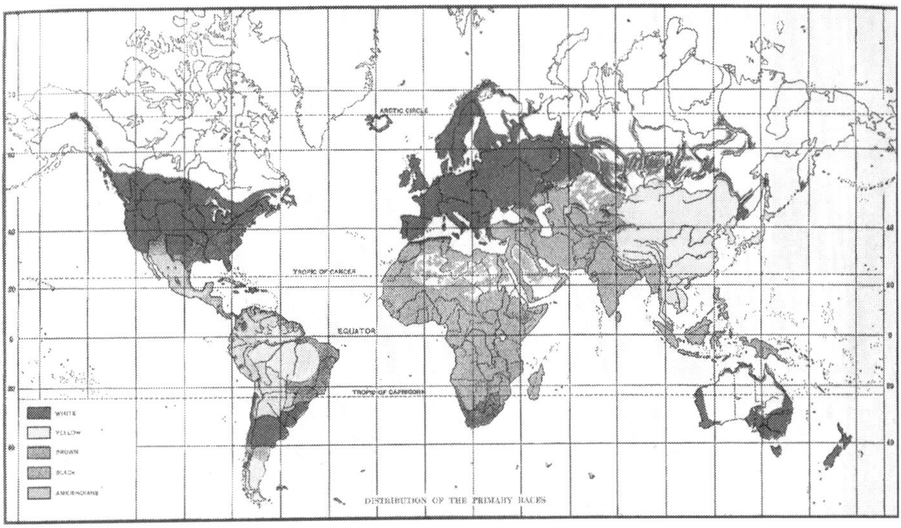

Figure 5.2. Lothrop Stoddard, "Distribution of the Primary Races," from *The Rising Tide of Color,* 1920.

theless allowed nativists to project individual biological difference onto a visual plane that immediately suggests social consequences. The visual rhetoric of maps modernized and objectified nativist and eugenicist political and cultural debate: maps rendered the "problem" of social change self-evident and irrefutable.

Madison Grant and his protégé Lothrop Stoddard drove much of the nativist agenda and supplied the movement with a eugenicist social program. In *The Rising Tide of Color against White World-Supremacy* (1920), Stoddard, in an echo of W. E. B. Du Bois, whom Stoddard cites disapprovingly, asserts that "the basic factor in human affairs is not politics, but race." He goes on to ask, "What assurance can the most impressive political panorama give us that the present [white-supremacist] world-order may not swiftly and utterly pass away?" and adds, "The force of this query is exemplified when we turn from the political map to the racial map of the globe. What a transformation! Instead of a world politically nine-tenths white, we see a world of which only four-tenths at the most can be considered predominantly white in blood, the rest of the world being inhabited mainly by the other primary races of mankind—yellows, browns, blacks, and reds." Stoddard's map "The Distribution of the Primary Races" (fig. 5.2) dramatically underscores his warning about the threat of a "rising tide" poised to wash out white influence in world politics. The most pressing danger, Stoddard argues, lies in immigration, particularly the immigration of Asians ("yellows") to areas of white control; the threat "infinitely transcends the peril of arms or markets, since it threatens not merely our supremacy or prosperity but our very race-existence, the well-springs of being, the sacred heritage of our children."[23]

Following the examples of Prescott F. Hall and Edward Alsworth Ross, his nativist comrades, Stoddard advocates stringent anti-immigration measures for areas under white control (particularly the United States) and the "scientific" practice of eugenics among existing white populations: "The immigrant tide must at all costs be stopped and America given a chance to stabilize her ethnic being."[24] Stoddard's unreconstructed paranoia registers not only in his verbal rhetoric but also in the visual rhetoric of his maps. He assigns sharply contrasting colors to each of the five "primary" races: red for the white race, yellow for the yellow race, brown for the brown, black for the black, and orange for the "Amerindians." Modern halftone printing technology, which dates to the 1880s, allows Stoddard to advocate on behalf of premodern (more accurately, fantasy-driven) racial boundaries.[25] Social modernity, the mingling of distinct racial groups, reveals itself where (for example) red and black dots overlap on Stoddard's map, tricking the eye to see a deep sienna, visual "proof" of racial coexistence and, more alarmingly from his standpoint, "evidence" of miscegenation. Halftone printing, because of its ability to offer a range of subtly shifting hues, approximates the fundamental metaphor of miscegenation, the intermixture of blood, more closely than the many available figures of speech for cultural pluralism, including the melting pot, mosaic, or crazy-quilt.

Although in *The Rising Tide of Color* Stoddard points out that the "black race" has a "distant outpost" in the Americas, and that the "superabundant animal vitality" of the "black man" leads to his "extreme fecundity," he nevertheless reserves most of his worry for the threat posed by Asian immigration to the United States.[26] In contrast, Stoddard's mentor and collaborator, Madison Grant, directly broaches the subject of miscegenation and the threat posed by growing numbers of African Americans in *The Conquest of a Content* (1933), a kind of American sequel to his study of the spread of "Nordic" influence in Europe and Asia, *The Passing of the Great Race* (1916). Grant concludes that "it is therefore the duty of all Americans . . . to face the problem boldly and to take all eugenic means to encourage the multiplication of desirable types and abate drastically the increase of the unfit and miscegenation by widely diverse races." He thus calls for the "*absolute* suspension of all immigration from all countries" along with the regulation of "births by depriving the unfit of the opportunity of leaving behind posterity of their own debased type."[27]

In two maps, "Negro Population, 1930" and "Negro Population Increase and Decrease, 1920–1930" (fig. 5.3), Grant employs black dots on a white map, thus providing visual signs of the peril of a mixed-race American society.[28] Grant refers to the rapid shift of the African American population from the rural South to the urban North, what we now call the Great Migration, and cautions against the dangers of modern, culturally plural urban life. Like many other pundits at the time, Grant associates the "Negro Problem" with the so-called Red Scare: "In the Negro section of Harlem a further problem is arising from crosses between Negroes and Jews and Italians. These and other Mulattoes are showing a tendency toward Communism."[29] Racial admixture, Grant argues, referring to a variety of pseudoscientific studies, tends toward racial degeneracy, and with it moral decay and political chaos. In other words, whenever white mixes with black, black features typically predominate, a most unfortunate "fact" of biology in the mind of a racist such as Grant. Instead of social modernization and interracial contact, Grant favors (if it were only feasible) the "gradual elimination of the Negro in America" by means of "repatriation" to Africa, strict birth control measures, forced sterilization, rigid anti-miscegenation statutes, and powerful taboos against black–white social commerce.[30] Eventually, he hopes, social engineering will rid the U.S. map of black dots.

I refer to the well-known, and hardly extraordinary, examples of Grant and Stoddard because they offer partial understanding of the verbal and visual context for urban social analysis of the Harlem Renaissance, including important gestures of self-understanding to emerge directly

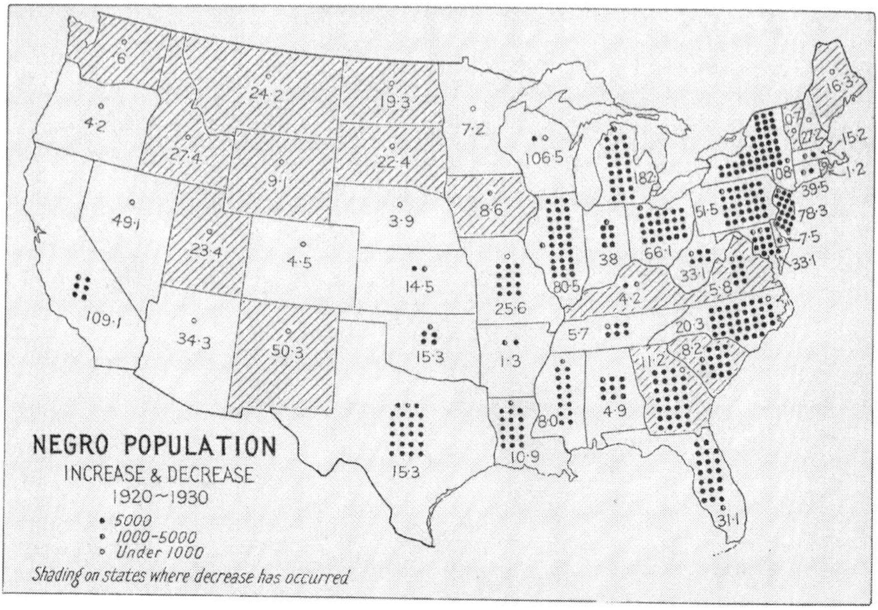

Figures in each State show the percentage of increase and decrease.

Figure 5.3. Madison Grant, "Negro Population Increase and Decrease, 1920–1930," from *The Conquest of a Continent,* 1933.

from the movement. Indeed, James Weldon Johnson appears to take direct aim at nativist paranoia. Johnson's *Black Manhattan* (1930) invites the now-familiar part-for-whole switch between black Harlem and the African American experience: Harlem represents a "city within a city"; it is the "intellectual and artistic capital of the Negro world." Significantly, Johnson repeatedly stresses that what makes Harlem so unique is its striking similarity to the rest of Manhattan, its all-Americanism in a time of Red Scare, with the obvious and important difference of race: "If you ride northward the length of Manhattan Island, going through Central Park and coming out on Seventh Avenue or Lenox Avenue at One Hundred and Tenth Street, you cannot escape being struck by the sudden change in the character of the people you see."[31]

Johnson reaches toward the language of racial essentialism, at least to the extent that it borrows from the overlapping discourses of psychology and morality ("character") to indicate a people's defining aspect. But as he continues, we recognize that we're witness not so much to deep-seated racial variations as to superficial distinctions among essentially similar peoples:

> In the middle and lower parts of the city you have, perhaps, noted Negro faces here and there; but when you emerge from the Park, you see them everywhere, and as you go up either of these two great arteries leading out from the city to the north, you see more and more Negroes, walking in the streets, looking from the windows, trading in the shops, eating in the restaurants, going in and coming out of the theatres, until, nearing One Hundred and Thirty-fifth Street, ninety per cent of the people you see, including the traffic officers, are Negroes. And it is not until you cross the Harlem River that the population whitens again, which it does as suddenly as it began to darken at One Hundred and Tenth Street. You have been having an outside glimpse of Harlem, the Negro metropolis.[32]

The "glimpse" offered here suggests that what makes Harlem so unique in the African American landscape is its sameness to the rest of Manhattan, give or take a shade or two of skin color. Perhaps with Mary White Ovington's habitual references to "Negro tenements" also in mind, Johnson's Harlem looks every bit the well-scrubbed, modern city. That "two great arteries" connect white Manhattan and black Manhattan further underscores that black and white share a single body politic.[33] The civic blood runs the same across the city. ("In Harlem," Fisher's narrator deduces, "black was white." King Solomon Gillis mumbles, "Even got cullud policemans.")[34] Still, what difference there is to be found, superficial though it may be, reveals itself in strict gradations of geography, so much so that Johnson can pinpoint the beginnings and endings of the geographic space known as Harlem with absolute, cartographic certainty. Johnson describes the contours of Harlem's boundaries in prose (essentially, upper Manhattan north of 110th Street) and offers side-by-side maps to illustrate the neighborhood's burgeoning African American population (fig. 5.4).

Johnson carefully points out that his maps represent the evolution of a population rather than static boundaries; he adds that "east of the Lenox Avenue boundary there are a score of mixed coloured and white population; and to the west of the Eighth Avenue boundary there is a solid Negro border, two blocks wide." His map illustrates "Negro" city blocks with black boxes, "White Population" city blocks with empty boxes, and

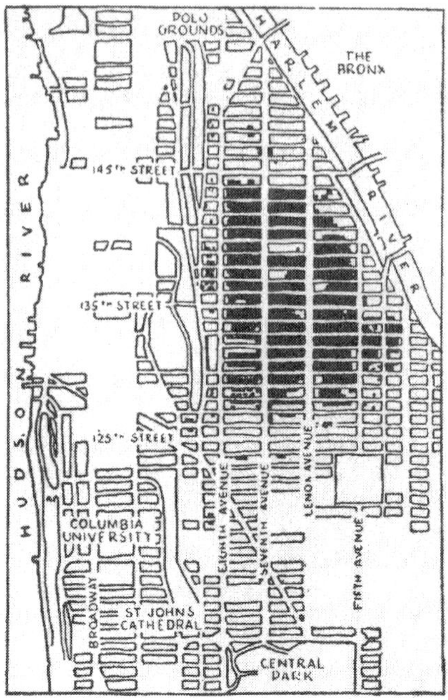

Negro Harlem 1925

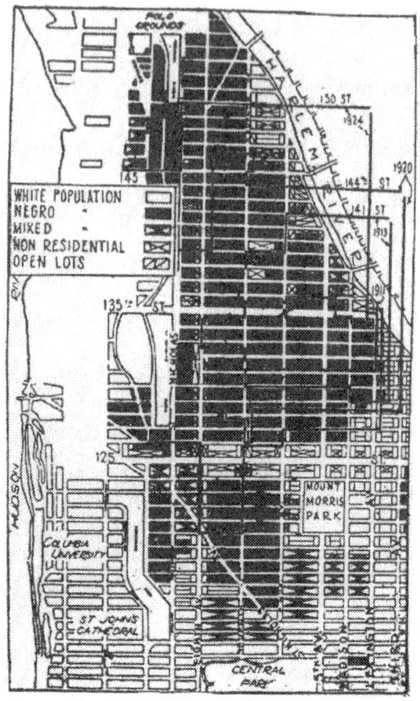

Negro Harlem 1930

Figure 5.4. James Weldon Johnson, "Negro Harlem 1925" and "Negro Harlem 1930," from *Black Manhattan,* 1930.

"Mixed" city blocks with a black-and-white checkered pattern. The side-by-side maps capture visually the competing (but hardly exclusive) messages of Johnson's population analysis: on the one hand, Harlem's population is in rapid flux, for the neighborhood's strongly African American "character" is "actually a development of the last fifteen years"; on the other hand, the "city within a city," with discrete physical boundaries (if not separate legal standing), boasts a population of "more than two hundred thousand Negroes, more to the square acre than any other place on earth."[35]

Black Harlem's density is wholly new and utterly unprecedented, and it's precisely measurable because the dividing line that Johnson identifies exactly corresponds to the census tract boundaries (CTs 186 and 216) created in 1910, the same boundaries that subsequently informed social-scientific analyses of the enclave. For these reasons as much as any other, Harlem represents for Johnson and many others the present-day lifestyles and forward-looking potential of the wider African American society. While Harlem bears but a small footprint geographically, it looms large in the American imagination. It has become, in the words of the anthropologist John L. Jackson Jr., a "Quotation-Marked-Off Place," a site whose symbolic value precedes and ultimately trumps the ability of an individual writer or reader to assign a stable meaning to "Harlem"; the place represents a "symbolic center for African American culture, a key reference point for blacks who seek to define themselves in relation to a certain canonized version of African American tradition and history."[36] Harlem's meaning both derives from and transcends its geography.

Significantly, Johnson borrows a recurrent trope in contemporaneous discussions of urban settlement, particularly as these pertained to analyses of immigration and social change. Social geographers have for at least a century coded Manhattan's racial and immigrant composition in a manner suggested to them by the science of epidemiology. In the years following the U.S. Civil War, according to the geographic historians Seymour I. Schwartz and Ralph E. Ehrenberg, "medical doctors used cartographic-statistical techniques to portray the geographical distribution of the different diseases" threatening the population, techniques that were popularized following the Census Bureau's publication of the first U.S. statistical atlas in 1874.[37] Rather than display the population density of specific racial groups, epidemiological maps illustrate the geographic range of mortality rates for such diseases as tuberculosis and malaria; the darker an area on the map, the deadlier the disease's effect on the population.

Following this logic, Johnson's maps suggest that the density of the African American population resembles waves of contagion spreading from Harlem across the wider landscape.[38] This approach to mapmaking, which Johnson merely borrows from widely accepted cartographic practice, stems in part from the nativist paranoia gripping the United States during the late nineteenth and early twentieth centuries, including the verbal and visual rhetorics of Grant and Stoddard.[39] But Johnson strategically reverses the traditional, xenophobic poles of nativist rhetoric, first by characterizing racist backlash as unwarranted paranoia, and then by revaluing the economic and especially the cultural contributions of the emergent African American population.

When African Americans "began to purchase the fine private houses between Lenox and Seventh" with the support of entrepreneurs such as Philip A. Payton and J. C. Thomas, Johnson writes, "in the eyes of the whites who were antagonistic, the whole movement took on the aspect of an 'invasion'—an invasion of both their economic and social rights. . . . Their conduct could be compared to that of a community in the Middle Ages fleeing before an epidemic of the black plague, except for the fact that here the reasons were not so sound."[40] It is a stubborn, "antagonistic" white population that represents social backwardness and a medieval worldview, Johnson argues, and African Americans who stand for economic vitality and cultural rejuvenation, who represent modernity in all its promise and glory.[41] *Black Manhattan* has played such a pivotal role in studies of the Harlem Renaissance—in a jacket blurb on a 1991 edition of the book, David Levering Lewis asserts that the "enduring cultural and scholarly significance of Johnson's classic work virtually speaks for itself"—because its careful attention to African American social customs, theater history, and popular music validate the notion that, at least for a brief moment, Harlem was indeed in vogue.

Johnson's tale of Harlem glory necessarily ends in 1930, just as the worst aspects of the Great Depression were beginning to take hold there as throughout the rest of the United States.[42] In subsequent years, when the Works Progress Administration sent a team of writers to record New York's African American history and social life, Harlem emerged not as a part-for-whole success story, but as the paradigmatic twentieth-century African American ghetto. The best known example of such an opinion belongs to Gilbert Osofsky, whose *Harlem: The Making of a Ghetto* (1966) influenced an entire generation's thinking about the monumental neighborhood and about African American urban life more broadly. According to Osofsky, the crushing "poverty, violence and segregation" experienced in Harlem during the late nineteenth and early twentieth centuries "were typical of the difficulties Negroes confronted in every major northern urban area in the twentieth century."[43]

We have already seen this paradox—that Harlem is at once exceptional and representative—in Johnson's study, but a similar view would routinely assert itself over the years in analyses that either celebrate or bemoan Harlem's fate, or both. The Harlem Renaissance has been and remains instrumental in the cultural historical interpretation of Harlem's status. Osofsky would go on to mention that "if the 1920's added anything to our knowledge of social conditions in Harlem, it presented a distorted or negative image of reality. . . . And, as the exotic vision of the twenties passed, a new image of Harlem emerged—a Harlem already known to stolid census-takers, city health officers and social workers."[44] The bright lights of the Harlem Renaissance, by this account, temporarily obscured from view an urban tragedy decades in the making.

The notion that Harlem can represent African American life in multiple ways—that it is both blacker than the rest of America and for that reason illustrative of black life throughout America—typically relies on two important social dynamics active during the early part of the twentieth century. First, because the space was so thickly populated with African Americans, not to mention other nationalities within the Afro-diaspora orbit, sheer density added to the "authenticity" of the African American experience in Harlem. Second, because a significant portion of Harlem's newly arrived population came from the rural South, even unprecedented urban density could not rob African Americans of their southern agrarian roots. A focus on the Harlem enclave allows social and cultural historians to have their corn cake and eat it, too.

E. Franklin Frazier, the leading sociologist of African American life during the middle part of the twentieth century, observes in his landmark *The Negro in the United States* (1949) that census data reveal a shift between 1910 and 1920 in the population sources of the Great Migration. Quoting Census Bureau statistics, he demonstrates that prior to 1910, two border states, Kentucky and Virginia, supplied 48 percent of the African American migrants to the North; the number of African American migrants from "cotton belt" states such as Alabama, Arkansas, Georgia, Florida, Louisiana, Mississippi, South Carolina, and Texas grew from 18.2 percent in 1910 to 40.5 percent in 1920.[45] Considered in this light, Johnson's maps of African American density in Harlem (fig. 5.4) closely resemble maps meant to convey a picture of the so-called Black

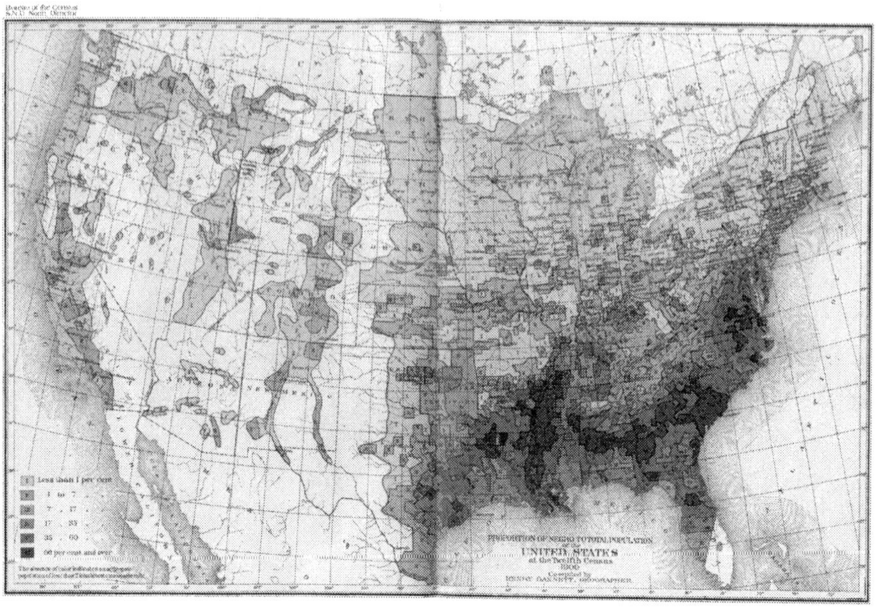

Figure 5.5. U.S. Census Bureau, "Proportion of Negro to Total Population of the United States at the Twelfth Census: 1900," from *Negroes in the United States,* 1904.

Belt, defined by the Census Bureau as southern counties at least one-half African American in population (fig. 5.5). In other words, as Harlem grew ever denser, it also became more "rural," more figuratively southern, a trend indicated in prose by Frazier and visually by Johnson. As the Duke Ellington standard "Drop Me Off in Harlem" (sung most memorably by Ella Fitzgerald) declares, "Harlem has those southern skies" and a "classy, uptown style." Or as Fisher would announce in the title of his influential Harlem vignettes, "The South Lingers On" (1925), even in the big city.[46]

In sharp contrast to Johnson's rosier view, for Frazier the rapid growth of Harlem, fueled by a relatively uneducated, unskilled population of migrants from the South, meant that newcomers were willing to occupy substandard housing abandoned by white tenants. These less fortunate new arrivals clustered at the heart of the neighborhood: "The expansion of the Negro population was associated with a process of selection and segregation of elements similar to that in the larger urban community. There has been a tendency for older persons and unmarried persons to be concentrated in the center of Harlem while married couples with children are found in the outer zones." Looking back from a 1930s perspective—and

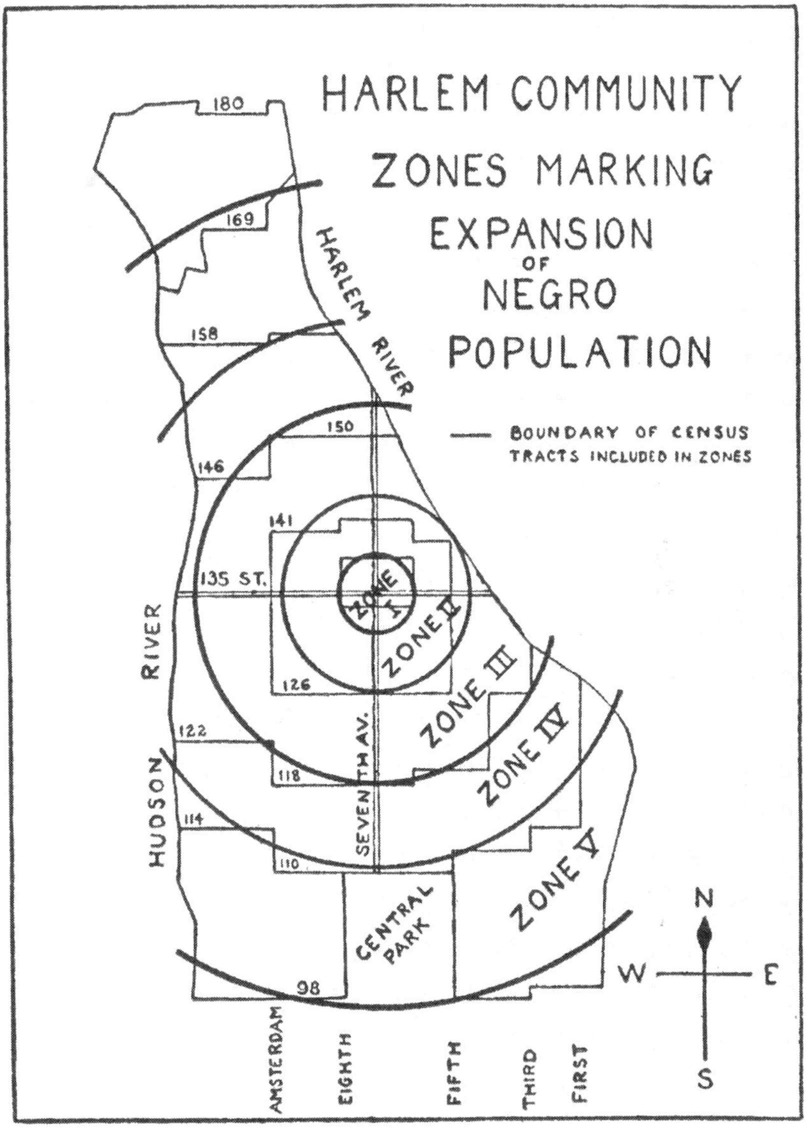

Figure 5.6. E. Franklin Frazier, "Harlem Community Zones Marking Expansion of Negro Population," from *The Negro Family in the United States,* 1939.

following the concentric zone model of the sociologist Ernest Burgess to assess Harlem human ecology—Frazier identifies several "zones" radiating outward from a central point (one might say a "target") located at the intersection of Seventh Avenue and 135th Street (fig. 5.6). The "radial expansion of the Negro population from the area about 135th Street and

Seventh Avenue may be represented ideally by drawing concentric circles about the census tract [CT 228] in which the intersection of these two main thoroughfares is located." Elsewhere Frazier clarifies that the "Negro population has not expanded to the same extent in all directions. It has been held in check until residential areas have deteriorated and have become accessible not only to Negroes but to Italians and Puerto Ricans as well. In other instances, white residential areas have put up a stubborn resistance even when surrounded by Negroes."[47]

Rather than indicate a complex set of motives and outcomes of polyethnic settlement patterns, Frazier's map suggests instead that Negro identity stems from a particular city, within a particular enclave, and at a particular intersection. Nowhere does Frazier mention that the corner of Seventh Avenue and 135th Street was known informally as the "campus" because, as Wallace Thurman records in fiction, "all the college boys hung out there when the weather permitted, obstructing traffic and eyeing the passerby professionally."[48] Frazier didn't mention, but could have, some of the prominent institutions located less than a block from this intersection: the *New York Age* and the *New York Amsterdam News,* key chroniclers of life in black Harlem; the Small's Paradise nightclub, where jazz leader Charlie Johnson entertained the masses; the Harlem branch of the YMCA, home for a while to Langston Hughes and Claude McKay; the Harlem branch of the New York Public Library, now known as the Schomburg Center for Research in Black Culture; the Urban League headquarters; and the headquarters of Marcus Garvey's Universal Negro Improvement Association. Nor does Frazier mention that this intersection happened to be James Weldon Johnson's home address, but he may as well have. The map's logic, which runs counter to Frazier's otherwise dispassionate social analysis, insists that Harlem is indeed Mecca of the New Negro.

Epilogue

Census Geography and the Burdens of Representation

The exhaustive survey work that informs E. Franklin Frazier's studies of human ecology could only occur at a national scale, as previously envisioned by W. E. B. Du Bois,[1] with the institutional reach and heft of the Census Bureau, and even then only once per decade. Not only did the Census Bureau directly investigate African American social life at a level of breadth and depth unimaginable before the twentieth century; the bureau also amassed and made available stores of data that have been studied and interpreted by third-party researchers, including Du Bois and Frazier, working within and beyond higher education. Harlem proved an enticing target for social science research into African American life because its density and its rapid social evolution virtually hypothesized themselves. This means that the Census Bureau's sometimes arbitrary census tract–level geographic boundaries quite literally shaped how social scientists and other intellectuals came to view Harlem.[2]

Frazier's theory of Harlem human ecology—that Harlem's Negro community developed radially, in concentric circles that were simultaneously less Negro and less dysfunctional as the five zones expanded outward—relied on census tract–level data and thus imagined Harlem as internally divided along census tract lines. For instance, Zone I, at the intersection of 135th Street and Seventh Avenue, differs greatly from Zone V, at Harlem's outer periphery (encompassing Central Park in the south and Washington Heights in the north). Frazier points to a wide array of demographic data (residential type, marriage rate, fertility, and so forth) to demonstrate that the outer zones are more stable, in terms of traditional family life, than the inner core of Harlem. Thus, the familiar "city within a city" refrain—the "Harlem Negro community," Frazier reports, "has assumed the same pattern of zones as a self-contained city"—takes on a dissonant undertone.[3]

There's a noteworthy problem with Frazier's geospatial analysis of the Harlem situation: his concentric zones are largely a product of the imagination, almost as fictional as one of Rudolph Fisher's sociological short stories. Frazier first introduced the concept of Harlem zones in 1937 in his "Negro Harlem: An Ecological Study," published in the *American Journal of Sociology*, the field's oldest and most influential outlet. To be more precise, there are at least two problems with Frazier's approach. First, and of little consequence, the table that complements the concentric zone map draws at different times from two distinct Manhattan census tracts (CTs 216 and 228) to supply data for the centermost part of the map, Zone I. (In 1910, the table reports Zone I data from CT 216 and in 1930 from CT 228.) The mismatched data skew the results, but only slightly; the overall trend, which shows a rapid shift in the Harlem population from white to black, remains indisputable.

A second, more impactful problem requires further explanation. Frazier admits that his "radial expansion" map "may be represented *ideally* by drawing concentric circles" around census tract 228; he also hints at a departure from the ideal by supplying angular lines to indicate the divide between census tracts. In a footnote to the 1937 article, one not reprinted in his later books, Frazier further clarifies that "statistical data from the federal census and other sources on the five zones are based on data for the census tracts which are included more or less in five zones as represented ideally on Map I. Data on Zone I are drawn from statistics on one census tract, No. 228; while data on the other four zones are based on statistics on the successive groups of census tracts encircling this central census tract."[4] Frazier's verbal slipperiness ("more or less," "ideally") has its visual analog: the map's right-angled lines hew much more closely to the concentric circles than do the actual census tract boundaries (see fig. 5.6).

The census tracts that Frazier identifies as Harlem in a decade's worth of social analysis—the same census tracts, more or less, that have consistently supplied social chroniclers, including this one, with empirical data about the neighborhood—follow the gridiron contours of the Commissioners' Plan of 1811 (see fig. 5.1). To the south, Central Park supplies one "natural" landmark, so that 110th Street demarcates Zone IV from Zone V, and 98th Street serves as the line between Harlem and the rest of Manhattan. North of this line are census tracts 168 and 185; south of the line are tracts 160 and 181. The Harlem River delineates Harlem's eastern and northern extents. The Hudson River represents Harlem's western extent, although Frazier repeatedly explains away statistical anomalies by referring to human institutions (such as the fashionable homes that line Riverside Drive) impeding the westward spread of the African American population.

A more faithful visual rendering of the census tracts applied to Frazier's zones would more closely resemble boxes surrounding boxes—concentric squares—rather than circles radiating outward from a central point. The urban grid and the census tracts that conform to its chessboard pattern allow Frazier to conceive of relevant comparative geographies, but the grid fails to supply his perfect circles. Zone I / census tract 228 looks instead like a chessboard square, and its neighboring zones would consist of the chessboard squares that enclose the first. Even so, Frazier's concentric circle zones proved a powerful sociological concept, particularly during the 1970s, when the now-familiar consensus view of the Harlem ghetto took firm hold in wider discussions of residential segregation. The sharply angled reality of census tract boundaries, particularly in Manhattan, did not fit precisely Frazier's portrayal of human ecology in Harlem, but it did enable the emergence of census tract–level data partitioning.

The census tract was born in 1906, when Walter Laidlaw, according to an official Census Bureau history in 1937, "became convinced that in order to study neighborhoods it was absolutely necessary to have population data for local areas smaller than boroughs or wards."[5] In his policy manifesto, "Federation Districts and a Suggestion for a Convenient and Scientific City Map System" (1906), Laidlaw decries mutable political boundaries and presents instead a case for fixed geospatial borders: "The scientific sociological study of Greater New York requires a 'dead language' boundary for tabulations. *Federation* respectfully suggests a scheme which does away both with ward and Assembly district outlines, and which can be permanent." Laidlaw proposed dividing each square mile of city geography into "quarter sections of 160 acres," and from this division the "nomenclature would then be (a) Blocks, (b) Quarter Sections, (c) Quarters, (d) Borough Sections, (e) Burroughs."[6] The right-angled grid of Manhattan would provide the basic building block of geosocial analysis. Later in 1906, Laidlaw took his idea to Washington, where he convinced Walter C. Hunt, the chief of the Division of Population at the Census Bureau, to deploy census tracts (known at the time as "districts") in New York City.

Thus the scheme set out by Laidlaw formed the blueprint for the census tract system first deployed in select parts of New York City in 1910, although the Census Bureau reported ward-level rather than tract-level data that year, leaving it to interested individuals and institutions to compile data for each of the 708 tracts.[7] (Of these, 415 tracts covering tenement areas conformed to Laidlaw's vision; the remainder consisted of legacy districts of varying size.) Laidlaw undertook the compiling effort himself, editing a two-volume, 800-page report underwritten with $60,000 from the New York Federation of Churches and Christian Workers, where Laidlaw served as executive secretary.[8]

To gear up for the next census in 1920, Laidlaw drew tracts for the entire city, 3,427 in all (later reduced to 2,463 when the Census Bureau adopted the boundaries). He also founded the Cities Census Committee to organize and support census compilation efforts in New York; of the

$65,000 raised by the committee, Laidlaw contributed $5,000 in personal funds.[9] In 1932, the committee published its *Population of the City of New York, 1890–1930,* a volume compiled and edited by Laidlaw and much used by social scientists and historians. Because of Laidlaw's efforts and his many connections among statisticians and government bureaucrats, together with the example of his editorial scholarship, the census tract system quickly spread to other cities and today spans the entire United States.

It is worth reflecting for a moment on why Laidlaw wished to study geospatial demographic patterns in New York City to begin with. Born in Ontario, Canada, and educated at the University of Toronto (MA) and New York University (BA and PhD), Laidlaw was an ordained Presbyterian minister in the Scottish tradition and the founding executive secretary of the New York Federation, a Protestant interdenominational association. Throughout its early existence, the group saw as its mission the sociological study of the New York City population to provide Christian congregations with strategic guidance. On the Federation's behalf, Laidlaw analyzed neighborhood population changes and predicted congregational viability based on these demographic shifts.

The group's research, regularly published in its journal, *Federation,* reveals a dynamic understanding of ethnic population change but a static understanding of ethnic religious identity. For example, if Scottish American families abandoned one particular neighborhood in favor of other parts of the city, then the Federation would recommend that the Reformed Presbyterian church consider relocation; if the same neighborhood became home to large numbers of Anglo-American families, then the prospects for an Episcopal church were deemed more promising, whether or not the families attended an Episcopal church across town. When, at the dawn of the twentieth century, white Moravians felt crowded out of their church by large numbers of black Moravian immigrants from the West Indies, the Federation suggested a suitable location on West Sixty-Third Street for a new, all-black Third Moravian Church of Manhattan. (A legacy Negro population cluster can be identified next to Central Park in fig. 3.1. This same church relocated to Harlem in 1954.) In a sense, the Federation functioned as an independent census bureau and interethnic arbiter for the city's religious institutions. Its motto, "Civic Evangelism," closely linked sociological knowledge with Christian service. Early *Federation* journal issues are brimming with statistical maps and population tables. Laidlaw, who led the group's survey teams, interpreted the results, and wrote most of the copy for *Federation,* stood at the center of the New York Federation's geosocial investigations.

Laidlaw clearly announces his belief in the interchangeability of ethnic and religious identities—and the geopolitical consequences of ethnic religiosity—in his *Federation* article "Religious Belief and Race Suicide" (1903). Unraveling data from Federation neighborhood surveys, Laidlaw compares family size by religious affiliation: "The average number of children in the Protestant families is 1.85, in the Roman Catholic 2.03, and in the Hebrew 2.54"; he further observes that "only 16.6 per cent. of the Hebrews are without children, whereas 28.3 per cent. of the Protestant are without children." From these figures, Laidlaw concludes that "Hebrews are freer from race suicide than Roman Catholics, Protestants or Agnostics"; sociological objectivity notwithstanding, his choice of phrase, borrowed from Theodore Roosevelt among others, indicates a negative assessment of the situation facing his fellow Protestants. Religious belief, Laidlaw adds, must be understood as "a contributing factor" to race suicide, "and President Roosevelt is a true Protestant, even if the honors, in the race suicide situation, lie with Hebrews more than with Christians, and with Protestants less than with Roman Catholics." Indeed, Laidlaw worries that Protestants (unlike Jews and Catholics) appear not to be heeding the Old Testament injunction to "be fruitful, and multiply and replenish the earth."[10] For Laidlaw, geospatial demography shines a bright light on a society that has fallen from the path of God.

Laidlaw was neither more nor less nativist than his era, and the census tracts that he conceived inevitably served interests that reacted to rapid social change with generosity or parsimony of human compassion. The census tract is thus a curious symptom of modern American identity scholarship and politics: it renders with surefire bureaucratic efficiency the tension inherent in multicultural (rather than strictly federalist) readings of the Great Seal motto, *E pluribus unum.* Out of many persons, the census tract gives us a shorthand version of one geographically defined social experience. The assembly of data into discrete census tracts has been instrumental in the comparative analysis of social attributes by race and ethnicity, particularly as these emerge from a context of segregated housing; as the sociologist Donald L. Foley pointed out at midcentury, "the research most directly promoted [by census tract data] has been that dealing with the differential characteristics of urban residential subareas within large cities."[11]

The census tract gave sociology the primary tool with which scholars could explore and illustrate human ecology, defined in 1926 by Frazier's Chicago School mentor Robert E. Park as "not man, but the community; not man's relation to the earth which he inhabits, but his relation to other men." Manhattan census tract 228, to return to our Zone I example, represents in Frazier's estimate the ultimate constellation of Harlem experiences. The census tract yields geographic data that insists upon comparative analysis deploying variables deemed important enough by the Census Bureau to collect and report. The variables have evolved over time, but as we have already seen, questions of racial identity and privilege loom large in our nation's bureaucratic history. And just as individuals sometimes bear the burden of representing a larger social identity, so too do census tracts. As Park observes, "Every local group exhibits a more or less definite constellation of the individual units that compose it."[12] As the spatial repository of the most complete set of readily available census data, the census tract is the part favored to represent the whole. Easily manipulated and tested for statistical reliability, census tract data remains the gold standard of demographic analysis.[13]

Census tract geography, as we see in Frazier's theory of concentric zones, has a tendency to accrue symbolic value as well. Harlem Renaissance literary history sides with Frazier in this regard. Rudolph Fisher explores the function of Manhattan's urban grid in imposing a kind of racial identity onto the exact same Zone I geography in his short story about intraracial violence, "Blades of Steel," first published in the *Atlantic Monthly* in 1927.

The story begins with a curious reference to the urban grid's too convenient symbolism: "Negro Harlem's three broad highways form the letter H, Lenox and Seventh Avenues running parallel northward, united a little above their midpoints by east-and-west 135th Streets." According to Fisher's clinically detached narrator, on Seventh Avenue there can be found a "promenade of high-toned dickties and strivers"; Lenox Avenue, on the other hand, is home to "unperfumed 'rats.'" The two social types come together, literally and symbolically, at the centermost point within Frazier's concentric circles: "These two highways, frontiers of the opposed extreme of dark-skinned social life, are separated by an intermediate any-man's land, across which they communicate chiefly by way of 135th Street. Accordingly 135th Street is the heart and soul of black Harlem; it is common ground; the natural scene of unusual contacts; a region that disregards class. It neutralizes, equilibrates, binds, rescues union out of diversity." The passage virtually groans under the weight of clichéd figures of speech, drawn from the lingo of westward expansion ("frontiers," "any-man's land"), pop cultural notions of selfless patriotism and racial essentialism ("heart and soul"), chemistry ("neutralizes, equilibrates, binds"), and of course Great Seal sloganeering ("union out of diversity"). The narrator makes equally painful exertions to render the story's two principal characters as absurd visual opposites; they are a cartoonish, albino "caricature" of "African ancestry" on the one hand, and a figure of absolute black with a "silhouette-like clean-cutness" on the other hand. The story features stock characters, settings (a barbershop and a 135th Street dance hall), Harlem slang, and even a "'low-down' orchestra," virtually the same contents that previously garnered disapproval for Fisher's friend and collaborator Carl Van Vechten.[14]

As one character in Van Vechten's infamous novel declares, "Nigger Heaven! That's what Harlem is. We sit in our places in the gallery of this New York theatre and watch the white world sitting down below in the good seats in the orchestra."[15] The spatial metaphor, which compares residential segregation in Manhattan to Jim Crow theater seating, allowed Van Vechten to project elements of class difference onto the black/white divide between Harlem and the rest of New York City, but all demographic subtlety was lost on most of his readers, then as now. Spatial metaphors tend toward bluntness. Harlem was at times known as "Little Africa," an exotic but easily grasped locale on a par with "Little Italy" or "Chinatown." Harlem itself has been understood primarily in terms of dissociative distance from the rest of New York City, and the census tract gives us plentiful data with which to tabulate and objectify the difference.

Human ecology as first conceived by Park invested heavily in notions of freedom of movement. As Park explained, "The fact that every individual is capable of movement in space insures him an experience that is private and peculiar to himself"; movement in space gives each of us our own, irreproducible identity. Similarly, Park understood human ecology to be shaped by social and cultural commerce that is mutually constitutive and evolutionary in nature. Anticipating the sociological concept transculturation, Park observed that social "communication involves not a translation of energies, such as seems to take place between individual social units . . . but rather communication involves a transformation in the individuals who thus communicate. And this transformation goes on unceasingly with the accumulation of individual experiences in individual minds."[16] Seen in this light, the census tract–level data that inform most studies of human ecology, including Frazier's seminal work in the field of Harlem studies, fails utterly to account for that which makes us most human. By fixing identity data points (race, gender, marital status, literacy, and the list goes on) in time and space, social chroniclers tend to inflict on individuals the same kind of too-certain, one-dimensional status that besets so many Harlem Renaissance fictional characters: Jake Brown, Helga Crane, Max Disher, Emma Lou Morgan, Angela Murray, 'Liza Jane Taylor. . . . And any census of Harlem Renaissance writers would uncover the recurring theme of individuals forced by American racial discourse into limited professional options and burdensome social responsibilities.

I offer no messianic pleas for a postracial understanding of the Harlem Renaissance; to do so would be to ignore five centuries' worth of discursive insistence—in law, in medicine, in politics, in culture—that race was a (if not *the*) crux of human social identity. But this book arrives at a moment that is animated by ongoing discussions of the racial nomenclature that will determine how some 335 million Americans define themselves on the 2020 census.[17] Throughout this book I have insisted on the value of census history as a lens through which we might view African American literary culture. Now is the time to turn the lens around and view social practices with all the nuance and generosity of a great work of literary art.

Appendix

Race/Color Categories Employed by the U.S. Census, 1790–2010

The following lists include two sets of race/color categories employed by the Census Bureau. The first set was found in census schedules used by enumerators (1790–1960) or census questionnaires completed by heads of household (1970–2010). The second set was published in official Census Bureau reports. The categories recorded and the categories reported do not always correspond exactly.

Source: First through Twenty-third Censuses of the United States (1790–2010). See also U.S. Census Bureau, *Measuring America: The Decennial Censuses from 1790 to 2000* (Washington, D.C.: Department of Commerce, 2002).

Census years: 1790, 1800, 1810

Race/color categories listed on census schedule: free white, other free, slaves
Race/color categories reported by Census Bureau: free white, other free, slaves
Marshal/enumerator instructions:
"marshals . . . are hereby authorized and required to cause the number of the inhabitants within their respective districts to be taken; omitting in such enumeration Indians not taxed, and distinguishing free persons . . . from all others; distinguishing also the sexes and colours of free persons"

Census year: 1820

Race/color categories listed on census schedule: free white, foreigners not naturalized, slaves, free colored persons, all others
Race/color categories reported by Census Bureau: free white, foreigners not naturalized, slaves, free colored persons, all others
Marshal/enumerator instructions:
Same as previous censuses

Census year: 1830

Race/color categories listed on census schedule: white, free colored, slaves
Race/color categories reported by Census Bureau: white, colored, free colored
Marshal/enumerator instructions:
Same as previous censuses

Census year: 1840

Race/color categories listed on census schedule: free white, free colored, slaves
Race/color categories reported by Census Bureau: free white, free colored, slaves
Marshal/enumerator instructions: Same as previous censuses

Census year: 1850

Race/color categories listed on census schedule: White, black, mulatto
Race/color categories reported by Census Bureau: white, free colored, slave
Marshal/enumerator instructions:
"Schedule No. 1—Free Inhabitants . . . Under heading 6, entitled *'Color,'* in all cases where the person is white, leave the space blank; in all cases where the person is black, insert the letter B; if mulatto, insert M. It is very desirable that these particulars be carefully regarded. . . .

Schedule 2—Slave Inhabitants . . . Under heading 5, entitled *'Color,'* insert, in all cases, where the slave is black, the letter B; where he or she is a mulatto, insert M. The color of all slaves should be noted."

Census year: 1860

Race/color categories listed on census schedule: White, black, mulatto
Race/color categories reported by Census Bureau: white, free colored, slave; black, mulatto
Marshal/enumerator instructions:
"Schedule No. 1—Free Inhabitants . . . Under heading 6, entitled '*Color,*' in all cases where the person is white leave the space blank; in all cases where the person is black without admixture insert the letter 'B;' if a mulatto, or of mixed blood, write 'M;' if an Indian, write 'Ind.' It is very desirable to have these directions carefully observed. . . .

Schedule No. 2—Slave Inhabitants . . . Under heading 5, entitled '*Color,*' insert, in all cases where the slave is black, the letter 'B.' When he or she is a mulatto insert 'M.' You are to note the color of every slave. Those who are in any degree of mixed blood are to be termed mulatto, 'M.'"

Census year: 1870

Race/color categories listed on census schedule: White, Black, Mulatto, Chinese, Indian
Race/color categories reported by Census Bureau: White, Colored, Chinese, Indian

Marshal/enumerator instructions:
"Color.—It must not be assumed that, where nothing is written in this column, 'White' is to be understood. The column is always to be filled. Be particularly careful in reporting the class Mulatto. The word is here generic, and includes quadroons, octoroons, and all persons having any perceptible trace of African blood. Important scientific results depend upon the correct determination of this class in Schedules 1 and 2."

Census year: 1880

Race/color categories listed on census schedule: White, Black, Mulatto, Chinese, Indian
Race/color categories reported by Census Bureau: White, Colored, Chinese, Japanese, Indian
Marshal/enumerator instructions:
"*Color.*—It must not be assumed that, where nothing is written in this column, 'white' is to be understood. The column is always to be filled. Be particularly careful in reporting the class mulatto. The word is here generic, and includes quadroons, octoroons, and all persons having any perceptible trace of African blood. Important scientific results depend upon the correct determination of this class in schedules 1 and 5."

Census year: 1890

Race/color categories listed on census schedule: white, black, mulatto, quadroon, octoroon, Chinese, Japanese, Indian
Race/color categories reported by Census Bureau: white, colored, Negro, mulatto, quadroon, octoroon, Chinese, Japanese, Indian
Marshal/enumerator instructions:
"Write *white, black, mulatto, quadroon, octoroon, Chinese, Japanese,* or *Indian,* according to the color or race of the person enumerated. Be particularly careful to distinguish between blacks, mulattoes, quadroons, and octoroons. The word 'black' should be used to describe those persons who have three-fourths or more black blood; 'mulatto,' those persons who have from three-eighths to five-eighths black blood; 'quadroon,' those persons who have one-fourth black blood; and 'octoroon,' those persons who have one-eighth or any trace of black blood."

Census year: 1900

Race/color categories listed on census schedule: No options printed; refer to instructions
Race/color categories reported by Census Bureau: white, Negro, Mulatto, Quadroon, Octoroon, Chinese, Japanese, Indian
Marshal/enumerator instructions:
"Color or race.—Write 'W' for white; 'B' for black (negro or of negro descent); 'Ch' for Chinese; 'Jp' for Japanese, and 'In' for Indian, as the case may be."

Census year: 1910

Race/color categories listed on census schedule: No options printed; refer to instructions

Race/color categories reported by Census Bureau: White, Negro (inc. black, mulatto), Indian, Chinese, Japanese, Other (incl. Hawaiian, Hindu, Korean, Filipino, Maori)

Marshal/enumerator instructions:

"Color or race.—Write 'W' for white; 'B' for black; 'Mu' for mulatto; 'Ch' for Chinese; 'Jp' for Japanese; 'In' for Indian. For all persons not falling within one of these classes, write 'Ot' (for other), and write on the left-hand margin of the schedule the race of the person so indicated. For census purposes, the term 'black' (B) includes all persons who are evidently full-blooded negroes, while the term 'mulatto' (Mu) includes all other persons having some proportion or perceptible trace of negro blood."

Census year: 1920

Race/color categories listed on census schedule: No options printed; refer to instructions

Race/color categories reported by Census Bureau: White, Negro (incl. black, mulatto), Indian, Chinese, Japanese, Other

Marshal/enumerator instructions:

"Write '*W*' for white; '*B*' for black; '*Mu*' for mulatto; '*In*' for Indian; '*Ch*' for Chinese; '*Jp*' for Japanese; '*Fil*' for Filipino; '*Hin*' for Hindu; '*Kor*' for Korean. For all persons not falling within one of these classes, write '*Ot*' (for other), and write on the left-hand margin of the schedule the race of the person so indicated. For census purposes the term 'black' (B) includes all Negroes of full blood, while the term 'mulatto' (Mu) includes all Negroes having some proportion of white blood."

Census year: 1930

Race/color categories listed on census schedule: No options printed; refer to instructions

Race/color categories reported by Census Bureau: White, Negro, Mexican, Indian, Chinese, Japanese, Filipino, Hindu, Korean, Hawaiian, Malay, Siamese, Samoan

Marshal/enumerator instructions:

"Write 'W' for white; 'Neg' for Negro; 'Mex' for Mexican; 'In' for Indian; 'Ch' for Chinese; 'Jp' for Japanese; 'Fil' for Filipino; 'Hin' for Hindu; and 'Kor' for Korean. For a person of any other race, write the race in full. A person of mixed white and Negro blood should be returned as a Negro, no matter how small the percentage of Negro blood. Both black and mulatto persons are to be returned as Negroes, without distinction. A person of mixed Indian and Negro blood should be returned a Negro, unless the Indian blood predominates and the status as an Indian is generally accepted in the community. A person of mixed white and Indian blood should be returned as Indian, except where the percentage of Indian blood is very small, or where he is regarded as a white person by those in the community where he lives. For a person reported as Indian in column 12, report is to be made in column 19 as to whether 'full blood' or 'mixed blood,' and in column 20 the name of the tribe is to be reported. For Indians, columns 19 and 20 are thus to be used to indicate the degree of Indian blood and the tribe, instead of the birthplace of father and mother. Practically all Mexican laborers are of a racial mixture difficult to classify, though usually well recognized in the localities where they are found. In order to obtain separate figures for this racial group, it has been decided that all persons born in Mexico, or having parents born in Mexico, who are not definitely white, Negro, Indian, Chinese, or Japanese, should be returned as Mexican ('Mex'). Any mixture of white and nonwhite should be reported according to the nonwhite parent. Mixtures of colored races should be reported according to the race of the father, except Negro-Indian."

Census year: 1940

Race/color categories listed on census schedule: No options printed; refer to instructions

Race/color categories reported by Census Bureau: White, Negro, Indian, Chinese, Japanese, Other

Marshal/enumerator instructions:

"*Color or Race.*—Write 'W' for white; 'Neg' for Negro; 'In' for Indian; 'Chi' for Chinese; 'Jp' for Japanese; 'Fil' for Filipino; 'Hin' for Hindu; and 'Kor' for Korean. For a person of any other race, write the race in full.

Mexicans.—Mexicans are to be regarded as white unless definitely of Indian or other nonwhite race.

Negroes.—A person of mixed white and Negro blood should be returned as a Negro, no matter how small the percentage of Negro blood. Both black and mulatto persons are to be returned as Negroes, without distinction. A person of mixed Indian and Negro blood should be returned as a Negro, unless the Indian blood very definitely predominates and he is universally accepted in the community as an Indian.

Indians.—A person of mixed white and Indian blood should be returned as Indian, if enrolled on an Indian Agency or Reservation roll; or if not so enrolled, if the proportion of Indian blood is one-fourth or more, or if the person is regarded as an Indian in the community where he lives.

Mixed Races.—Any mixture of white and nonwhite should be reported according to the nonwhite parent. Mixtures of nonwhite races should be reported according to the race of the father, except that Negro-Indian should be reported as Negro."

Census year: 1950

Race/color categories listed on census schedule: "White (W), Negro (Neg), American Indian (Ind), Japanese (Jap), Chinese (Chi), Filipino (Fil), Other race—spell out"

Race/color categories reported by Census Bureau: White, Negro, Indian, Japanese, Chinese, All other

Marshal/enumerator instructions:

"Determining and entering race.—Write 'W' for white; 'Neg' for Negro; 'Ind' for American Indian; 'Chi' for Chinese; 'Jap' for Japanese; 'Fil' for Filipino. For a person of any other race, write the race in full. Assume that the race of related persons living in the household is the same as the race of your respondent, unless you learn otherwise. For unrelated persons (employees, hired hands, lodgers, etc.) you must ask the race, because knowledge of the housewife's race (for example) tells nothing of the maid's race.

Mexicans.—Report 'white' (W) for Mexicans unless they are definitely Indian or other nonwhite race.

Negroes.—Report 'Negro' for Negroes and for persons of mixed white and Negro parentage. A person of mixed Indian and Negro blood should be returned as Negro, unless the Indian blood very definitely predominates and he is accepted in the community as an Indian.

American Indians.—Report 'American Indian' (Ind) for persons of mixed white and Indian blood if enrolled on an Indian Agency or Reservation roll; if not so enrolled, they should still be reported as Indian if the proportion of Indian blood is one-fourth or more, or if they are regarded as Indians in the community where they live. In those counties where there are many Indians living outside of reservations, special care should be taken to obtain accurate answers to item 9.

Special communities.—Report persons of mixed white, Negro, and Indian ancestry living in certain communities in the Eastern United States in terms of the name by which they are locally known. The communities in question are of long standing and are locally recognized by special names, such as 'Croatian,' 'Jackson White,' 'We-sort,' etc. Persons of mixed Indian and Negro ancestry and mulattoes not living in such communities should be returned as 'Negro.' When in doubt, describe the situation in a footnote.

Mixed parentage.—Report race of nonwhite parent for persons of mixed white and nonwhite races. Mixtures of nonwhite races should be reported according to the race of the father.

India.—Persons originating in India should be reported as 'Asiatic Indians.'

Census year: 1960

Race/color categories listed on census schedule: "Is this person—White, Negro, American Indian, Japanese, Chinese, Filipino, Hawaiian, Part Hawaiian, Aleut, Eskimo, (etc.)?"

Race/color categories reported by Census Bureau: White, Negro, Indian, Japanese, Chinese, Filipino, All other

Marshal/enumerator instructions: No instructions printed; refer to schedule

Census year: 1970

Race/color categories listed on census questionnaire: "Fill one circle. If 'Indian (American),' also give tribe. If 'Other,' also give race. White, Negro or Black,

Indian (Amer.) [Print tribe], Japanese, Chinese, Filipino, Hawaiian, Korean, Other [Print race]"

Race/color categories reported by Census Bureau: White, Negro, Indian, Japanese, Chinese, Filipino, All other

Instructions to respondent: No instructions printed; refer to questionnaire

Census year: 1980

Race/color categories listed on census questionnaire: "Is this person— *Fill one circle.* White, Black or Negro, Japanese, Chinese, Filipino, Korean, Vietnamese, Indian (Amer.) [*Print tribe*], Asian Indian, Hawaiian, Guamanian, Samoan, Eskimo, Aleut, Other [*Specify*]"

Race/color categories reported by Census Bureau: White, Black, American Indian, Eskimo, Aleut, Japanese, Chinese, Filipino, Korean, Asian Indian, Vietnamese, Hawaiian, Guamanian, Samoan, Other

Instructions to respondent:

"Fill the circle for the category with which the person most closely identifies. If you fill the Indian (American) or Other circle, be sure to print the name of the specific Indian tribe or specific group."

Census year: 1990

Race/color categories listed on census questionnaire: "Race: Fill ONE circle for the race that the person considers himself/herself to be. If Indian (Amer.), print the name of the enrolled or principal tribe. If Other Asian Pacific Islander (API), print one group, for example: Hmong, Fijian, Laotian, Thai, Tongan, Pakistani, Cambodian, and so on. If Other race, print race"

Race/color categories reported by Census Bureau: White, Black, American Indian, Eskimo, Aleut, Chinese, Filipino, Japanese, Asian Indian, Korean, Vietnamese, Cambodian, Hmong, Laotian, Thai, Bangladeshi, Burmese, Indonesian, Malayan, Okinawan, Pakistani, Sri Lankan, All other Asian, Hawaiian, Samoan, Guamanian, Tongan, Tahitian, Northern Mariana Islander, Palauan, Fijian, All other Pacific Islander, Other race

Instructions to respondent:

"Fill one circle for the race each person considers himself/herself to be.

If you fill the Indian (Amer.) circle, print the name of the tribe or tribes in which the person is enrolled. If the person is not enrolled in a tribe, print the name of the principal tribe(s).

If you fill the Other API circle under Asian or Pacific Islander (API), only print the name of the group to which the person belongs. For example, the Other API category includes persons who identify as Burmese, Fijian, Hmong, Indonesian, Laotian, Bangladeshi, Pakistani, Tongan, Thai, Cambodian, Sri Lankan, and so on.

If you fill the Other race circle, be sure to print the name of the race.

If the person considers himself/herself to be White, Black or Negro, Eskimo or Aleut, fill one circle only. Please do not print the race in the boxes.

The Black or Negro category also includes persons who identify as African-American, Afro-American, Haitian, Jamaican, West Indian, Nigerian, and so on. All persons, regardless of citizenship status, should answer this question"

Census year: 2000

Race/color categories listed on census questionnaire: "What is Person 1's race? Mark one or more races to indicate what this person considers himself/ herself to be. White; Black, African Am., or Negro; American Indian or Alaska Native [*Print name of enrolled or principal tribe.*]; Asian Indian; Chinese; Filipino; Other Asian [*Print race.*]; Japanese; Korean; Vietnamese; Native Hawaiian; Guamanian or Chamorro; Samoan; Other Pacific Islander [*Print race.*]; Some other race [*Print race.*]"

Race/color categories reported by Census Bureau: White, Black or African American, American Indian and Alaska Native, Asian, Native Hawaiian and Other Pacific Islander, Some other race, Two or more race

Instructions to respondent: No instructions printed for respondent; refer to questionnaire; see also *Nonresponse Followup Enumerator Manual*

Census year: 2010

Race/color categories listed on census questionnaire: "What is Person 1's race? Mark one or more boxes. White; Black, African Am., or Negro; American Indian or Alaska Native [*Print name of enrolled or principal tribe.*]; Asian Indian; Chinese; Filipino; Other Asian [*Print race, for example, Hmong, Laotian, Thai, Pakistani, Cambodian, and so on.*]; Japanese; Korean; Vietnamese; Native Hawaiian; Guamanian or Chamorro; Samoan; Other Pacific Islander [*Print race, for example, Fijian, Tongan, and so on.]*; Some other race [*Print race.*]"

Race/color categories reported by Census Bureau: White, Black or African American, American Indian and Alaska Native, Asian, Native Hawaiian and Other Pacific Islander, Some other race, Two or more races

Instructions to respondent: No instructions printed for respondent; refer to questionnaire; see also *2010 Census Nonresponse Followup Enumerator Manual*

Notes

Introduction

1. Qtd. in Jonathan Elliot, ed., *The Debates in the Several State Conventions, on the Adoption of the Federal Constitution,* 5 vols. (Washington, D.C.: Printed for the editor, 1836), 2:237. In *The Federalist* number 54, Hamilton or James Madison expands upon the necessity to strike a balance between treating slaves as either property or persons. Although Hamilton and Madison opposed slavery, both were politically pragmatic and cautious advocates for a gradual, compensated emancipation. Thadious M. Davis argues convincingly that the ironic tensions built into the Constitution's handling of slavery spill over into the tortured reasoning behind the *Dred Scott* (1857) decision and the *U.S. v. Army* (1859) decision and even into the twentieth-century American cultural imagination. See Thadius M. Davis, *Games of Property: Law, Race, Gender, and Faulkner's "Go Down Moses"* (Durham: Duke University Press, 2003).
2. The phrase "long Harlem Renaissance" has recently begun to circulate so that the adjective might expand the place name's range of associations, both chronologically and geographically. Cherene Sherrard-Johnson, for example, indicates a "long Harlem Renaissance" period from the 1890s to the 1930s; this book pushes the boundaries even further, with a look at African American cultural formations from the Reconstruction era to the mid-twentieth century. Cherene Sherrard-Johnson, ed., *A Companion to the Harlem Renaissance* (Chichester, U.K.: Wiley Blackwell, 2015), 2–5.
3. Unless otherwise noted, all demographic data that I cite in this book are drawn from the relevant decennial census. Online editions of decennial census reports, from the first census of 1790 to the twenty-third census of 2010, can be accessed at www.census.gov/prod/www/decennial.html.
4. Prior to the publication of Hughes's *The Big Sea* (1940), the Harlem Renaissance was known strictly as the "Negro Renaissance," a phrase that predates the movement itself. I trace the history of both phrases in *The Modernist Nation: Generation, Renaissance,*

and Twentieth-Century American Literature (Tuscaloosa: University of Alabama Press, 2004), chap. 2.

5. Brent Hayes Edwards, *The Practice of Diaspora: Literature, Translation, and the Rise of Black Internationalism* (Cambridge: Harvard University Press, 2003), 3.
6. John L. Jackson Jr., *Harlemworld: Doing Race and Class in Contemporary Black America* (Chicago: University of Chicago Press, 2001), 19.
7. Roi Ottley, *"New World A-Coming": Inside Black America* (Cleveland: World, 1943), v.
8. Benedict Anderson, *Imagined Communities: Reflections on the Origin and Spread of Nationalism,* rev. ed. (London: Verso, 1991), xiv, 188.
9. For an overview of U.S. census questionnaires, see U.S. Census Bureau, *Measuring America: The Decennial Census from 1790 to 2000* (Washington, D.C.: Department of Commerce, 2002).
10. The Census Bureau defines "census tracts" as "small, relatively permanent statistical subdivisions of a county or equivalent entity. . . . The primary purpose of census tracts is to provide a stable set of geographic units for the presentation of statistical data." See "Geographic Terms and Concepts—Census Tract" at www.census.gov/geo/reference/gtc/gtc_ct.html.
11. Kenneth W. Warren, *What Was African American Literature?* (Cambridge: Harvard University Press, 2011).
12. Soto, *Modernist Nation,* chap. 2.
13. It is worth taking the Senegalese writer Léopold Sédar Senghor at his word when he claims that "the discovery of black values and recognition for the Negro of his situation—was born in the United States of America." Qtd. in T. Denean Sharpley-Whiting, ed., *Negritude Women* (Minneapolis: University of Minnesota Press, 2002), 13.
14. Anderson, *Imagined Communities,* 170.
15. I address the theoretical and practical difficulties posed by social research in much greater detail in chapter 3.
16. Theodor Adorno, "Commitment," trans. Francis McDonagh, in *Aesthetics and Politics* (London: Verso, 1977), 194.
17. David Levering Lewis, *When Harlem Was in Vogue* (New York: Penguin, 1997), xvi.
18. Simone de Beauvoir, *The Second Sex,* trans. H. M. Parshley (New York: Vintage, 1974), 267.
19. The growing body of scientific literature about the emergence of skin color variation in early humans has been deftly summarized by Nina G. Jablonski, *Living Color: The Biological and Social Meaning of Skin Color* (Berkeley: University of California Press, 2012).
20. I hesitate to use the word "miscegenation" given its racist origins and given its imprecision—after all, vastly different groups have always interbred, a practice that goes back at least to early interaction between *Homo sapiens* and Neanderthals.
21. Vera M. Kutzinski poses an intriguing question in relation to this very example of transliteration: "One need not to subscribe to Walter Benjamin's view of original and translation as so many shards of a greater language to imagine some semantic overlap between the Spanish noun *negro* and its English counterparts. Such overlap has invited much theoretical speculation on kinship relations among the cultural formations of the African diaspora in the Americas. But can a 'spic' really be a 'Negro,' even a

'nigger,' and vice versa?" Vera M. Kutzinski, *The Worlds of Langston Hughes: Modernism and Translation in the Americas* (Ithaca: Cornell University Press, 2012), 56.

1. Measure for Measure for Measure

1. Francis Bicknell Carpenter, *Six Months at the White House with Abraham Lincoln* (New York: Hurd and Houghton, 1866), 10–11, 90.
2. Ibid., 217, 218.
3. The office was later renamed the U.S. Coast and Geodetic Survey. Today it is known as the Office of Coast Survey, housed since 1970 within the National Oceanic and Atmospheric Administration.
4. Carpenter, *Six Months at the White House,* 215–16.
5. Ibid., 216.
6. Susan Schulten, *Mapping the Nation: History and Cartography in Nineteenth-Century America* (Chicago: University of Chicago Press, 2012), 139.
7. Ibid., 140–41.
8. Paul D. Escott, *"What Shall We Do with the Negro?": Lincoln, White Racism, and Civil War America* (Charlottesville: University of Virginia Press, 2009), chap. 1; Eric Foner, *The Fiery Trial: Abraham Lincoln and American Slavery* (New York: Norton, 2010); George M. Frederickson, *Big Enough to Be Inconsistent: Abraham Lincoln Confronts Slavery and Race* (Cambridge: Harvard University Press, 2008), chap. 3.
9. Foner, *Fiery Trial,* 17.
10. Henry Louis Gates, ed., *Lincoln on Race and Slavery* (Princeton: Princeton University Press, 2009), 223.
11. Ibid., 226–27.
12. Frederickson, *Big Enough to Be Inconsistent,* 125.
13. Lincoln's views on race are paradoxical even in Carpenter's generous account. Carpenter quotes Douglass's magnanimous description of his much-publicized White House visit, but elsewhere Carpenter indicates that Lincoln was not above deploying a racist joke to spice up a conversation. Carpenter, *Six Months at the White House,* 204, 158–59.
14. Abraham Lincoln, *Collected Works,* ed. Roy P. Brasler, 8 vols. (New Brunswick: Rutgers University Press, 1953), 5:371.
15. See, for example, Frederickson, *Big Enough to Be Inconsistent,* chap. 2.
16. Melissa Nobles, *Shades of Citizenship: Race and the Census in Modern Politics* (Stanford: Stanford University Press, 2000). See also Jennifer L. Hochschild and Brenna Marea Powell, "Racial Reorganization and the United States Census 1850–1930: Mulattoes, Half-Breeds, Mixed Parentage, Hindoos, and the Mexican Race," *Studies in American Political Development* 22.1 (2008): 59–96.
17. U.S. Census Bureau, *Eighth Census* (Washington, D.C.: G. W. Bowman, 1860), x, xi, xii.
18. Jean Toomer, *Cane* (1923), ed. Rudolph P. Byrd and Henry Louis Gates Jr. (New York: Norton, 2011), lxx.
19. Rudolph P. Byrd and Henry Louis Gates Jr., "Jean Toomer's Conflicted Racial Identity," *Chronicle of Higher Education,* February 6, 2011; Felicia R. Lee, "Scholars Say Chronicler of Black Life Passed for White," *New York Times,* December 26, 2010.
20. George Hutchinson, "Jean Toomer and the 'New Negroes' of Washington," *American Literature* 63.4 (1991): 686–87.

21. Joel Williamson, *New People: Miscegenation and Mulattoes in the United States* (New York: Free Press, 1980), 114. It is worth noting that according to Williamson's logic, all white people must also look alike to the Census Bureau.
22. Michael North, *The Dialect of Modernism: Race, Language, and Twentieth-Century Literature* (New York: Oxford University Press, 1994), 163; Rachel Farebrother, *The Collage Aesthetic in the Harlem Renaissance* (Surrey, U.K.: Ashgate, 2009), 94.
23. Byrd and Gates, introduction to *Cane,* lxvi, lxvi–lxvii, lxvii. Curiously, Byrd and Gates reproduce a later copy (dated October 28, 1932) of Toomer's marriage certificate rather than the original filed a year earlier (lxxvii). Much of the personal information, including racial identities, on Toomer's original State of Wisconsin marriage certificate was typed by an unknown person on the state's form 503 1/2 and issued by the county clerk, H. R. Tongen, on October 28, 1931. Daniel Corrigan, who officiated the wedding, completed the remaining information on October 30, 1931. R. Klinert and Marion R. S. Rogers witnessed the certificate. Neither Toomer nor Latimer wrote on the document. If anyone were ever to pressure Toomer to identify as Negro in Wisconsin, one of the few states never to pass an anti-miscegenation law, it may well have been Corrigan, then the Episcopal rector of St. John's Church in Portage and later an important figure in the U.S. civil rights movement. Corrigan was present, for example, at Martin Luther King Jr.'s "I Have a Dream" speech; after his retirement, he campaigned vigorously for the ordination of women clergy. The Beinecke Rare Book and Manuscript Library at Yale University has reproduced the original Latimer–Toomer marriage certificate online: http://brbl-dl.library.yale.edu/vufind/Record/3837788.
24. Byrd and Gates, introduction to *Cane,* lxvii–lxviii.
25. See National Archives and Records Administration document numbers 927 and 929 for lists of data collected on World War I and World War II (Fourth Registration) draft cards.
26. Digital copies of microform census schedules from 1920 and 1930 can be found on the Internet Archive website, https://archive.org/.
27. Caroline F. Ware, *Greenwich Village, 1920–1930: A Comment on American Civilization in the Post-war Years* (Boston: Houghton Mifflin, 1935), 11–12.
28. Ibid., 15–23.
29. Qtd. in David Levering Lewis, *W. E. B. Du Bois: A Biography* (New York: Henry Holt, 2009), 235.
30. W. E. B. Du Bois, "The Twelfth Census and the Negro Problems," *Southern Workman* 29.5 (1900): 307, 308.
31. Du Bois's volume on the Negro farmer was a highly condensed version of the manuscript that he originally submitted. Much of Du Bois's historical commentary was struck from the published work because the Census Bureau director felt that historical interpretation lay outside the bureau's purview and because the subject was potentially controversial. Letter from the United States Census Office to W. E. B. Du Bois, March 7, 1904, W. E. B. Du Bois Papers (MS 312), Special Collections and University Archives, University of Massachusetts Amherst Libraries (hereafter cited as Du Bois Papers).
32. Du Bois, "Twelfth Census," 307.
33. For inclusion among the "Special Committee for the Study of the Negro Problems," Du Bois suggests five Negro leaders (including Francis J. Grimké, Kelly Miller, and Booker T. Washington) who also favored strategic, intraracial cooperation.

34. U.S. Census Bureau, *Negroes in the United States* (Washington, D.C.: Government Printing Office, 1904), 15, 17, 15.
35. W. E. B. Du Bois, *The Souls of Black Folk: Authoritative Text, Contexts, Criticism*, ed. Henry Louis Gates Jr. and Terri Hume Oliver (New York: Norton, 1999), 72.
36. For a thorough discussion of the politics and policies behind census racial categories, see Nobles, *Shades of Citizenship*, esp. chap. 2. See also Sharon M. Lee, "Racial Classifications in the U.S. Census: 1890–1990," *Ethnic and Racial Studies* 16.1 (1993): 75–94; and Clara E. Rodríguez, *Changing Race: Latinos, the Census, and the History of Ethnicity in the United States* (New York: New York University Press, 2000). On the subject of mixed-race census data, the Census Bureau report for the Eleventh Census (1890) concluded, "These figures are of little value. Indeed as an indication of the extent to which the races have mingled, they are misleading." Qtd. in Nobles, *Shades of Citizenship*, 60.
37. The census of 1960 collected primarily enumerator-designated racial data, but it introduced for the first time a subset of self-reported racial data.
38. U.S. Census Bureau, *Negro Population, 1790–1915* (Washington, D.C.: Government Printing Office, 1918), 207.
39. Qtd. in Rodríguez, *Changing Race*, 81.
40. Qtd. in Nobles, *Shades of Citizenship*, 68–69. According to the Census Bureau's "Through the Decades" website, there were 70,286 enumerators in 1910 and 87,234 in 1920. See www.census.gov/history/www/through_the_decades/. The website does not indicate the racial identities of enumerators. In a letter to Du Bois dated January 17, 1922, Census Bureau director William Mott Steuart claimed that there were over 2,000 Negro enumerators deployed in 1910 and none in previous censuses or 1920 (Du Bois Papers). The letter also anticipates subsequent conclusions regarding Negro enumerators and the mulatto population count. *Crisis* magazine reported in 1911 that the previous year's census required 55,000 enumerators, of whom 1,605 were Negro, including 1,295 in the South. "Along the Color Line," *Crisis* 1 (January 1911): 8.
41. For example, the ordering of the racial categories throughout the appendix follows the example of the census schedules themselves, which claim a priori to list the categories according to numerical significance. Obviously, the practice might easily be shown to reflect social as well as numerical hierarchies.
42. A search of *Crisis* archives at the Modernist Journal Project website (http://modjourn.org/) quickly reveals the extent of the magazine's debt to census data.
43. It is likely that Du Bois knew Hall, at least professionally, through their mutual friend Kelly Miller. (Miller also served as Du Bois's *Crisis* assistant editor.) Hall's professional and social exploits were the occasional subject of *Crisis* commentary.
44. See, for example, David I. Kertzer and Dominique Arel, "Censuses, Identity Formation, and the Struggle for Political Power," in *Census and Identity: The Politics of Race, Ethnicity, and Language*, ed. Kertzer and Arel (Cambridge: Cambridge University Press, 2002). In 1936, LULAC successfully lobbied congressional leaders and the Census Bureau to eliminate the "Mexican" racial category and to count all persons of Mexican descent as "white." See Patrick D. Lukens, *A Quiet Victory for Latino Rights: FDR and the Controversy over "Whiteness"* (Tucson: University of Arizona Press, 2012).
45. Barack Obama, *Dreams from My Father: A Story of Race and Inheritance* (New York: Random, 2004), xx.
46. Abigail Thernstrom, "Obama's Census Identity," *Wall Street Journal*, April 9, 2010; Patricia J. Williams, "Not-black by Default," *Nation*, May 10, 2010.

2. Harlem Society

1. I am deeply indebted to George Koppelman at Cultured Oyster Books in New York for sharing with me high-quality reproductions of the first-edition dust jacket and cloth cover. As he points out to me (in an email dated June 10, 2011), Macaulay paid rare attention to visual detail in the jacket and cover design, which feature matching illustrations by the key Harlem Renaissance illustrator Aaron Douglas, who was a friend of Thurman.
2. Wallace Thurman, *The Blacker the Berry* (1929; New York: Scribner, 1996), 21.
3. Qtd. in David Levering Lewis, *When Harlem Was in Vogue* (New York: Penguin, 1997), 236.
4. Alain Locke, "Both Sides of the Color Line," *Survey* 62 (June 1, 1929): 325.
5. "Harlem Negroes," *New York Times,* March 17, 1929.
6. Emily Bernard, "Unlike Many Others: Exceptional White Characters in Harlem Renaissance Fiction," *Modernism/modernity* 12.3 (2005): 416.
7. Bernard W. Bell, *The Afro-American Novel and Its Tradition* (Amherst: University of Massachusetts Press, 1987), 146.
8. Qtd. in Eleonore Van Notten, *Wallace Thurman's Harlem Renaissance* (Amsterdam: Rodopi, 1994), 212. Amritjit Singh provides a rare example of unabashed praise for Thurman's novel. Singh labels *The Blacker the Berry* "among the better achievements of the Harlem Renaissance . . . both for what it achieves and for what it does not." Amritjit Singh, *The Novels of the Harlem Renaissance: Twelve Black Writers, 1923–1933* (University Park: Pennsylvania State University Press, 1976), 106.
9. Shaun P. Hargreaves Heap and Yanis Varoufakis, *Game Theory: A Critical Introduction* (London: Routledge, 1995), 1–2.
10. Battle of the sexes is a two-player coordination game in which (usually) a husband and wife cannot recall whether they planned to meet at the opera (the wife's preference) or at a football match (the husband's preference); each must decide which to attend without consulting the other. The prisoner's dilemma involves two prisoners, kept apart by their interrogators, who must separately decide whether or not to sell out their coconspirator. The princess and monster game locates us in a dark room where a princess must find the best strategy for evading a monster for the longest possible time. In all three of these examples, the separate agents receive higher or lower payoffs depending not only on their choices, but also on the choices of their fellow agent, with whom they do not communicate.
11. Robert J. Leonard, *Von Neumann, Morgenstern, and the Creation of Game Theory: From Chess to Social Science, 1900–1960* (New York: Cambridge University Press, 2010).
12. See Michael Suk-Young Chwe, *Jane Austen, Game Theorist* (Princeton: Princeton University Press, 2013); and Thadious M. Davis, *Games of Property: Law, Race, Gender, and Faulkner's "Go Down Moses"* (Durham: Duke University Press, 2003). Much as Chwe and Davis assert regarding Austen and Faulkner, both Thurman's and (as I discuss below) Hurston's explorations of game theory derive from amateur interests in human behavior rather than theoretical interests in economic motives.
13. Thurman, *Blacker the Berry,* 47, 48, 49.
14. Ibid., 24, 36, 54.
15. Ibid., 95.
16. Ibid., 60.

17. Ibid., 64–65.
18. In her unpublished memoir, Louise Thompson Patterson, Thurman's ex-wife, observes that Thurman "mocked the phenomenon of up and coming black men having to have light-skinned women in order to get ahead, although he, in a way, was doing the same thing" in choosing the light-skinned Patterson as a mate. "Memoirs: chapter 3," box 19, folder 20, Louise Thompson Patterson papers, Stuart A. Rose Manuscript, Archives, and Rare Book Library, Emory University, Atlanta, Ga.
19. U.S. Department of Labor, *The Negro Family: The Case for National Action* (Washington, D.C.: Government Printing Office, 1965), 5.
20. W. E. B. Du Bois, *The Philadelphia Negro: A Social Study* (New York: Benjamin Blom, 1967), 67, 193.
21. E. Franklin Frazier, *The Negro in the United States,* rev. ed. (New York: Macmillan, 1957), 313.
22. E. Franklin Frazier, *The Negro Family in the United States* (Chicago: University of Chicago Press, 1939), 285.
23. On Moynihan's complicated debt to Frazier, see Tony Platt, "E. Franklin Frazier and Daniel Patrick Moynihan: Setting the Record Straight," *Crime, Law and Social Change* 11.3 (1987): 265–77.
24. Frazier, *Negro in the United States,* 318.
25. Before the 1840s, when the transatlantic slave trade exerted an influence on slave demography, African American men outnumbered African American women, and "head of household" was an anachronism within the dehumanizing plantation system.
26. When he refers to an "unhealthy tone" in "social intercourse," Du Bois has in mind the notion that a scarcity of men results in a lowering of social standards to admit a sufficient number of men at middle-class gatherings. Elsewhere, Du Bois notes that the "unusual excess of females . . . has not often been noticed, and has not been given its true weight as a social phenomenon." Du Bois, *Philadelphia Negro,* 55, 53. Additional early discussions of an imbalanced sex ratio among African Americans include Kelly Miller's 1905 essay, "Surplus Negro Women," in *Race Adjustment: Essays on the Negro in America* (New York: Neale, 1908); and Mary White Ovington's 1911 study, *Half a Man: The Status of the Negro in New York* (New York: Schocken, 1969).
27. Mary White Ovington, a cofounder of the NAACP, observes, "In their hours of leisure the surplus women are known to play havoc with their neighbors' sons, even with their neighbors' husbands, for since lack of men makes marriage impossible for about a fifth of New York's colored girls, social disorder results." Ovington, *Half a Man,* 148.
28. Miller, "Surplus Negro Women," 170.
29. U.S. Department of Labor, *Negro Family,* 19. For a broad overview of the reaction to the Moynihan Report, including the feminist response, see Daniel Geary, *Beyond Civil Rights: The Moynihan Report and Its Legacy* (Philadelphia: University of Pennsylvania Press, 2015).
30. Harlem is not a separately incorporated entity (as it was briefly in the Dutch colonies); as a result, its boundaries are necessarily artificial and slightly arbitrary. I am following the social historian Cheryl Lynn Greenberg's sound example in identifying 28 census tracts in upper Manhattan that define the geographic extent of the Harlem enclave. Greenberg singled out the 28 census tracts because in 1930 their Negro population was proportionally higher than the Negro population for Manhattan overall. See Cheryl Lynn Greenberg, *"Or Does It Explode?": Black Harlem in the Great Depression* (Oxford:

Oxford University Press, 1991). Because I have extended my analysis backward in time, many of these same census tracts had very small Negro populations in 1920; one (CT 204) had a Negro population of zero in that year.

31. Basic statistical analysis of arc sine conversions of the proportions that comprise figure 2.1 (percent Negro and sex ratio converted to percent female) shows a moderate positive correlation ($r = 0.3828$) across all 28 Harlem census tracts.
32. The sex ratios of New York City census tracts also correlated positively with the percentage of native-born white women ($r = 0.355$) and negatively with the percentage of foreign-born white men ($r = -0.302$).
33. The historian of ethnicity Joel Perlmann describes ethnic intermarriage as "American as apple pie." Joel Perlmann, "Multiracials, Intermarriage, Ethnicity," *Society* 34.6 (1997): 20.
34. I hesitate to use a hypothetical example that some might find patronizing, but similar examples were used in early twentieth-century discussions of an African American sex imbalance. Kelly Miller, for example, when considering the imbalance in urban areas, writes, "If every Negro male in these cities should be assigned a helpmeet there would still remain eighteen left-over females for every one hundred couples." Miller, "Surplus Negro Women," 170.
35. These sex ratios are based on data found in Nettie Pauline McGill and Ellen Nathalie Matthews, *The Youth of New York City* (New York: Macmillan, 1940), 8.
36. U.S. Census Bureau, *Negroes in the United States, 1920–1932* (Washington, D.C.: Government Printing Office, 1935), 79.
37. Although most Harlem Renaissance novels about working women shed light on the professional classes, domestic workers made up 86 percent of the African American women's workforce in 1910 and 71.5 percent in 1920. Louise Venable Kennedy, *The Negro Peasant Turns Cityward: Effects of Recent Migrations to Northern Centers* (New York: Columbia University Press, 1930), 90. For a full discussion of employment opportunities available to Harlem women at this time, see Greenberg, *"Or Does It Explode?,"* chap. 3.
38. Frazier, *Negro in the United States,* 182.
39. Marcia Guttentag and Paul F. Secord, *Too Many Women? The Sex Ratio Question* (Beverly Hills: Sage, 1983), 199, 207. More recently, sociologists have added to this list higher rates of male African American incarceration. Some analysts, including Moynihan, attribute a significant portion of the African American sex imbalance within official population figures to census undercounts, which disproportionately affect the African American male population.
40. See Mark A. Fossett and K. Jill Kiecolt, "Mate Availability and Family Structure among African Americans in U.S. Metropolitan Areas," *Journal of Marriage and the Family* 55.2 (1993): 288–302; Cynthia M. Cready, Mark A. Fossett, and K. Jill Kiecolt, "Mate Availability and African American Family Structure in the U.S. Nonmetropolitan South, 1960–1990," *Journal of Marriage and the Family* 59.1 (1997): 192–203; and Scott J. South and Kim M. Lloyd, "Marriage Opportunities and Family Formation: Further Implications of Imbalanced Sex Ratios," *Journal of Marriage and the Family* 54.2 (1992): 440–51.
41. Fossett and Kiecolt, "Mate Availability and Family Structure," 297.
42. McGill and Matthews, *Youth of New York City,* 26.
43. Deborah McDowell, *"The Changing Same": Black Women's Literature, Criticism, and Theory* (Bloomington: Indiana University Press, 1995), xii, xiii.

44. Charles W. Chesnutt, "A Matter of Principle," in *The Wife of His Youth and Other Stories of the Color Line* (Boston: Houghton Mifflin, 1901), 98–99.
45. Similar analyses might easily extend into the late twentieth and twenty-first centuries. A number of popular novels and films during this period (the work of Terry McMillan offers perhaps the best-known examples) dramatize the social pressures faced by African American professional women.
46. Von Neumann and Morgenstern address the prospects for economic game theory in terms of the need to quantify "rationality": "The individual who attempts to obtain these respective maxima is also said to act 'rationally.' But it may safely be stated that there exists, at present, no satisfactory treatment of the question of rational behavior. There may, for example, exist several ways by which to reach the optimum position; they may depend upon the knowledge and understanding which the individual has and upon the paths of action open to him. A study of all these questions in qualitative terms will not exhaust them, because they imply, as must be evident, quantitative relationships. It would, therefore, be necessary to formulate them in quantitative terms so that all the elements of the qualitative description are taken into consideration. This is an exceedingly difficult task, and we can safely say that it has not been accomplished in the extensive literature about the topic." John Von Neuman and Oskar Morgenstern, *Theory of Games and Economic Behavior* (Princeton: Princeton University Press, 1947), 9.
47. Elise Johnson McDougald, "The Task of Negro Womanhood," in *The New Negro: An Interpretation,* ed. Alain Locke (1925; New York: Atheneum, 1992), 379.
48. Claude McKay, *Home to Harlem* (Lebanon, N.H.: Northeastern University Press, 1987), 68.
49. Of Fauset, Nathan Irvin Huggins writes: "Jessie Fauset tried to project the Negro image in very conventional terms. Indeed, it was her intended purpose in writing novels to place the Negro in the context of standard American life"; she "delineates middle-class Negro life, contrives problems to generate the stories." Nathan Irvin Huggins, *Harlem Renaissance* (New York: Oxford University Press, 1971), 146. Lewis, in what's meant to be a sympathetic sketch of her life, sums up Fauset's position upon her arrival in New York in 1920 as follows: "she was already an unmarried, proper, thirty-eight-year-old Washington schoolteacher." Lewis, *When Harlem Was in Vogue,* 122.
50. As William J. Maxwell observes (following Hazel Carby), Hurston serves as the key figure in the postmodern reappraisal of a romanticized rural South as the "imaginary homeland of black America." The conceptual gesture, Maxwell adds, mirrors the ongoing demographic reversal of the early twentieth-century Great Migration. William J. Maxwell, "'Is It True What They Say about Dixie': Richard Wright, Zora Neale Hurston, and Rural/Urban Exchange in Modern African-American Literature," in *Knowing Your Place: Rural Identity and Cultural Hierarchy,* ed. Barbara Ching and Gerald W. Creed (New York: Routledge, 1997), 71. For an overview of recent Hurston short fiction recovery efforts and a thoughtful appraisal of two short stories, see M. Genevieve West, "'Youse in New Yawk': The Gender Politics of Zora Neale Hurston's 'Lost' Caroline Stories," *African American Review* 47.4 (2014): 477–93.
51. Zora Neale Hurston, "Story in Harlem Slang," *American Mercury* 55 (July 1942): 85, 87.
52. Ibid., 88–89. The *American Mercury* published Hurston's "Glossary of Harlem Slang" as part of the short story; it is worth pointing out that much of the story's relevant street language (including "pimp" and "putting out") is not included in the glossary.

53. Zora Neale Hurston, "Monkey Junk: A Satire on Modern Divorce," *Pittsburgh Courier,* March 5, 1927.
54. Ibid.
55. Glenda R. Carpio and Werner Sollors, "The Newly Complicated Zora Neale Hurston," *Chronicle of Higher Education,* January 7, 2011.
56. Hurston, "Monkey Junk."
57. James Weldon Johnson, ed., *The Book of American Negro Poetry* (New York: Harcourt, Brace, 1931), 9.
58. Tendencies within social realist writing have been handled expertly by Stacy I. Morgan, *Rethinking Social Realism: African American Art and Literature, 1930–1953* (Athens: University of Georgia Press, 2004).
59. According to Lewis, David Belasco's play *Lulu Belle* "was a racially exploitative farce that pretended to depict Harlem street life. It virtually jump-started the rush of sightseeing Caucasians to those parts of Harlem where people of color were predominant." David Levering Lewis, *W. E. B. Du Bois: A Biography* (New York: Henry Holt, 2009), 173.
60. Thurman, *Blacker the Berry,* 120.
61. Neal A. Lester makes a mostly convincing case that it's possible to read Hurston's "Story in Harlem Slang" as an example of "veiled homoeroticism" between the provocatively named Jelly and Sweet Back; the short story dramatizes "the reality of heterosexual passing" and it "challenges black cultural perceptions that demand, particularly from black males, a performance that contradicts their true desires." Neal A. Lester, "Sounds of Silent Performances: Homoeroticism in Zora Neale Hurston's 'Story in Harlem Slang: Jelly's Tale,'" *Southern Quarterly* 36.3 (1998): 18.
62. Wallace Thurman, *Infants of the Spring* (1932; Boston: Northeastern University Press, 1992), 186, 187.
63. Vincent Kang Fu and Nicholas H. Wolfinger, "Broken Boundaries or Broken Marriages? Racial Intermarriage and Divorce in the United States," *Social Science Quarterly* 924 (2011): 1102, 1097; Zhenchao Qian and Daniel T. Lichter, "Changing Patterns of Interracial Marriage in a Multiracial Society," *Journal of Marriage and Family* 73.5 (2011): 1067.

3. Harlem Diversity

1. Rachel Farebrother, *The Collage Aesthetic in the Harlem Renaissance* (Surrey, U.K.: Ashgate, 2009), 16.
2. The polyglot, international cast of characters in *Quicksand* renders our preferred contemporary phrase "African American" suspect.
3. Nella Larsen, *Quicksand* and *Passing,* ed. Deborah E. McDowell (New Brunswick: Rutgers University Press, 1986), 49, 35, 104, 53, 111, 25.
4. Ann E. Hostetler, "The Aesthetics of Race and Gender in Nella Larsen's *Quicksand,*" *PMLA* 105.1 (1990): 35.
5. Larsen, *Quicksand,* 2, 50, 71, 86, 89.
6. Ibid., 59. A large plurality of Larsen scholars see *Quicksand* as a direct repudiation of the primitivist vogue exemplified by Van Vechten's career and long associated with the Harlem Renaissance.
7. Ibid., 59–60.
8. Ibid., 60.

9. Marjorie Perloff, "Collage and Poetry," in *Encyclopedia of Aesthetics,* ed. Michael Kelly, 4 vols. (Oxford: Oxford University Press, 1998), 1:384.
10. Mary Esteve, "Nella Larsen's 'Moving Mosaic': Harlem, Crowds, and Anonymity," *American Literary History* 9.2 (1997): 279.
11. When considering the alternatives offered by the cabaret versus the church crowds, the novel's Danish interlude takes on an interesting geographic symbolism. As Larsen's biographer George Hutchinson notes, "Larsen drew upon a fairly wide experience and intimate knowledge of [Copenhagen] at a particular moment," right down to the novel's reference to a specific street address where her aunt and uncle live, Maria Kirkeplads number 2. As Hutchinson points out, this small street near the train station contained a "row of bourgeois apartment buildings facing a small church off Istegrade," the Mariakirken, or St. Mary's Church. George Hutchinson, *In Search of Nella Larsen: A Biography of the Color Line* (Cambridge: Harvard University Press, 2006), 69. It is especially worth adding that St. Mary's was founded at the end of the nineteenth century, in a building that had previously been used as a dance hall.
12. At one point Jake forgets the words to a ballad, causing the narrator to confess, "But [Jake] could not remember most of the words, therefore Bullocky Bill cannot be presented here." Claude McKay, *Home to Harlem* (1928; Lebanon, N.H.: Northeastern University Press, 1987), 293.
13. McKay, *Home to Harlem,* 28, 29, 31, 33, 55, 56, 58, 63, 65, 66, 84, 91, 105, 106, 113, 141, 146, 165, 190, 196, 219, 236, 249, 282, 289, 291, 318, 320, 55, 318.
14. Ibid., 320.
15. Michael Soto, *The Modernist Nation: Generation, Renaissance, and Twentieth-Century American Literature* (Tuscaloosa: University of Alabama Press, 2004), chap. 4.
16. McKay, *Home to Harlem,* 57–58.
17. Werner Sollors, *Neither Black nor White Yet Both: Thematic Explorations of Interracial Literature* (New York: Oxford University Press, 1997), appendix A.
18. For a full discussion of the rise of "renaissance rhetoric" in early twentieth-century African American letters, see Soto, *Modernist Nation,* chap. 2.
19. Schuyler qtd. in David Levering Lewis, *When Harlem Was in Vogue* (New York: Penguin, 1997), 131.
20. Walter White, "The Paradox of Color," in *The New Negro: An Interpretation,* ed. Alain Locke (1925; New York: Atheneum, 1992), 336.
21. James Weldon Johnson, "Harlem: The Culture Capital," in Locke, *The New Negro,* 301.
22. Roi Ottley and William J. Weatherby, eds., *The Negro in New York: An Informal Social History* (New York: New York Public Library, 1967), 190.
23. W. A. Domingo, "Gift of the Black Tropics," in Locke, *The New Negro,* 341.
24. Census tracts were deployed in New York City for the first time with the 1910 census. Historical census data at the tract level is incomplete for 1910, however, and tract boundaries were refined after the 1910 census (thus rendering longitudinal analysis invalid). For a brief overview of the rise of the census tract, see the epilogue.
25. U.S. Census Bureau, *Thirteenth Census of the United States,* vol. 3 (Washington, D.C.: Government Printing Office, 1913), 211. The same phrasing is repeated multiple times throughout the volume as part of individual state census reports.
26. Ira De A. Reid, *The Negro Immigrant, His Background, Characteristics, and Social Adjustment, 1899–1937* (1939; New York: AMS Press, 1968), 12.
27. The rationale for the Bureau of Immigration and Naturalization at the time was to

protect the jobs of native-born Americans, which explains its bureaucratic headquarters; after the functions of the bureau were split between the Commerce Department and the Labor Department in 1913, it was finally merged once again and transferred to the Justice Department in 1940.

28. Negro immigrants from Puerto Rico or the Virgin Islands, because they were U.S. colonial subjects, were counted among native-born Negroes. By 1930, there were 17,625 Negroes from these territories. We might also consider the fact that in 1930 there were an additional 83,361 U.S.-born Negroes of foreign or mixed parentage. Reid, *Negro Immigrant,* 42.
29. On the rise and role of restrictive quota policies in U.S. immigration history, see Aristide R. Zolberg, *A Nation by Design: Immigration Policy in the Fashioning of America* (Cambridge: Harvard University Press, 2006).
30. G. E. Cumper, "Preliminary Analysis of Population Growth and Social Characteristics in Jamaica, 1943–60," *Social and Economic Studies* 12.4 (1963): 401.
31. One thinks, for example, of the Afro-Cuban visual artist Wifredo Lam, the Cuban-born son of a Chinese immigrant and a mulatto Cuban woman. Although Lam sometimes exhibited in the United States—his masterwork, *The Jungle* (1943), resides in New York at the Museum of Modern Art—he never called it home; his wanderings more often found him in Europe and Latin America. On the Afro-Chinese presence in the South, see James C. Cobb, *The Most Southern Place on Earth: The Mississippi Delta and the Roots of Regional Identity* (Oxford: Oxford University Press, 1992), chap. 7; and James W. Loewen, *The Mississippi Chinese: Between Black and White,* 2nd ed. (Long Grove, Ill.: Waveland, 1988), chap. 6.
32. James Weldon Johnson, *The Autobiography of an Ex-Colored Man* (New York: Sherman, French, 1912), 1, 74.
33. Ibid., 65, 69.
34. Ibid., 65. It is perhaps ironic that slavery was not ended in Cuba until 1886, when a Spanish royal decree outlawed the practice. As Suzanne Bost recounts, abolitionist and anti-imperial sentiment in Cuba often intertwined in unexpected ways; ultimately, the "independent Cuban culture united black and white based on their shared rejection of Spanish authority," but only after the question of abolition was long settled. Suzanne Bost, *Mulattas and Mestizas: Representing Mixed Identities in the Americas, 1850–2000* (Athens: University of Georgia Press, 2003), 102.
35. I certainly don't wish to imply that Cuban reality lived up to the egalitarian rhetoric of its independence movement. For a full discussion of the Afro-Cuban role in the island's independence, see Alejandro de la Fuente, *A Nation for All: Race, Inequality, and Politics in Twentieth-Century Cuba* (Chapel Hill: University of North Carolina Press, 2001).
36. Brian Russell Roberts, "Passing into Diplomacy: U.S. Consul James Weldon Johnson and *The Autobiography of an Ex-Colored Man,*" *Modern Fiction Studies* 56.2 (2010): 307.
37. Amanda M. Page, "The Ever-Expanding South: James Weldon Johnson and the Rhetoric of the Global Color Line," *Southern Quarterly* 46.3 (2009): 30.
38. Johnson, *Autobiography of an Ex-Colored Man,* 207.
39. The elder Gómez was instrumental in establishing a long-term connection between Cuba and the Tuskegee Institute. For a full discussion of the Afro-Cuban presence at Tuskegee, see Frank Andre Guridy, *Forging Diaspora: Afro-Cubans and African Americans in a World of Empire and Jim Crow* (Chapel Hill: University of North Carolina Press, 2010), chap. 1.
40. Johnson, *Autobiography of an Ex-Colored Man,* 80–81.

41. James Weldon Johnson, *Along This Way: The Autobiography of James Weldon Johnson* (1933; New York: Penguin, 1990), 60.
42. Johnson, *Autobiography of an Ex-Colored Man,* 74. In *Along This Way*, Johnson had a less sanguine recollection of the Jacksonville of his adult life: "Jacksonville is today a one hundred percent Cracker town, and each time I have been back there I have marked greater and greater changes." Johnson, *Along This Way*, 45.
43. Johnson, *Autobiography of an Ex-Colored Man,* 74, 76. Johnson's sociocultural excurses appear less clunky if we consider the book's original publication status as autobiographical nonfiction.
44. The historian Frank Andre Guridy describes the growth in U.S.–Cuban travel, including the rise of Afro-Cuban travel to the United States and African American travel to Cuba, during the early part of the twentieth century. Guridy, *Forging Diaspora,* chap. 4.
45. Johnson, *Along This Way,* 88–89.
46. Guridy points out that whenever large delegations of Afro-Cubans traveled the U.S. South, they faced predictable difficulties navigating the Jim Crow landscape until well into the twentieth century. Guridy, *Forging Diaspora,* chap. 4.
47. Larsen, *Passing,* 150. The Afro-Latino motif has a historical basis as well. As the historian Martha Hodes points out regarding the antebellum South, "a claim of Spanish or Portuguese nationality could erase counter-claims of blackness." Martha Hodes, "The Mercurial Nature and Abiding Power of Race: A Transnational Family Story," *American Historical Review* 108.1 (2003): 103.
48. Valerie Popp, "Where Confusion Is: Transnationalism in the Fiction of Jessie Redmon Fauset," *African American Review* 43.1 (2009): 132.
49. Jessie Redmon Fauset, *Plum Bun: A Novel without a Moral* (1928; Boston: Beacon, 1990), 287, 290.
50. Fauset, *Plum Bun,* 14, 196.
51. The IBGE's race labels are neatly summarized by the sociologist Edward E. Telles: "Since 1950, the IBGE has employed the categories white (*branco*), brown (*pardo*), black (*preto*), Asian (*amarelo*), and since 1991, indigenous (*indígena*). . . . While white and black refer to the ends of the continuum, the census's brown category (*pardo*) serves as an umbrella category for the various mixed-race terms used in popular discourse." Edward E. Telles, *Race in Another America: The Significance of Skin Color in Brazil* (Princeton: Princeton University Press, 2004), 81.
52. Stanley R. Bailey, *Legacies of Race: Identities, Attitudes, and Politics in Brazil* (Stanford: Stanford University Press, 2009), 42. Telles and José Luis Petrucelli, an IBGE researcher, point out that a majority of Brazilians refer to themselves along the lines suggested by the official color/race categories listed on IBGE census schedules. For the comprehensive list of unofficial terms, see José Luis Petrucelli, *A cor denominada: estudos sobre a classificação étnico-racial* (Rio de Janeiro: DP&A, 2007).

4. Harlem Modernity

1. Emmett Jay Scott, *Negro Migration during the War* (New York: Oxford University Press, 1920), 3. In fact, Scott's concluding chapter is simply a compendium of newspaper clippings that offer multiple perspectives on the effects of the Great Migration.
2. "Harding Says Negro Must Have Equality in Political Life," *New York Times,* October 27, 1921.

3. "Harding Supports New Policy in South," *New York Times,* October 27, 1921. Marcus Garvey understood Harding's speech as a direct repudiation of Du Bois and thus an implicit endorsement of Garvey's separatism. David Levering Lewis, *W. E. B. Du Bois: A Biography* (New York: Henry Holt, 2009), 426–27.
4. A large plurality of animal great migration references addresses the flight patterns of birds; the work of the turn-of-the-century English ornithologist Charles Dixon offers one example rich with references to great migrations. See also the work of the influential English naturalist Richard Lydekker, who mentions great migrations of antelopes, elephants, and rhinoceroses. Nineteenth-century American naturalists routinely wrote about great migrations of bison (often in the past tense, just as the species threatened to disappear from the landscape).
5. Christopher Wills includes a chapter titled "The Great Migration" on the movement of humans from Africa to the four corners of the globe. Christopher Wills, *The Darwinian Tourist: Viewing the World through Evolutionary Eyes* (Oxford: Oxford University Press, 2010). The science reporter Guy Gugliotta described the venture into Europe this way: "Modern humans eventually made their first forays into Europe only about 40,000 years ago, presumably delayed by relatively cold and inhospitable weather and a less than welcoming Neanderthal population. The conquest of the continent—if that is what it was—is thought to have lasted about 15,000 years, as the last pockets of Neanderthals dwindled to extinction. The European penetration is widely regarded as the decisive event of the great migration, eliminating as it did our last rivals and enabling the moderns to survive there uncontested." Guy Gugliotta, "The Great Human Migration," *Smithsonian* 39.4 (2008): 62. Until well into the twentieth century, many archaeologists and anthropologists, who often saw Africans as a polygenetic branch of the human tree or as devolved from a shared primal ancestor, mistakenly believed that human origins could be traced to Europe or the Middle East. Ironically, some refer to a great migration of early humans *into* Africa. Twenty-first-century investigations into the genetic connections between primitive hominids (including Neanderthals) and modern humans, including the extent to which *Homo sapiens* interbred with their prehistoric companions, bear an uncanny resemblance to eighteenth- and nineteenth-century discussions about whether or not the distinct races constituted separate species. On the race/species debate, see Werner Sollors, *Neither Black nor White Yet Both: Thematic Explorations of Interracial Literature* (New York: Oxford University Press, 1997), chap. 2. Modern science generally agrees that most Neanderthals had lighter skin than their human counterparts. See Nina G. Jablonski, *Living Color: The Biological and Social Meaning of Skin Color* (Berkeley: University of California Press, 2012), 44–45. Genetic overlap between contemporary humans and Neanderthals is discussed in Kate Wong, "Our Inner Neanderthal," *Scientific American* 303.1 (2010): 18–20.
6. Madison Grant, *The Conquest of a Continent; or, the Expansion of Races in America* (New York: Scribner's, 1933), 82. Writing about George Washington's ancestors, Woodrow Wilson, then on the faculty at Princeton University, gave a rare example of great migration discourse applied to southern Cavaliers: "It was in these years Virginia got her character and received her leading gentry for the time to come—the years while the Commonwealth stood and royalists despaired, and the years immediately following the Restoration, when royalists took heart again and Englishmen turned with a new ardor to colonization as the times changed. Among the rest in the great

migration came two brothers, John and Lawrence Washington, of a stock whose loyalty was as old as the Conquest." Woodrow Wilson, "In Washington's Day," *Harper's* 92 (January1896): 174.

7. "Anthropological Society of Washington," *Journal of the Washington Academy of Sciences* 3.3 (1913): 91.
8. U.S. Census Bureau, *Negro Population, 1790–1915* (Washington, D.C.: Government Printing Office, 1918), 17, 31, 32.
9. The earliest example that I have found is a July 10, 1915, article in the *Washington Bee.* The article reports on efforts by the National League on Urban Conditions Among Negroes (later the National Urban League) "to check the great migration to cities, and to help those who migrate to towns to learn how to live and survive there and become like other citizens." "Checking Migration of Negroes to Cities," *Washington Bee,* July 10, 1915. As this report suggests, National Urban League leadership thought it best for the largest numbers of African Americans to remain in the South lest northern African American enclaves deteriorate into slums. Perhaps more than any other publication, Robert Abbott's *Chicago Defender,* which boasted a nationwide circulation, popularized the "Great Northern Drive" of southern African Americans. The *Defender* encouraged southerners to create migration clubs and arranged for group discounts on Chicago-bound trains. See Milton C. Sernett, *Bound for the Promised Land: African American Religion and the Great Migration* (Durham: Duke University Press, 1997), 42. For an overview of Great Migration scholarship from 1918 to the 1980s, see Joe William Trotter, "Introduction: Black Migration in Historical Perspective: A Review of the Literature," in *The Great Migration in Historical Perspective: New Dimensions of Race, Class, and Gender,* ed. Trotter (Bloomington: Indiana University Press, 1991).
10. U.S. Department of Labor, *Negro Migration in 1916–17* (Washington, D.C.: Government Printing Office, 1919), 7.
11. Woodson defines "bulldozing" as "a rather vague term, covering all such crimes as political injustice and persecution." Carter G. Woodson, *A Century of Negro Migration* (Washington, D.C.: Association for the Study of Negro Life and History, 1918), 167, 168–69, 126.
12. Scott notes in particular that "wages in the North were double and treble those received in the South. Women who received $2.50 a week in domestic service could earn from $2.10 to $2.50 a day and men receiving $1.10 and $1.25 a day could earn from $2.50 to $3.75 a day in the various industries in the North." Scott, *Negro Migration during the War,* 13, 17. According to the sociologists Daniel M. Johnson and Rex R. Campbell, "In the first 14 years of the century, more than 12 million immigrants had arrived in the United States. In 1914 alone, more than one million immigrants arrived. But the following year, the number of immigrants declined to about one-third that number, in 1916 to about one-fourth, and by 1918, there were only 110,000 new arrivals to the United States. At the same time, almost 100,000 emigrated from the United States to their European homeland." Daniel M. Johnson and Rex R. Campbell, *Black Migration and America: A Social Demographic History* (Durham: Duke University Press, 1981), 71–72. It should also be noted that during the early twentieth century, the African American population declined in the rural West, Midwest, and New England; this pattern suggests that a more abstract urbanization played a large role in the African American population shift.
13. David Levering Lewis, *When Harlem Was in Vogue* (New York: Penguin, 1997), xxviii.

14. See, for example, Woodson, *Century of Negro Migration,* 183–84. There's scant evidence, apart from the appointment of prominent African Americans to posts within the Republican administration, that the Great Migration resulted in any lasting political improvement. One coveted political post went to Emmett Jay Scott, who in 1917 became special assistant to Secretary of War Newton D. Baker. Scott's assignment was to improve the morale of African American servicemen and to press for the just application of Selective Service regulations.
15. Werner Sollors, *Beyond Ethnicity: Consent and Descent in American Culture* (New York: Oxford University Press, 1986), 57.
16. Albert J. Raboteau, "African Americans, Exodus, and the American Israel," in *Religion and American Culture: A Reader,* ed. David G. Hackett (New York: Routledge, 1995), 81, 84.
17. James Weldon Johnson, *God's Trombones: Seven Negro Sermons in Verse* (1927; New York: Penguin, 1990), 52.
18. Some scholars have made the case that Hurston subverts the Old Testament narrative by introducing a wide range of discursive intricacies: *Moses, Man of the Mountain* has been read as gothic farce, Boasian cultural analysis, Oedipal tragedy, fascist nightmare, and liberation theology. As Erica R. Edwards points out, Hurston marshals these varied possibilities to complicate the Old Testament's model of nation building via charismatic male leadership. Erica R. Edwards, "Moses, Monster of the Mountain: Gendered Violence in Black Leadership's Gothic Tale," *Callaloo* 31.4 (2008): 1084–1102.
19. Zora Neale Hurston, *Moses, Man of the Mountain* (1939; New York: Harper, 1991), 190.
20. Ibid., 127; Johnson, *God's Trombones,* 46.
21. High-quality images of odd-numbered panels are available online from the Phillips Collection at www.phillipscollection.org/migration_series. For an excellent print catalog of the entire Migration Series, see Elizabeth Hutton Turner, ed., *Jacob Lawrence: The Migration Series* (Washington, D.C.: Rappahannock Press, 1993).
22. Qtd. in Sharon F. Patton, *African-American Art* (Oxford: Oxford University Press, 1998), 156.
23. Patricia Hills, "Jacob Lawrence's *Migration Series:* Weavings of Pictures and Texts," in Turner, *Jacob Lawrence,* 144.
24. Christopher Capozzola, "Jacob Lawrence: Historian," *Rethinking History* 10.2 (2006): 291–95.
25. Martha Nadell, "Visual Art of the Harlem Renaissance," in *Teaching the Harlem Renaissance: Course Design and Classroom Strategies,* ed. Michael Soto (New York: Peter Lang, 2008), 57.
26. In an illuminating study of "The Wife of His Youth," Earle V. Bryant focuses on the title's biblical allusion (to Malachi 2, Proverbs 5, and Isaiah 54) to explore parallels between religious and racial loyalty. Earle V. Bryant, "Scriptural Allusion and Metaphorical Marriage in Charles Chesnutt's 'The Wife of His Youth,'" *American Literary Realism* 33.1 (2000): 57–64.
27. Charles W. Chesnutt, *The Wife of His Youth and Other Stories of the Color Line* (Boston: Houghton, Mifflin, 1901), 1, 2.
28. Chesnutt, *Wife of His Youth,* 7. The language of "absorption" and "extinction" flows freely in nineteenth- and twentieth-century nativist rhetoric. Even the Eighth Census (1860) lamented that the mulatto "is doomed to comparatively rapid absorption

and extinction" into the dominant racial groups. U.S. Census Bureau, *Population of the United States in 1860; Compiled from the Original Returns of the Eighth Census* (Washington, D.C.: Government Printing Office, 1864), xii.

29. Chesnutt, *Wife of His Youth,* 8, 7.
30. See, for example, Judith R. Berzon, *Neither White nor Black: The Mulatto Character in American Fiction* (New York: New York University Press, 1978); and Sollors, *Neither Black nor White Yet Both.* Additional examples of "blue vein" literature not discussed here include Chesnutt's "A Matter of Principle" (1899) and Sutton E. Griggs's *Overshadowed* (1899). A similar example, obviously without the same racial overtones, can be found in Shakespeare's *Antony and Cleopatra,* in which Cleopatra refers to her "bluest veins" (II.v).
31. The historian Willard B. Gatewood writes of "blue veinism" in a number of U.S. cities, finding a close connection between blue veinism and communities of free blacks with long histories prior to emancipation. Willard B. Gatewood, *Aristocrats of Color: The Black Elite, 1880–1920* (Bloomington: Indiana University Press, 1990), chaps. 5 and 6.
32. Chesnutt, *Wife of His Youth,* 1. Gatewood writes, "In possessing a reputation for a 'blue-vein element,' few cities equaled that of Cleveland. Throughout the late nineteenth and early twentieth centuries references to its existence regularly appeared in print." Gatewood, *Aristocrats of Color,* 159. It should be noted that the sources cited by Gatewood predate "The Wife of His Youth," suggesting that the story's popularity did not spur the blue vein references.
33. Wallace Thurman, *The Blacker the Berry* (1929; New York: Scribner, 1996), 6.
34. Katherine Davis Chapman Tillman, *The Works of Katherine Davis Chapman Tillman,* ed. Claudia Tate (Oxford: Oxford University Press, 1991), 196.
35. Bernard W. Bell, *The Afro-American Novel and Its Tradition* (Amherst: University of Massachusetts Press, 1987), 146.
36. Thurman, *Blacker the Berry,* 6, 7. Much has been written about the nineteenth century's association of dark skin and working-class status, followed by the twentieth century's association of a suntan and leisure activity. See, for example, Kerry Segrave, *Suntanning in 20th Century America* (Jefferson, N.C.: McFarland, 2005).
37. See, for example, William Ross Wallace's encomium to the American landscape, "Rest of the Nation," which compares a river to "a blue vein on sleeping Beauty's breast." William Ross Wallace, *Meditations in America* (New York: Scribner, 1851), 135. William Gilmore Simms extended Shakespeare's notion that Cleopatra displayed a "blue vein" on the "heaving wave" of her breast in his blank verse drama *The Death of Cleopatra* (1852). William Gilmore Simms, *Poems,* 2 vols. (Charleston, S.C.: John Russell, 1853), 2:332. Elizabeth Barrett Browning refers to a blue-veined brow in her "Aurora Leigh" (1864). In his epic *Clarel: A Poem and Pilgrimage in the Holy Land* (1876), Herman Melville curiously represents an ascetic monk's blue-veined feet.
38. See, for example, the American-born geographer and physician John Mitchell's "An Essay upon the Causes of the Different Colours of People in Different Climates," *Philosophical Transactions of the Royal Society* 43.472–77 (1746): 102–50, which includes a section titled "The Skins of Negroes Are of a Thicker Substance, and Denser Texture, Than Those of White People, and Transmit No Colour thro' Them." The essay later served as the basis for Mitchell's 1748 election to the Royal Society. Today he is remembered for the famous Mitchell Map (1755) of North America.

39. Segrave, *Suntanning in 20th Century America,* 181.
40. Jo M. Martin et al., "Changes in Skin Tanning Attitudes: Fashion Articles and Advertisements in the Early 20th Century," *American Journal of Public Health* 99.12 (2009): 2143, 2144.
41. Finsen focused on the treatment of lupus vulgaris, but similar procedures were soon developed to treat "anemia, Hodgkin's disease, chronic renal disease, syphilis, and septic wounds." Henry W. Randle, "Suntanning: Differences in Perceptions throughout History," *Mayo Clinic Proceedings* 72.5 (1997): 462, 463. Segrave's *Suntanning in the 20th Century* reproduces a number of early twentieth-century print advertisements for sunlamps.
42. George S. Schuyler, *Black No More* (1931; New York: Modern Library, 1999), 11.
43. Sollors, *Neither Black nor White Yet Both,* 75. For a thoughtful discussion of *Black No More* in light of contemporaneous racial discourse, see Jane Kuenz, "American Racial Discourse, 1900–1930: Schuyler's *Black No More,*" *Novel* 30.2 (1997): 170–94.
44. Schuyler, *Black No More,* 150, 177, 178.
45. Ibid., 179–80. The science historian Carolyn Thomas de la Peña argues that Schuyler's model for Crookman was Dr. Henry Pancoast, an X-ray scientist who in 1904 was erroneously credited with turning the skin of Negroes white. Pancoast strenuously denied that he ever engaged in such efforts. See Carolyn Thomas de la Peña, "'Bleaching the Ethiopian': Desegregating Race and Technology through Early X-Ray Experiments," *Technology and Culture* 47.1 (2006): 27–55.
46. Chesnutt, *Wife of His Youth,* 3–4, 5.
47. Because there was no practical way of reproducing color illustrations, the medieval and early modern blazon, typically found in catalogs of nobility, described the heraldic symbols rather than picturing them. The French and Anglo-Norman terminology used to describe blazons, according to Gerard J. Brault, was formalized by the end of the thirteenth century. Gerard J. Brault, *Early Blazon: Heraldic Terminology in the Twelfth and Thirteenth Centuries with Special Reference to Arthurian Heraldry* (Woodbridge, U.K.: Boydell Press, 1997).
48. Chesnutt, *Wife of His Youth,* 10.
49. Ibid., 9.
50. The Arthurian parallel in "The Wife of His Youth" would place Ryder in the position of Guinevere: he must choose between loyalty to his spouse or romantic fulfillment. If we extend the analogy, Molly Dixon plays the role of Lancelot and 'Liza Jane improbably plays the role of Arthur. Unlike Arthurian legend (including Tennyson's), "The Wife of His Youth" restores the sanctity of "Arthurian" genealogy by reuniting Ryder and 'Liza Jane. Curiously, Clyde O. De Land's illustration for the story ("This is the Woman, and I am the Man") depicts 'Liza Jane in a manner virtually identical to the Blue Vein women also seen in the picture.
51. Alain Locke, ed., *The New Negro: An Interpretation* (1925; New York: Atheneum, 1992), 48.
52. Baker credits Chesnutt with a "mastery of form" in his "ability to give the trick to white expectations, securing publication for creative work that carries a deep-rooted African sound." Houston A. Baker, *Modernism and the Harlem Renaissance* (Chicago: University of Chicago Press, 1987), 49. I agree with Baker on the question of Chesnutt's literary self-fashioning; however, I think that in his use of the blazon (among other

devices), Chesnutt also qualifies as one who explicitly and aggressively reworks literary raw material.

53. Jean Toomer, *Cane* (1923), ed. Rudolph P. Byrd and Henry Louis Gates Jr. (New York: Norton, 2011), 30.

54. See, for example, Susan Gubar, *Racechanges: White Skin, Black Face in American Culture* (New York: Oxford University Press, 1997); George Hutchinson, "Jean Toomer and American Racial Discourse," *Texas Studies in Literature and Language* 35.2 (1993): 226–50; and Charles Scruggs and Lee VanDemarr, *Jean Toomer and the Terrors of American History* (Philadelphia: University of Pennsylvania Press, 1998). Contemporaneous reviews of *Cane* tend not to address "Portrait in Georgia."

55. Walter Benn Michaels, *Our America: Nativism, Modernism, and Pluralism* (Durham: Duke University Press, 1995), 62.

56. Ezra Pound, *Literary Essays of Ezra Pound* (New York: New Directions, 1935), 6.

57. The measurement is called the "paper bag test": the color of a commonly used brown paper grocery bag serves as the dividing line between light-skinned persons who can pass for white and dark-skinned persons who cannot pass. See, for example, Audrey Elisa Kerr, *The Paper Bag Principle: Class, Colorism, and Rumor in the Case of Black Washington, D.C.* (Knoxville: University of Tennessee Press, 2006). For a detailed analysis of Charles B. Davenport's outlandish experiments with a spin-top color wheel made by the toy and board-game company Milton Bradley, see Sollors, *Neither Black nor White Yet Both*, chap. 4.

58. Charles W. Chesnutt, "What Is a White Man?," *Independent* 41 (May 30, 1889): 5–6.

59. In South Carolina in 1830, slaves made up 54.3 percent of the state's total population (315,401 out of 581,185).

60. H. Bailey, *Reports of Cases Argued and Determined in the Court of Appeals of South Carolina, on Appeal from the Courts of Law,* 2 vols. (Charleston, S.C.: A. E. Miller, 1834), 2:559.

61. Ariela J. Gross, "Litigating Whiteness: Trials of Racial Determination in the Nineteenth-Century South," *Yale Law Journal* 108.1 (1998): 126.

62. W. R. Hill, *Reports of Cases at Law, Argued and Determined in the Court of Appeals, of South Carolina,* 3 vols. (Charleston, S.C.: McCarter, 1857), 2:614. A leading booster of John C. Calhoun's nullification movement, Harper would write a lengthy apology for slavery in the years following his *Cantey* decision. See William Harper, *Memoir on Slavery, Read before the Society for the Advancement of Learning, of South Carolina, at Its Annual Meeting at Columbia, 1837* (Charleston, S.C.: J. S. Burges, 1838).

63. On the social constructionist tendencies of nineteenth-century racial jurisprudence, see Daniel J. Sharfstein, "The Secret History of Race in the United States," *Yale Law Journal* 112.6 (2003): 1473–1509.

64. Charles W. Chesnutt, *The House behind the Cedars* (Boston: Houghton, Mifflin, 1900), 168, 172.

65. Ibid., 160, 167. At this same point in the novel Judge Straight pulls out a legal volume and reads from *State v. Davis.*

66. Chesnutt criticism routinely and often disparagingly assigns the "tragic mulatto" label to *The House behind the Cedars.*

67. Kenneth W. Warren, *What Was African American Literature?* (Cambridge: Harvard University Press, 2011), 1, 42.

5. Harlem Geography

1. Even today's scholars of the Harlem Renaissance who mention the parade tend to ignore or quickly move past the Red Summer riots later in 1919.
2. Houston A. Baker, *Modernism and the Harlem Renaissance* (Chicago: University of Chicago Press, 1987), 49, 91.
3. James de Jongh, *Vicious Modernism: Black Harlem and the Literary Imagination* (Cambridge: Cambridge University Press, 1990), appendixes 1 and 2.
4. Rudolph Fisher, *The City of Refuge: The Collected Stories of Rudolph Fisher*, ed. John McCluskey Jr. (Columbia: University of Missouri Press, 2008), 35.
5. Fisher opens yet another *Atlantic Monthly* short story, "The Promised Land" (1927), by bringing modern Harlem into contact with religious antiquity: "At a certain level of the airshaft two songs, issuing from opposite windows, met, mingled in minor refrains, and rose together toward Negro Harlem's black sky; two futile prayers which spent themselves like a mist ere they reached the roof. The one was a prayer for the love of man, the other a prayer for the love of God: 'blues,' and a spiritual." Ibid., 48. In 1938, Louis Armstrong performed a similar fusion when he recorded "Jonah and the Whale," a song that found its way into the album *Louis and the Good Book* (1958).
6. Ibid., 35.
7. Edwin G. Burrows and Mike Wallace, *Gotham: A History of New York City to 1898* (New York: Oxford University Press, 1999), xviii.
8. John W. Reps, *The Making of Urban America: A History of City Planning in the United States* (Princeton: Princeton University Press, 1965), 295–96; for a wonderfully illustrated discussion of the diffusion of the urban grid in U.S. urban planning, see chaps. 9–11. For a brief overview of the grid pattern from antiquity to the early modern era, see Dan Stanislawski, "The Origin and Spread of the Grid-Pattern Town," *Geographical Review* 36.1 (1946): 105–20.
9. An excellent assortment of maps can be found in Paul E. Cohen and Robert T. Augustyn, *Manhattan in Maps, 1527–1995* (New York: Rizzoli, 1997). The most comprehensive printed collection of New York maps remains I. N. Phelps Stokes, *The Iconography of Manhattan Island, 1498–1909: Compiled from Original Sources and Illustrated by Photo-intaglio Reproductions of Important Maps, Plans, Views, and Documents in Public and Private Collections*, 6 vols. (New York: R. H. Dodd, 1915–1928).
10. Cohen and Augustyn, *Manhattan in Maps*, 64; Reps, *Making of Urban America*, 296.
11. For a full discussion of the Commissioners' Plan of 1811, see Edward K. Spann, *The New Metropolis: New York City, 1840–1857* (New York: Columbia University Press, 1981), chaps. 5–8.
12. Lewis Mumford, *The Culture of Cities* (1938; New York: Harcourt, 1970), 183, 185, 184, 126.
13. Ibid., 5.
14. Oswald Spengler, *The Decline of the West*, trans. Charles Francis Atkinson, 2 vols. (New York: Knopf, 1926–1928), 2:100, 99.
15. Le Corbusier, *When the Cathedrals Were White: A Journey to the Country of Timid People*, trans. Francis E. Hyslop Jr. (New York: Reynal and Hitchcock, 1947), 47–48.
16. Le Corbusier, *The City of Tomorrow and Its Planning*, trans. Frederick Etchells (Cambridge: MIT Press, 1971), part 3.
17. Le Corbusier, *When the Cathedrals Were White*, 50.
18. Mumford, *Culture of Cities*, 188.

19. Beginning in 1939, however, Gunnar Myrdal conducted the research for his famous study, *An American Dilemma* (1944), out of the Chrysler Building's 46th floor. David Levering Lewis, *W. E. B. Du Bois: A Biography* (New York: Henry Holt, 2009), 623.
20. Fisher, *City of Refuge,* 115.
21. Ulla Ehrensvärd, "Color in Cartography: A Historical Survey," in *Art and Cartography,* ed. David Woodward (Chicago: University of Chicago Press, 1987), 138. In the seventeenth and eighteenth centuries, art instruction manuals recommended the hand painting of printed maps as a useful means for the ruling class to learn geographic markers and boundaries.
22. Jacob A. Riis, *How the Other Half Lives: Studies among the Tenements of New York* (New York: Scribner's, 1890), 25.
23. Lothrop Stoddard, *The Rising Tide of Color against White World-Supremacy* (New York: Scribner's, 1920), 5, 251.
24. Ibid., 266.
25. On the invention of the halftone, see David Clayton Phillips, "Art for Industry's Sake: Halftone Technology, Mass Photography, and the Social Transformation of American Print Culture, 1880–1920" (PhD diss., Yale University, 1996). A full-color version of Stoddard's map can be found at the Wikimedia Commons website, https://commons.wikimedia.org/wiki/File:Stoddard_race_map_1920.jpg.
26. "There is no immediate danger of the world being swamped by black blood," Stoddard concedes. "But there is a very imminent danger that the white stocks may be swamped by Asiatic blood." He adds that "with the development of cheap and rapid transportation, nature's barriers are down. Unless man erects and maintains artificial barriers the various races will increasingly mingle, and the inevitable result will be the supplanting or absorption of the higher by the lower types." Stoddard, *Rising Tide of Color,* 87, 90, 301, 302.
27. Madison Grant, *The Conquest of a Continent; or, the Expansion of Races in America* (New York: Scribner's, 1933), 352, 348, 351.
28. The line print technology deployed in the reproduction of Grant's maps is fairly primitive; however, the use of maps in statistical interpretation was still a recent development. The statistical analysis of racial identity in the United States, where the practice was pioneered, had been in use only since the U.S. Civil War. See introduction.
29. Grant, *Conquest of a Continent,* 283. Grant was hardly alone in associating the larger civil rights movement with the communist threat. For example, A. Mitchell Palmer, who served as U.S. attorney general from 1919 to 1921, routinely (if usually incorrectly) linked African American intellectuals and groups with international socialism and communism.
30. Ibid., 286.
31. James Weldon Johnson, *Black Manhattan* (1930; New York: Da Capo, 1991), 147.
32. Ibid., 145.
33. In the undated text of a speech titled "Harlem, the Negro Metropolis," Fisher, a medical doctor by training and trade, presented Seventh Avenue in similar fashion, calling it "Harlem's transverse aorta." Fisher, *City of Refuge,* 330. Le Corbusier lamented that the world's "great capitals have no arteries; they have only capillaries." Le Corbusier, *City of Tomorrow,* 13.
34. Fisher, *City of Refuge,* 36.

35. Johnson, *Black Manhattan,* 146, 147.
36. John L. Jackson Jr., *Harlemworld: Doing Race and Class in Contemporary Black America* (Chicago: University of Chicago Press, 2001), 9.
37. Seymour I. Schwartz and Ralph E. Ehrenberg, *The Mapping of America* (New York: Harry N. Abrams, 1980), 298, 303.
38. In "The Making of Harlem," his contribution to the Harlem number of the *Survey Graphic* (1925), Johnson introduced many of the same ideas that he deploys in *Black Manhattan.* He also reproduces a map that very closely resembles his "Negro Harlem 1925" map shown in this chapter. And while Johnson stresses that, unlike African American enclaves in most U.S. cities, Harlem is not a ghetto, he also includes photographs of densely peopled Harlem street scenes, which bear some resemblance to the oft-printed photographs of urban ghettos, the type popularized in the late nineteenth century by Jacob Riis and found in contemporaneous discussions of immigration. Johnson's Harlemites, it must be stressed, tend to dress professionally in suits and hats rather than the usual shabby immigrant garb.
39. In Stoddard's words: "The whole course of modern urban and industrial life is disgenic [*sic*]. . . . [M]odern civilization has been one-sided, abnormal, unhealthy—and nature is exacting penalties which will increase in severity until we either fully adapt or *finally perish.*" Stoddard, *Rising Tide of Color*, 302, 303.
40. Johnson, *Black Manhattan,* 150. Most historians of New York point out that African Americans began to settle in the neighborhood well before Payton founded his Afro-American Realty Company in 1904; however, the efforts of Payton and others (including several African American churches) dramatically accelerated African American settlement in Harlem during the 1910s and '20s.
41. E. Franklin Frazier similarly wrote that "the sudden descent of this vast human tide upon a few northern cities constituted a flight, replete with dramatic episodes, from medieval to modern America." E. Franklin Frazier, *The Negro Family in the United States* (Chicago: University of Chicago Press, 1939), 291.
42. The Harlem historian Cheryl Lynn Greenberg makes a convincing case that in reality Harlem bore all the hallmarks of a depressed urban community as early as the 1910s. See Cheryl Lynn Greenberg, *"Or Does It Explode?": Black Harlem in the Great Depression* (Oxford: Oxford University Press, 1991).
43. Gilbert Osofsky, *Harlem: The Making of a Ghetto, 1890–1930* (New York: Harper, 1966), ix.
44. Ibid., 179, 187.
45. E. Franklin Frazier, *The Negro in the United States,* rev. ed. (New York: Macmillan, 1957), 192.
46. A parallel debate took shape surrounding the "Americanness" of New York City during the early part of the twentieth century. As Angela M. Blake demonstrates, nativists, promoters of tourism, and a host of additional voices during this time clashed over the true meaning of the city's ethnic pluralism: were ethnic enclaves harbors of potentially subversive difference, or were they picturesque settings worthy of a tourist's time and money? See Angela M. Blake, *How New York Became American, 1890–1924* (Baltimore: Johns Hopkins University Press, 2006).
47. Frazier, *Negro in the United States,* 265, 262, 264.
48. Wallace Thurman, *The Blacker the Berry* (1929; New York: Scribner, 1996), 214.

Epilogue

1. See chapter 1.
2. The Census Bureau developed guiding principles for determining census tract boundaries in 1934, long after Harlem's census tracts came into existence.
3. E. Franklin Frazier, "Negro Harlem: An Ecological Study," *American Journal of Sociology* 43.1 (1937): 74. Frazier's earlier study, *The Negro Family in Chicago* (1932), deploys census data using a similar methodology. But Frazier's Chicago zones extend linearly, from north to south between Twelfth and Seventy-First Streets; thus they lack the radial patterning that defines his Harlem zones. Frazier's Chicago study also develops a geospatial argument about mulattoes, who cluster in the better-off southern zones; the geographic distribution of mulattoes does not enter into his Harlem discussion. It is also worth noting that the Harlem concentric-zones analysis, subsequently featured in *The Negro Family in the United States*, has proven far more influential on subsequent scholarship; in a search done in early 2016 Google Scholar identified 369 citations of *The Negro Family in Chicago* and 1,790 citations of *The Negro Family in the United States*.
4. Frazier, "Negro Harlem," 75.
5. Howard Whipple Green and Leon E. Truesdell, *Census Tracts in American Cities: A Brief History of the Census Tract Movement, with an Outline of Procedure and Suggested Modifications* (Washington, D.C.: Bureau of the Census, 1937), 1.
6. Walter Laidlaw, "Federation Districts and a Suggestion for a Convenient and Scientific City Map System," *Federation* 4.4 (1906): 5.
7. The Census Bureau did not publish tract-level data until the 1940 census. Even then, it favored publishing data by assembly districts or wards in its most widely disseminated reports.
8. Arthur L. Swift, "Doctor Laidlaw's Vision: The Early Years," in *Golden Anniversary of Census Tracts, 1956* (Washington, D.C.: American Statistical Association, 1956), 4–5.
9. Ibid., 5.
10. Walter Laidlaw, "Religious Belief and Race Suicide," *Federation* 3.1 (1903): 34, 37, 40, 38.
11. Donald L. Foley, "Census Tracts and Urban Research," *Journal of the American Statistical Association* 48 (1953): 733–34.
12. Robert E. Park, "The Urban Community as a Spatial Pattern and a Moral Order," in *Urban Community*, ed. E. W. Burgess (Chicago: University of Chicago Press, 1926), 3.
13. This is not to say that all demographers find the census tract beyond improvement; see, for example, Barrett A. Lee et al., "Beyond the Census Tract: Patterns and Determinants of Racial Segregation at Multiple Geographic Scales," *American Sociological Review* 73.5 (2008): 766–91. Because the census tract has been in existence in some areas for over a century, however, few if any demographers would sacrifice the ability to compare geographic data over time by replacing the census tract as the basic unit of census geography.
14. Rudolph Fisher, *The City of Refuge: The Collected Stories of Rudolph Fisher*, ed. John McCluskey Jr. (Columbia: University of Missouri Press, 2008), 159, 160, 161, 164. As Emily Bernard reports, Fisher was one of a handful of writers who reviewed the manuscript of *Nigger Heaven* prior to its 1926 publication. Emily Bernard, *Carl Van Vechten and the Harlem Renaissance: A Portrait in Black and White* (New Haven: Yale University Press, 2012), 114.

15. Carl Van Vechten, *Nigger Heaven* (1926; Urbana: University of Illinois Press, 2000), 149.
16. Park, "Urban Community," 15, 13.
17. As of 2016 the Census Bureau plans to drop "Negro" from its racial nomenclature and to continue allowing respondents to indicate multiple racial identities simultaneously. (The American Community Survey of 2014 was the first not to include "Negro.") The most contentious debate in anticipation of the 2020 census centers on the question of whether or not to consider Hispanic/Latino a "racial" category.

Index